THE
Unbroken Field

THE POWER OF
INTENTION IN HEALING

Dr. Michael Greenwood

1st edition

Published by
PARADOX Publishers
1980 Cromwell Rd.
Victoria, B.C. V8P 1R5

If not available at your local bookstore, this book may be ordered from the
publisher. Send the cover price plus four dollars for shipping.

Printed in Canada

National Library of Canada Cataloguing in Publication

Greenwood, Michael, 1949-
   The unbroken field: the power of intention in healing / Michael T.
Greenwood; editor, Susan Clark.

Includes bibliographical references and index.

ISBN 0-9695822-2-6

   1. Mental healing. 2. Meditation—Therapeutic use. 3. Mind and body.
I. Clark, Susan, 1954- II. Title.

R733.G745 2004   615.8'51   C2003-907001-8

Typeset by the Vancouver Desktop Publishing Centre

Printed by Hignell Printing (Winnipeg)

Cover illustration by Miles Lowry, www.mileslowry.ca

Inside illustrations by Richard Greenwood, www.richardgreenwood.ca

all I need to be well
lives deeply within me.
the healer who comes
is a midwife
who helps to birth
my original self.
it is from this place
I am ready to be
where I have never been, before.
able now to know,
may be for the first time
The Unbroken Field

—*Cherie Greenwood*

CONTENTS

ABOUT THE AUTHOR

Michael Greenwood trained at St. John's College, Cambridge and St. Mary's Hospital, London and practised Family Medicine in Victoria for many years. His interest in deep healing arose out of his own experience of chronic pain, which began with a motorcycle accident while he was a medical student. The pain, unresponsive to all that conventional medicine could offer, forced him to face the limits of his own medical training. His search for an answer led him on a fascinating journey to a new understanding of health and illness, stress and deep inner tensions and how they affect our lives. Many of those insights were recorded in Michael's first book, *Paradox and Healing: medicine, mythology and transformation*, co-authored with Dr. Peter Nunn and first published in 1992.

Michael's explorations into alternative approaches led him to study Chinese medicine, Ayurveda and meditation before they became generally fashionable. He was one of the founding staff-members of the Canadian College of Chinese Studies where, in addition to teaching, he initiated a research study into the use of acupuncture for post-motor-vehicle accident chronic pain. That research gradually evolved into the highly successful residential program at the Victoria Pain Clinic. His second book, *Braving the Void: journeys into healing*, arose out of his experiences at the Pain Clinic, where he developed many of the interactive techniques discussed more fully in *The Unbroken Field: the power of intention in healing*.

In 1993, Michael gave up his Family Practice to devote his time to people suffering from chronic pain and other chronic illnesses. Currently, he teaches East-West Medicine at the

International College of Traditional Chinese Medicine, and is the Medical Director of the Victoria Pain Clinic.

More information on Dr. Greenwood's various books and articles can be found at:

www.paradoxpublishing.com or www.michaeltgreenwood.com.

ACKNOWLEDGEMENTS

This book could never have been written without the opportunity to work extensively with many people in the retreat setting of the Victoria Pain Clinic. To the staff there, past and present, I owe a huge debt of gratitude.

First and foremost to my wife, Cherie, whose tireless support over the years has now expanded to her becoming an integral part of VPC. She now often works closely with me, holding the space in which we work, and providing enormous safety for people to take their journeys into the void. But more than that, her accurate intuitive perceptions, and uncompromising commitment to the truth has kept me from drifting off into my own petty concerns. To her, I am eternally grateful.

To my colleagues at the clinic: Ken White, who takes care of everything to do with the business, Tracey Nigro, who does craniosacral therapy and various muscular stretching techniques; Darwyn Rowland, who is so skilful at Hellerwork that everyone wants to take him home with them; to Elizabeth Hartney, who warms everyone's hands and hearts with biofeedback; to Linda Wyness, who is the backbone of the program, and who is without a doubt one of the best and most experienced chronic pain counsellors around; and to my former colleague, Mary-Joan Zakovy, who helped me to open my mind to many new perspectives on healing.

My thanks also to Dr. Peter Nunn, who first inspired me to begin writing, to Miles Lowry, who contributed his vision to the cover art, to my sons Richard, who did all the interior graphics, and Mischa, who has further inspired me to follow the path of the Heart; to Susan Clark, who put enormous time and energy into exploring the fine nuances of Chinese medicine as she skilfully edited the manuscript; and to Michael and Tony Gregson, who helped bring the whole project to completion.

DISCLAIMER

Although the vignettes in *The Unbroken Field: the power of intention in healing* are based on the experiences of actual people, the names and many specific details of each case have been altered to protect the identity of those involved.

INTRODUCTION

Although chronic illness and pain are not very glamorous, they nevertheless have an enormous amount to teach us. This book you hold in your hands represents my desire to share as vividly and as clearly as possible some of the things they have taught me.

I offer no miracle cure. Any understanding I may have of the nature and meaning of chronic illness has arisen out of my own personal experience of pain, out of my experiences in daily meditation and out of the interactive explorations of others' pain in which I have been privileged to participate.

The dynamic and interactive approach to acupuncture and bodywork that you will hear much about in the coming pages is not just a clever new way of suppressing symptoms. Rather, at its foundation lies a practice of intentionally *moving toward* symptoms that is very much the antithesis of our habitual approach of shunning or masking our discomforts. At its core is an insistence that, in order to heal deeply, we must give up any hope of a *fix* and choose instead to encounter rather than hide from our pain, to *integrate* rather than exile our symptoms. In my view, this is the true meaning of holism.

THEORY AND PRACTICE:
FROM COMPLEXITY TO SIMPLICITY

To allow whatever needs to happen, to trust the body and to keep one's perception fresh, to hold simplicity as dear as knowledge and to value *not-doing* as highly as *doing* are among the most important of the tasks of this integration.

Over the past couple of decades, as my theoretical and experiential understanding of Western, Chinese and Ayurvedic medicine has grown, simplicity has proven difficult at times to honour.

Each of these medical traditions has built its understandings of the body, mind and spirit over centuries if not millennia and it has been a daily challenge to continue to work intuitively, as I try to do, by their lights; to be guided but not blinkered in the moment of interaction by such awesome stores of subtle knowledge.

But, after all, there is always more simplicity than we imagine. For instance, once you take away the labels, most diseases can be reduced to a handful of bodily discomforts, including fatigue, pain, depression and disability. Unfortunately, chronic illness, which tends by its nature to be complex and layered, attracts the sort of diagnosis that is frequently no more than a label, and one that neither means very much nor clarifies useful treatment options. In fact, our obsession with trying to pinpoint a diagnosis takes our attention from the simple fact that our illness is not a replication of something countless others have had before us, nor an accident of fate unrelated to ourselves but is in fact the opposite: a message *from* our deepest selves. And it is a message that is by and large not being heard.

Thus, beyond diagnosis, illness can be a call to rediscover our original alignment, to re-establish our essential wholeness; and chronic illness or pain is a particularly insistent caller. This realization saves a lot of energy! If, instead of encountering illness in ourselves as a call to arms in a psychic war against bits and pieces of our bodies and minds, we attempt to understand our symptoms in the light of the whole of our being, suddenly the question is no longer the primarily academic one of finding a label for a particular pattern of discomforts but rather one of a feeling investigation into our judgements and fears and the way they restrict our life energies. Instead of asking, *What disease do I have?* the question becomes, *Why do I restrict energy in the particular way that I do?* In other words, just *who is it* that is hurting?

KILLING THE MESSENGER

It is hard, however, to listen to a message that is being delivered in the language of unrelenting pain, disability and discomfort. In fact, no matter how sophisticated we grow, our desire to avoid confronting our pain never seems to waiver and our compulsion to rid ourselves of it remains unquestioning.

But suppose you took your car to a mechanic because the oil warning light was on and she offered to fix the problem for you by cutting the wires to the warning light. What would you think of that kind of a mechanic? Probably not much, yet most of us think nothing of treating our bodies this way. We take a painkiller for a headache, an anti-depressant when we feel down or an anxiolytic when we are strung out, without a second thought. But we, just like our unwise mechanic, have only killed the messenger. In fact, we have merely rid ourselves of our *awareness* of our pain and have mistaken this lack of awareness for wellness.

And we as individuals are not alone in this anxious rush to erase the messages from our deeper selves. The fact is, the tantalizing offer of a quick fix also answers our society's materialist demands of us, unfortunately supporting most of us in our desire to live out the greater part of our lives cut off from the darker, richer, less rational parts of our natures so that we do not fail the system. It is almost as if we must not falter, dare not stumble, lest we confront the fact that we are not machines after all but mortal flesh, embodied spirit.

Sadly, over the last century or more, our entire health care system has come to reflect this fundamental misapprehension. For — going back to my car analogy for a moment — we the owners know that if we were to allow the mechanic to cut the wires to the warning light, we might drive another mile or two in blissful ignorance but our bliss will be bought at great price as, sooner or later, our car's engine will seize up.

In my view, it should not take too much deep study to figure out that much the same thing is likely to happen in the human body. Ignoring, suppressing or removing symptoms might give us the sense that all is well for a year or two, perhaps even longer, but sooner or later we are going to have to face a bigger problem. Symptoms are by definition symptoms *of* something; they are not in and of themselves illness but pointers to some underlying malaise of body, mind and spirit. Erase them and you have merely succeeded in cutting the wires to the warning light!

Why this is not obvious to all of us I do not know. It certainly seems obvious to me now but I admit it took me twenty years of medical practice, many years of exploration and a long struggle with my own chronic pain before I really understood the enormity of the implications of this simple truth. In fact, I now believe that if this one fundamental error could be exposed, it would herald the end of medicine as we know it. Were we no longer driven to cast out the demons of our illnesses, we might be willing to learn from them instead. Without the fear and hostility with which we currently encounter our symptoms, we might accept them for the teachers they really are. For the fascinating thing about chronic illness is that it *demands an expansion of consciousness* before it will yield. It refuses to leave us until we have embraced it fully and understood its urgent message.

PAIN AS TEACHER

In fact, pain may be the greatest teacher we will ever know: it provides exquisitely sensitive feedback on our advancement, calls our attention to the moments when we fall off the path and never gives up on us, even when we are at our most slothful, our most inattentive, our most imperceptive, our most obstinate. What better teacher could there be? So when illness comes unbidden, we would do well to treat it with the respect due such a teacher.

Of course, pain is not a pleasant experience. And so all the powers of the ego resist it. Indeed, I might even define pain as an *ego boundary* — a psychological line that marks the place beyond which the ego cannot go. This gut reaction is so strong, I have known people who have given up their lives rather than risk putting their egos aside in order to encounter their pain. I have even known people who *knew* that exploration of their pain might lead them to the freedom they so desperately wanted, yet who chose destruction anyway.

We glibly talk of holism yet refuse to risk our core assumptions. Instead, we hope that alternative medicine is just another way to get rid of a problem, one that is perhaps not quite as dehumanizing as conventional approaches. But if we take a herb instead of a drug, or pop vitamins instead of drinking coffee for a boost of energy, we are not much closer to opening ourselves to the real import of our illness — which lies in our minds and in our hearts and in our spirits.

So let's respect our pain and what it offers. Let's explore our symptoms without judgement, not as a mental abstraction but really, actively, in our stomachs and in our chests and in our intestines and in our hearts, and listen to what they have to tell us. Such a down-to-earth approach is the essence of the dynamic interactive acupuncture/bodywork (DIA) and meditative practices presented in the coming pages.

NOTES

(For technical language, see the glossary)

Chinese medicine (CM): I will be using the term Chinese medicine (CM) throughout the book rather than the more familiar Traditional Chinese Medicine (TCM) in order to be more inclusive of the different styles of Chinese medicine.

Capitalization: I will be using capitalization throughout to mark an important distinction in Chinese medicine between the organ (e.g. the heart, liver, blood) and the energy of the whole organ meridian (e.g. Heart, Liver, Blood), the energy and attributes of which are *not limited to the physical organ.*

Explorer: Explorer is the term I will use to describe those seeking healing not as subjects of a process imposed from the outside but as participants in a healing journey, the itinerary of which cannot be known at the outset. The traditional term, *patient*, has an unfortunate history wedded to the hierarchies of early modern medicine; and *client* — introduced some time ago in our society as a neutral and therefore progressive alternative — unfortunately invokes a relationship of transaction: we assume that we will be given some thing, or some service by someone in exchange for money. Neither term falls anywhere near the mark, so, awkward as the term explorer may seem at first, it seems a more accurate description than either of the two more familiar options.

Witness: Witness is the correlate of explorer, as described above. The witness supports the explorer by her presence, intention, experience and skills in facilitating integration of trans-rational (void) experiences. But most importantly, the witness takes a stance of not-knowing and not-doing, of allowing the *whatever* that is so often the crucial and surprising, unforeseeable key to discovery and integration.

Language and the body: Attempting to express in writing the intuitive, dynamic, personal and interpersonal processes that are integral to the healing explorations I have been involved in has, sadly, brought me face to face on many occasions with the significant poverty of our language when it comes to describing holistic concepts and experiential healing. As a stark example, it is nearly impossible to discover a non-pejorative way to speak of pain, fear or illness, or, as noted above, to find a way to describe the relationship between people exploring such things interactively.

Case studies: Interspersed throughout the book are a number of brief vignettes, most of which have been chosen to illustrate a point rather than attempt to fully describe a particular individual's healing journey. (Those readers who are interested in such stories may want to look at my previous book, *Braving the Void: journeys into healing.*)

Victoria Pain Clinic (VPC): For those readers who may not know of the Victoria Pain Clinic (VPC), it is centred around a residential program designed to help people explore their symptoms experientially in a retreat setting over ten days. The program includes DIA, Hellerwork (deep tissue massage and structural realignment), biofeedback, counselling, cranial-sacral therapy, relaxation instruction, lectures and group interaction — an experiential immersion grounded in an integrated therapeutic philosophy. As you read the vignettes, it is worth remembering that many of them describe people who are in such a residential immersion. Their experiences with DIA have therefore been supported and enabled by all the other aspects of the ten-day program.

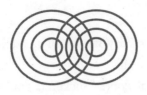

CHAPTER 1

THE FIELD OF ENERGY

Out beyond ideas of wrongdoing
and rightdoing there is a field.
I'll meet you there.
When the soul lies down in that grass,
the world is too full to talk about.
Ideas, language, even the phrase 'each other'
doesn't make any sense.

— Rumi

*T*he gentle invitation of the great Sufi poet, mystic, passionate friend and beloved teacher, Jelaluddin Rumi, quoted above, appears nonchalant in its reference to a field that lies beyond the very idea of judgement. His invitation implies that this field is a real place where you and I might meet and further hints that where the narrow strictures of rationality and conventional wisdoms end is not nothing but in fact a kind of open space.

This image of the field — open, welcoming, perhaps verdant, perhaps wild and beyond our ideas of right and wrong — is precious. It embodies our own profound intuition that there is a wider, sweeter realm of real understanding beyond our habitual, restless ways of thinking and beyond the fear of the unknown that holds us to our limited views. And it speaks directly to our intuition that the mind can let go of its customary modes of operation and its structures without annihilating itself.

This insight has of course flickered within humankind everywhere and all through the ages — wherever minds and hearts have sought to free themselves. Suddenly and slowly, individuals and at times whole civilizations have let go of old understandings of what they are; and have seen in such moments of collective or individual re-cognition that the mind is paradoxically both what enabled these radical shifts in understanding and what inhibited them.

Is it a terrifying leap that leads us to this field beyond judgement and so beyond our normal understanding? Not necessarily, say those — like Rumi — who invite us, almost casually, to join them there. In some deep part of us, too, most of us wrestle with the recognition that every day of our lives our minds are able to understand as they did not the day before, limited only by fear and our core beliefs — our dearest safeguards against the shock and challenge of new awareness.

But hearts can be as tremulous as they can be courageous, so let us begin by cutting ourselves some slack and briefly exploring the more familiar terrain of Western science, charting its own recent progress 'out beyond' its former beliefs.

ENERGY FIELDS: MODERN SCIENCE CATCHES UP WITH THE 'PRIMITIVE'

Because an understanding of the human body, mind and spirit as an energy field is integral to the experiential and interactive healing practices I want to try to articulate in this book, I would like to begin by mapping the relevant science — what this field is and how it relates to the way we experience our world, our chronic pain, our illness and our healing.

What is most immediately striking when we turn our attention to modern science, however, is how very few of us have caught up with the latest developments. For instance, most of us still conduct our lives as though we believe the world to be filled with solid and distinct entities, even though those whose job it is to know that world best — contemporary physicists and a growing number of leading scientists in other disciplines — now routinely speak of energy fields rather than solid objects when they describe physical reality.

It seems we have gone the long way around to discover what other medical traditions (Chinese medicine, Ayurveda, homeopathy and shamanism, for example) have long taken as fundamental: that our universe is made of energy rather than matter, of flows rather than beings. Traditional wisdom and contemporary physics agree that even the familiar solidity of our own bodies is simply our habitual interpretation of what is really an energy field manifesting a particular kind of static. In other words, the persons we identify as I, you and she are much less solid and much less distinct from one another than we have supposed.

Unfortunately, most of us find it impossible to experience ourselves this way, day to day! Although we may welcome such news with curiosity or with reverent amazement, our practical everyday understanding of the world and ourselves usually alters very little. However hard we try, until we have direct personal experience of it — as a result of a near-death experience, an imbalance in our brain chemistry, an unusual empathic or intuitive capacity, or long and rigorous meditation — our understanding of this information tends, at best, to be intellectual and a bit strained.

However, as just this sort of vivid personal experience of the self as an energy field is the place from which we can do our best work with chronic pain, depression and other illness, let us take a quick, layperson's look at the phenomenon of an energy field in action, using a simple visual metaphor. Imagine jiggling two sticks in a still pond a few inches apart. Almost immediately, two sets of expanding concentric rings will meet and overlap and what is known as an interference pattern of waves and troughs will develop, rather like the image of overlapping circles at the beginning of the chapter.

This interference pattern is an energy field. It is a pattern whose chief characteristics are: that although it is moving and shifting, it remains fairly constant; and that even when the interference pattern we see in the waves is no longer being created by our imaginary sticks moving in the water, the pattern reflects the sticks' energy in such a way that an interpretation of the pattern could infer just those sticks moving in just the way they did in just this water — would in other words infer the pattern's so-called originating conditions exactly.[1]

ENERGETICS

Popular science writers have been working with field theories for years. Rupert Sheldrake's morphogenic fields, Fritjof Capra's self-organizing systems, Karl Pibram's holographic mind and David Boehm's theory of implicate order have all lodged in the common mind. But the origins of modern energy and field theories go back much further: Einstein developed his theory of relativity in the early part of the last century, just as Newtonian science began to loosen its hold on our perceptions. Now, almost a hundred years later, researchers generally agree that the apparently solid and separate phenomena around us are in fact all manifestations of an underlying non-material field.

That Western medicine has not yet embraced modern field

1 It might be worth holding in mind as you move through the next few chapters that one way to conceive of acupuncture's effects on the body-mind's originating conditions is to imagine the acupuncture needle as a kind of third stick wiggled in the pond of the body's energy field.

theories as fundamental and transforming speaks to a bureaucratically and economically driven medical system, an entrenched politics and a professional conservatism. Nevertheless, there has been an explosion of research just outside the precinct of conventional medicine that is based on the body as an energy field, affirming that the material structure of the body is a secondary phenomenon of the primary and generative energy field that sustains it. Some recent research goes so far as to propose that our human consciousness can, in some respects, be considered *the field becoming aware of itself*.

These sophisticated theories suggest a new description of disease as a field disturbance first and foremost, manifesting only secondarily as a pathology. In other words, illness arises from the field before it manifests in the material structure of the body. So if we really wish to understand the problem of illness, and want to effect real change in our health, it is at the field level — the energy level — that we must begin.

THE FIELD ORGANIZATION

Basic chemistry teaches that energy radiates from every charged particle in the body — whether it be sodium, potassium, inorganic ions or macro-molecular ions such as proteins. What the chemistry student may not know is that these charged oscillators emit waves of electromagnetic radiation in very wide frequency ranges and that these waves travel through the body influencing every structure they come across. Some decay, some are emitted, some are refracted by skin, bones and nerves. So, to continue with our water imagery, the body's field can be understood to represent the sum total of all the tiny energy fields surrounding each individual molecule and atom in the body and the interference patterns — rather like the myriad patterns on the surface of the ocean — that their infinitely complex overlappings create.

These patterns are not restricted to their physical or material confines but stretch out infinitely into the surrounding medium. In other words, the body's energy field extends into the space beyond what we see as its physical limits. Although the potency of the field falls off quite rapidly as one moves away from the body, the field is always there — it has no limits and is detectable given sufficiently sensitive instruments.

An instrument called a SQUID magnetometer has revolutionized the whole area of inquiry.[2] The SQUID has made it possible to image the presence of the body's electromagnetic (or biomagnetic) field and to transfer the information to another medium and permanently record it. Newer instruments can not only measure but also analyze the fields, producing a readout on a computer screen that can then be used to suggest homeopathic or other vibrational treatment regimens.

Despite the subtlety of its design and instrumentation, there is much more to the body's biomagnetic field than is apparent from the SQUID or the newer instruments. Wondrous as these devices may be, there is no substitute for acute human sensitivity. To experience oneself and others as energy is to initiate transformation and harmonization — without external aids or prescriptions.

THE SHAPE OF THE FIELD

Wisdom traditions — whether from ancient India, Asia, North America, Africa or Europe — all refer to several kinds or densities of energy in and around the body that become subtler as they extend out into space, just as the planet's atmosphere becomes thinner the farther one is from Earth.

---

2   The SQUID, or Super Conducting Quantum Interference Device, was developed by J.E. Zimmerman in the 1970s. It is sensitive to extremely small energy fields.

Most traditions speak of these densities as layers, or fields, or bodies of energy. The physical body stands at the centre, the least subtle and most visible of the fields. Next, the etheric or energy body is an energetic double of the physical body that extends a few inches from the visible surface of the body. Beyond that is a protective layer that Chinese medicine refers to as the *wei qi*. Beyond this is the astral body — a more rarefied field still, extending several feet from the body, that interpenetrates the physical, etheric and protective planes. This field is often called the aura and it has been described as a cocoon-like oval or egg of coloured light that is responsive to desires and emotions.

Beyond the aura are even more rarefied fields — the mental realm of thoughts, memories and ideas (known in Chinese medicine as *Heart yang*), the soul or Atman (known as *Heart yin*) and finally the causal level, some of whose names are Brahman, Absolute Spirit, God, Sat-Chit-Ananda and the Tao (Dao).

The aura forms the bulk of the detectable biomagnetic field and so is the one that naturally attracts most of our attention and interest. This field radiates out of the top of the head and circles around to enter the feet — somewhat like the magnetic field around a magnet. If we could see the lines of force, it might look something like the picture in figure 1.

ENERGY CENTRES

The cocoon-like image in figure 1 is not the smooth, homogeneous field the picture might suggest. Within it are energy foci — areas of high-energy intensity — that remain remarkably consistent in their location. The best known of these centres are the chakras, which run up the front of the body from the perineum to the crown of the head or just above it (see figure 2).

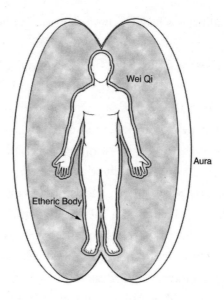

Figure 1: The general shape of the body's energy field

Most systems recognize seven main chakras, as follows:

1. The first, or ground, or root, chakra — located in the perineum
2. The second, or sexual, chakra — just above the pubic bone
3. The third, or power, chakra — in the solar plexus area
4. The fourth, or heart, chakra — at the centre of the chest
5. The fifth, or throat, chakra — over the Adam's apple
6. The sixth, or forehead, chakra, or *third eye* — between and just above the eyebrows
7. The seventh, or crown, chakra — at, or just above, the top of the head

Of course, there are many more energy centres — probably an infinite number. For example, chakras have been described in such places as the palms and soles, over the spleen (in the left upper abdomen), over the elbows and the knees, and so on. Such centres

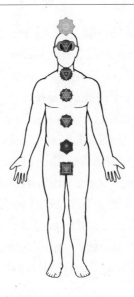

Figure 2: The seven chakras

have been noted, mapped and grouped in many traditional medicines. In Ayurveda they are collectively called *nadis* and in Chinese medicine, they are the acupuncture points.

THE HEART AND THE HEAD

SQUID recordings have shown that the heart and the brain radiate the largest electromagnetic fields in the body. Consequently, they are generally regarded as the main informational field generators that, like metronomes, set the rhythms or frequencies that organize the wave patterns in the field.

But of the two, it is the field around the heart that is stronger — several thousand times stronger, in fact.[3] This remarkable finding means that our hearts, not our brains, are the energetic centres of

3 To put it into actual figures, the field around the heart measures 50,000 femtoteslas (a measure of electromagnetic field intensity) while the field around the brain is only in the region of 10 femtoteslas.

our bodies. (As noted at the end of the introduction, readers should be aware that it is the Heart's energy field — not the physical heart — we are talking about, an important difference).

The energetic primacy of the Heart centre is a core assumption of the five-element tradition of Chinese medicine, which I will go into in more detail later. So it is interesting to see that modern science may again be confirming the intuitive knowledge of millennia. Nevertheless, one of the hallmarks of the last few hundred years of Western civilization has been a shift away from the Heart — in the sense of intuitive understanding — toward the head, in the sense of logical or analytical understanding. As we shall see later, this shift from feeling-thought to analysis lies hidden behind many modern diseases.

The difficulty — aside from the waste of the Heart's intelligence — is that the brain is not suited to the task of directing our destinies. The brain is able to plan, to think through mathematical problems and make practical, day-to-day decisions, but it does not have the strength to grasp the entirety of our spiritual and emotional selves, which extend far beyond the visible limits of time, space, flesh and bone — that whole I refer to in this book as the field. Indeed, if the brain tries to imitate or replace the rich, broad sweep of intuition's understanding with its step-by-step reasoning and its deductive logic, it will simply exhaust itself; and sooner or later, it will stop functioning.

This energetic depletion of the brain, brought on by our habit of thinking in circumstances where feeling and intuition are called for, may well be creating a precondition for degenerative brain diseases such as Alzheimer's and dementia. If at the same time, the vibrational function of the heart is suppressed and the Heart energy congested, this may create a precondition for coronary artery disease. Perhaps tellingly, both these conditions are almost epidemic in modern Western culture.

COHERENCE, ENTRAINMENT AND THE MEISSNER EFFECT

Many people who have lost connection to their Heart — to their intuition, to their emotional intelligence, to their spirit and to their compassion for themselves — become chronically ill. Re-connecting to Heart is crucial to healing for these people. In fact, it is often all that is needed to begin a healing journey and must ordinarily come before all else, for lack of access to the Heart's enormous energy leaves the body's self-healing responses starved for sufficient energy to do their work. And where a strong Heart centre promotes balanced energy in our bodies, allowing the field to gradually reach coherence, too much energy in our heads renders our energy field fragmented and incoherent.

Meditation can have profound effects on the energy field and can lead to the unlocking of the Heart centre. Regular practice leads to increasing field awareness and coherence through a process of coupling or entrainment of various body rhythms. Entrainment is the tendency of vibrational phenomena to adopt the same or related frequencies when they are near one another. A familiar example of this can be found in the grandfather clock phenomenon: the tendency for adjacent clocks to adopt the same frequency. And musicians are familiar with resonance: the tendency of one string to vibrate in harmony with an adjacent string.

The development of coherence in the physiology leads to a remarkable phenomenon known in physics as the Meissner Effect, in which the energy field shows an increasing resistance to outside interference that can seem almost miraculous. However, it is not so much a miracle as an observable property peculiar to highly ordered systems — an example of which is superconductance, a phenomenon observed when semiconducting crystals are brought into a highly ordered state by being cooled to very low temperatures. And biological systems such as ours are chock-full of semi-conducting systems. So it is perhaps no surprise that such coherence can bring about increased well-being, a strengthened immune system and a remarkable resistance to disease. In Chinese medicine and in the martial arts, this super-resistant, coherent energy state is called *zhen qi* (or true *qi*, or energy).

FEELING YOUR ENERGY FIELD

It is actually not difficult to feel the energy field around your body. Almost everyone can feel some heat coming off their hands or other parts of their bodies, though few will realize that it is their body's energy field they are feeling. Of course, the field does not only manifest as heat. There are other sensations that can take more practice to recognize. Some common ones are tingling, shaking, hot or cold sensations, and magnetic attractions and/or repulsions.

If you put your hands in front of you, palms facing each other, four to six inches apart, then move your hands gently back and forth or side to side, you may feel a magnetic sensation, or an odd feeling of pulling pizza dough. It can take a few tries to get this sensation but almost everyone eventually feels it. If necessary, the sensations can be amplified by rubbing your hands together a few times, massaging the palms or taking a few deep breaths.

FEELING YOUR ENERGY FIELD INTERNALLY

Internally, the field is accessed through the sense of touch. And again, it is relatively easy for most people to feel the field this way. Sustained attention to internal sensations of movement and change reveal minute currents of flow, tingling and shimmering. The increased awareness of the field engendered through such attention makes the field real, expanding our awareness from a simple game with the hands to a profound experience of life itself, in whatever form, *as* an energy flow.

If you close your eyes for a moment and pay attention to the sensations in your body, you will get a taste of what I am talking about. There is a general sense of presence and, within that presence, you will notice places of tension, aches or pains, itches, little irritations and whatnot. As you tune in to this informational matrix, you may notice a fluidity, a sense of change, fluctuation and flow, a world of constant movement. You are experiencing your body as a field of energy. What appeared objectively as structure now appears subjectively as a field of energy, or mind. You will immediately notice that body and mind are not separate but simply different modes of perception: if we look (objective perception), we see the body; if we feel (subjective perception), we experience mind.

CYTOSKELETON AS VIBRATIONAL APPARATUS

Notwithstanding their ultimate oneness, energy fields and the physical structures we use to do the shopping and walk the dog are clearly different orders of reality. So, what is the relationship between energy and structure? Cell biologists increasingly regard the body as an energy transmitter or a carrier of vibrational information. They talk of a cytoskeleton — the body's bone and myofascial structure[4] — which has the ability to transmit or carry a variety of different wave forms. And the brain, the organ we generally regard as a thinker and organizer, they see as

4 Myofascial is a term used to refer collectively to the body's muscle (*myo*) and connective tissue (*fascia*).

a kind of transducer that creates three-dimensional pictures out of the interference patterns in the field. In other words, the brain interprets the field to produce images of a three-dimensional reality, which we then take to be real.

More exciting still is their idea that the tissue cytoskeleton is really a whole system matrix whose fibres percolate everywhere in the body. It appears that fascial tissue is not just a useless artefact of muscular packaging but rather is a continuous system capable of transmitting vibrational information everywhere in the body — right down to the intracellular compartments and the DNA. In other words, the cytoskeleton is intimately involved in the coherence and entrainment phenomena previously mentioned.

The implication is this: the body is an integrated system — a receiver, a recorder and a carrier of vibrational information, the interpretation of which is our reality, and the totality of which is the field.

HOW THE FIELD INFLUENCES STRUCTURE

Every experience, whether physical, mental, emotional or spiritual, has a vibrational influence on the field. Everything that has ever happened is registered, even the smallest thing. Whatever can be allowed to flow freely will create minimal lasting disturbance. However, trauma is often resisted and such resistance can increase the depth and intensity of the vibrational impact on the field. Any obstruction to the free flow of a wave sets up an energy trap: the obstructed wave must somehow be accommodated by the structure if it is to be contained.

For example, following trauma, mechanical energy flows away from the site of impact — like a wave on the surface of our hypothetical pond — as a vibration throughout the cytoskeleton. If the individual resists the free flow of energy by, for example, bracing against the impact, the kinetic energy of the impact is stored as potential energy in the myofascial tissue and experienced as tension. Since the tension arises from the impact, its perpetuation can be understood as body or cellular memory. The greater the trauma, the more likely it is that experiences remain on permanent record as mechanical deformations. Over time, these deformations lead to observable changes of body structure, including the restricted flexibility and reduced resilience often interpreted as due simply to ageing.

Emotional traumas and unexpressed feelings can get stored as well. For example, chronically held fear, grief or anger often leave people with characteristic attitudes and behaviours. We will explore this idea further in a subsequent chapter but, for the moment, let us just note that restricted emotions lead to restricted physical movement in such a way that the emotion is visibly and palpably somatized, or embodied. Over time, the expression of the emotion becomes blunted or distorted until, eventually, people can no longer feel the emotion at all, experiencing it instead as a physical symptom that may then be interpreted as a disease.

Thus, disease and chronic pain arise as the result of layers of energetic experiences superimposed over time on our unique individual natures and constitutions. Unfortunately, our society often encourages us to leave whatever trauma we encounter unexplored. And because most of us are also unaware of our habitual emotional repressions, we tend to disown our symptoms as intrusive, senseless, mysterious or cruel.

But it has been said that a problem can never be solved at the level at which it manifests, and nowhere is this truer than in the case of chronic pain (and many other chronic illnesses). No matter what we do, such illnesses repeatedly defy a solution at the physical level, which is the arena of conventional medicine. To meet the challenge, we must remember ourselves, return to the deeper levels of mind and heart and spirit where illness first arises as an energetic distortion, long before it ever appears on the physical level. When we are willing to honour our symptoms in this way, and return our attention to the field (or energy body), then a door opens to a different and powerful approach, to the extraordinary potential of working directly with the field.

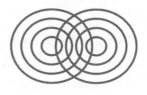

CHAPTER 2

FRAGMENTATION OF THE FIELD

Through the process of Maya, of dualistic thought, we introduce illusory dualities or divisions, creating two worlds from one. These divisions are not real, but only seeming, yet man behaves in every way as if they were real.

— Ken Wilber

*F*ragmentation of that luminous integrity of the body-mind-spirit we have been referring to as the field is unfortunately so common in the West it is nearly the norm. How did this come to be? Our cultural assumptions — which confuse the important psychological process of *individuation* with the political notion of *individualism*, narrowly understood as a kind of stoic self-reliance and competitiveness — pervert our understanding of our place in the world and in community almost before we take our first step and often remain as the foundation on which the rest of our lives are built.

In other words, our destiny may be shaped, as the ancient text puts it, before the cloth for our first garment is cut. Our wholeness is fractured by the assumption that our individual identity is based on our separateness and uniqueness. This belief is so pronounced in the West that we perhaps need look no further than our Freudian egos for an explanation of our angst. And, while Chinese medicine does address various blocks and separations between mind and spirit, mind and heart, or mind and body, I sometimes wonder whether the ancients ever imagined the degree to which those blocks would one day be inscribed in the bedrock of a culture.

The Westerner's strong ego, combined with his materialist understanding of his body as a machine, to be repaired like a machine, has contributed to our disconnection from and misunderstanding of our bodies at all levels. That is why our healing quests must generally begin with a defragmentation process so that we begin to feel our bodies and our symptoms more fully and less fearfully, and so that we begin to connect with our bodies' innate healing potential.

After all, if our health is reliant on a balanced and smooth flow of energy, it is important that we be aware of the presence or absence of that quality of energy in ourselves. If we have become so distanced from our bodies that we cannot feel these flows at all, we face a daunting task in attempting to integrate and balance ourselves.

Unbalanced and unintegrated energies create what are known as blocks both in energy medicine and in psychotherapy. These blocks are many and diverse and will vary from person to person in location and severity, of course. However, as a society, and as human beings whose minds tend to work by differentiation and objectification, we position ourselves to live out the implications of some very profound, but ultimately artificial, divisions, to the detriment of our bodies, our minds and our spirits. So, for example, while health and illness or good and bad can certainly be differentiated in our minds, they are never absolute in our lived experience but part of a continuum. Fixation on attributes and a lack of appreciation for the greater whole is ultimately what distorts the smooth flow of *qi*.

These artificial dualities, blocks or splits have been noticed and broadly classified by Western thinkers who follow in the footsteps of those ancient geniuses of energy medicine in the East, whose work we are only beginning to be able to appreciate. In the West, the blocks are usually defined as: *existential, life/death, mind/body* (and sometimes, more broadly, *mind/nature*) and, finally, *personal/ shadow*. I will explore these four in this chapter. Two others — *love/sex* and *Heart/Mind* — are often left out of this classification. I will discuss them as separate phenomena, however, because I believe strongly that their impact on health is significant.

THE EXISTENTIAL DUALISM: ALIENATION FROM PARADISE

The existential dualism is so fundamental in us that it seems to emanate from the very depths of our Western minds and haunts our most potent myths. For example, the Old Testament book of Genesis resonates through our assumption that our physical birth is an alienation from the primeval Eden of the womb to an outside in which it is necessary, as an act of self-defence, to build an ego, a separate self.

That this sense of birth as an exit from paradise is not universal is shown by contrasting it with Taoism, which sees no possibility of such an outside. On the contrary, the Tao is all-encompassing; and humans simply take the place of the primal *chong qi*, which mediates the seamless flow of energy between Heaven and Earth, or *yin* and *yang*, in which everything is connected to everything else.

The price of valuing ourselves as separate individuals, it seems, is that we are made to feel the subtle terror of our separation from our first moments until our last. The downside of our excessive self-consciousness and tendency to make distinctions — as Genesis illustrates so well in its story of our arrival at the knowledge of good and evil — is alienation, exile from paradise, angst, hardship and toil, and the fear of hunger, violence, strife and death. If, on the other hand, instead of considering ourselves to be born into an alienated state, we knew ourselves to be truly part of a larger, interdependent whole, we might be able to let *qi* flow smoothly in and around us.

But the sense of alienation and uncertainty at the core of our being is for most of us no abstract philosophical tenet. It makes itself felt in daily life as a persistent low-level unease some have called *existential anxiety*. Few of us escape it. In my opinion, it lies behind many of our epidemic chronic illnesses: from addictions to insomnia to depression. The tragedy is that the anxiety we suffer and try to escape — through addictions, medications and perhaps even depression itself — is in fact our very life current. It is painful because we misinterpret it as a threat to our egos and resist it at every turn. No doubt much of our frenetic, stress-inducing daily activity has its origin in this angst. Seeing problems wherever we look, we act to fix whatever we think is wrong.

It seems to me that the resisted energy we all hold in some degree is likely the origin, when it reaches critical proportions, of chronic illness; and if that is true, then any approach that ignores or tries to medicate or suppress this existential angst is bound to fail in the long run. On the other hand, it is astonishing to watch troublesome symptoms spontaneously resolve when the sufferer learns how to surrender to, rather than resist, the flow of her life current.

Angst, stress, seeing problems instead of accepting *what is* all disrupt the natural flow of *qi* through us and around us. *Qi* then flows erratically, or becomes distorted in some way. Repressed in the body, this distortion blocks or stagnates energy flows, leading to the condition known in Chinese medicine as *stagnant qi*. At the other end of the spectrum, excessive activity generated by anxiety wastes available energy and eventually leads to exhaustion — a condition known as *empty fire*, or *deficient yin*.

Briefly put: *Energy flowing creates wellness and a sense of well-being; energy resisted creates illness and anxiety.*

℞ *MEL*: LIFE IS A PROBLEM

Mel was a fifty-five-year-old psychotherapist who had wanted to come to a residential session to work on his depression. Although much of his career had been devoted to helping people clarify their thoughts and feelings and resolve their existential angst, he was anything but clear or integrated himself. Almost before he sat down in our initial interview, he presented me with a written description of his condition that included symptoms such as chronic hopelessness, fear, paranoia, alienation and the inability to feel joy.

Mel had probably had more therapy than most of us but, perhaps because of his training, he was convinced he still 'had a problem' and felt he had no choice but to keep working to fix it. Despite twenty years of what seemed to him failed cures, he had never entertained the possibility that nothing could cure him because nothing was wrong, that there was no problem — other than his own life-distorting conviction that there was one.

For whatever reason, Mel never came to work with us. Perhaps he took up the suggestion that he stop seeing his life as a problem and had no more trouble. But I doubt it. Existential angst does not usually yield to such simple solutions, even though the solution really is that simple. For most people, it takes many years to break the strange hold of illusion, or *Maya*, which holds us trapped in alienation. I trust that, in time, Mel will find what he is looking for.

THE LIFE / DEATH DUALISM

One manifestation of our sense of alienation or disconnection from wholeness is our fear of death. Nearly as soon as we realize we exist as a separate entity, we realize we must die. So, although we often choose to ignore or deny it for as long as possible, the stark inevitability looms larger as life goes on; and as we get older, our fear of death can often dwarf any actual illness we might be suffering from.

Sadly, this fear of death sets the stage for the nightmarish eleventh-hour deathbed interventions and their attendant moral dilemmas which characterize modern medicine like nothing else. Our hospitals are full of death-defying medicines and machines and these are in demand daily by anxious patients, their families and their physicians (who also tend to deal with death by avoidance and denial, cloaking their fear in the profession's oath to preserve life at all costs). I found this denial very difficult to accept during my training but, not daring to question authority as a student, I often found myself involved in life-saving actions, many of which I found morally repugnant — such as violent and useless attempts at cardiac resuscitation on elderly patients — simply because no-one was able to let them go, to face what we call *the end*.

Fear of the end is often foreshadowed in our younger years by an inability to let go — of objects, ideas, projects, relationships, status — in the normal ebb and flow of life. Instead, our life energy is dammed up, as if to hold it might be a means of preserving it. Unfortunately, it is just the opposite. Without vital flow, yang energy becomes separated from yin and the flow back to yin is also blocked, which only increases anxiety and jeopardizes our health. As yin becomes deficient, the body-mind suffers increasing anxiety (or, as mentioned above, what Chinese medicine calls *empty fire*), while the inability to let go gives rise to energy stagnation.

Going largely unrecognized, these two factors loom larger with increasing age, and contribute to the depression, obsessive states and bowel problems often seen in the elderly. When patients and their physicians focus on suppressing these symptoms and ignore the underlying energetic imbalance, their interventions are at best stopgaps or diversions.

℞ *BROCK*: A LIFE/DEATH SITUATION

Terminal cancer provokes the fight and flight response like possibly no other diagnosis. That is fight *and* flight — rather than fight *or* flight — as what is customarily called fighting the cancer is usually in fact trying to run from it.

I recall Brock, a First Nations abuse counsellor, who came to my office one day with a pleural effusion (a build-up of fluid around the lungs) caused by secondary tumours from a cancer whose primary site was unknown. He had been told that there was no treatment available to him and was desperately looking for alternatives. The only thing conventional medicine had to offer him was a trial regimen involving Taxol — an antineoplastic derived from the Pacific yew. Although well aware of the minuscule five-year survival rates for someone in his situation, Brock insisted he was going to beat the disease.

As we talked that first morning, he told me a remarkable story. Some years earlier, he had made friends with a band elder who had encouraged him to take part in a ritual that involved, among other things, making a traditional Native medicine from the Pacfic yew. Because collecting the bark was part of the ritual, Brock had scoured a forested area for the rare tree and eventually found a couple of specimens. However, as he approached them, he had been overcome by an inexplicable anxiety that had stopped him in his tracks.

Not sure what to do next, Brock felt he should ask permission from the trees to proceed, and ask it from a place of vulnerability and surrender. So without a second thought, he took off his clothes, plunged into a nearby river and asked, 'May I take some of your bark?' To his enormous surprise, an answer came back immediately: 'Yes, you must take some now!' And with the reply he felt a kind of inner explosion that confounded him completely.

After a few days, Brock put his strange experience aside and thought little more of the yew trees. Perhaps it was just too much for him; perhaps he was working with it more deeply than he knew. In any case, the episode had been absent from his conscious mind until we talked. I remember the room going silent for a moment as the significance of his story sank in for both of us. Brock had distinctly heard, many years before his cancer was discovered, the yew trees practically pleading with him to use their bark — the same bark that is used to make the cancer drug Taxol — as medicine. In the end, I suggested that Brock go back to the elder rather than work with me and see what he could do to further integrate his experiences by meditating on death.

I saw him a few months later, two weeks before he died, and found him in an astonishing state of grace, grateful for his life and looking forward to whatever was coming next.

THE MIND / BODY DUALISM:
BODIES SHOULD BE SEEN AND NOT HEARD

For many of us, identity feels like a little man or woman located somewhere behind our eyes, a Wizard of Oz figure operating the machinery of our bodies like a puppet. Perhaps it is our tendency to recognize each other and ourselves by our faces that leads us to lodge our sense of identity in our heads. From the safety of our cerebral observation post, we gaze out at a threatening world and try to figure out how to stay safe.

Unfortunately, this *self* in our heads comes to understand everything, including the body it rides around on, as foreign territory, and a dumping ground for energies it cannot deal with. The ego views the body as a shaky foundation and at the same time displaces its free-floating anxiety there. And because it feels in the body all that it cannot acknowledge, its suspicion and alarm at the unreliability of the body increases with every little symptom.

It is a classic vicious cycle: we fear the symptoms that threaten the self we have isolated in an indistinct area of our heads, when they are in fact the language of our body-mind trying to communicate important information. Moreover, once the ego decides that the body's language cannot be trusted — denying the unflattering reflection of itself there — it cuts itself off from the body as much as possible, disrupting and preventing communication through muscular armouring.

So we sit in our heads and divert, contain and dissociate energies in such a way as to guarantee we never have to feel pain or anxiety. And unfortunately, the strategies work. Cut off from the physical body, the ego imagines it is truly separate and self-sustaining.

In other words, if I refer to my body as 'me' but distrust its sensations, its language, its needs; if I say 'my body' but do not experience the body as a part of the 'I', it's a very convenient place to dump my grief, fear, rage, anxiety, shame, guilt and sorrow. I have then only to suppress my awareness of the movement of these energies in it and they appear to be gone. By the time I get sick from this dissociation, I am genuinely puzzled at my misfortune, which seems to fall upon me like a bolt out of the blue.

THE MIND / NATURE DUALISM:
NATURE WITH A CAPITAL 'N'

Echoing and amplifying the mind/body block is the mind/Nature block — Nature meaning roughly not-us, whatever we have neither created nor owned. We tend to spell this Nature, tellingly, with a capital 'N', as if it were a discrete object, nearly another being, whereas in fact it is what is — it is all around us, is us. As nothing comes of nothing, we can be quite sure there is nothing that exists outside this Nature — even machinery, which we like to exempt from nature, still works in gravity, in air, via electrical, petroleum or other energy derived from nature. This mind/Nature, or self/Nature dualism allows us to knowingly pollute the Earth that sustains us; and to passively witness the abuse and despoiling of that Earth by others and feel powerless, without authority to stop it.

COMPARTMENTALIZATION:
THE ORIGINAL PANDORA'S BOX

Now that we have glanced at some of the major blocks, I want to take a quick look at one of the chief strategies we use to contain difficult or forbidden energies. After cutting the mind from the body, the ego, like a skilful surgeon, begins by a process of *containment* and *dissociation* to, in a sense, cut the body off from itself in a desperate attempt to further distance its own anxiety.

To do this, the ego constructs body-mind compartments: mental and physical walls of tension built to resist the movement of forbidden energies. The body armour we mentioned earlier is a good example. A block at the level of the neck and jaws represents a manifestation of the mind/body dualism; three further bands — in the pelvis, the diaphragm and the upper chest/shoulders — demarcate the areas known in Chinese medicine as the *triple-heater*, or *three body heaters* (or *jiao*s). Each zone has its own kind of energy (or heat): the pelvic zone contains the energies of sexuality, urinary function and defecation. The mid-zone contains the diaphragm and digestive energies. And the upper zone contains the heart and lungs — the heart energy being the mediator of the body's field, while the lung energy connects us to the outside through the breath.

To further complicate this picture, a traumatic experience will superimpose its own compartment, or restricted area, on any preexisting one. For example, an arm injury may lead to a containment/dissociation phenomenon in which the entire limb is first compartmentalized and then summarily dissociated from our sense of self. Since zones of tension contain different psychic as well as physical energies, they can enable the existence of distinct personas within a single individual.

For example, someone with habitual pelvic tension may have contained and compartmentalized her sexual energy there. Once this is accomplished, her sexual energy will only be accessible to her through an altered state of consciousness, or distinct persona. Although at first glance this may sound extreme and outlandish, from an energetic perspective, such splitting of psyche and soma is common. One way or another, significant mind/body or body/body blocks are present in almost everyone and, in fact, nearly all of us have multiple selves, each dependent on a particular context for its expression.

The hallmark of these blocks is an undue suspicion of bodily symptoms, combined with a desire to figure out what is wrong. Sometimes the compartments can be identified by differences in body temperature on either side of the tension bands. In an extreme mind/body dualism, the head and neck may be hot to the touch while the rest of the body is distinctly cold. Severe headaches or migraines also seem to describe or call attention to the situation of energy trapped in the head. Blocks in any zone will produce altered sensation across the block, with symptoms above, below, inside or outside the block.

Addressing the mind/body block requires more than just opening it in the course of a therapeutic session: it requires that we understand how we contain and dissociate energies. To do this, we have to take responsibility for ourselves, our emotions and our habitual repressions. Without such understanding, we will simply re-establish the energetic configuration that is most familiar, the status quo.

Like it or not, if mind and body are one, then a symptom is not something we have but something we are. Energetically, we do not get or have an illness as something extrinsic and extra, *we are the illness*.

☋ *KAREN*: MIND OVER MATTER

Karen was a long-time Vipassana (insight meditation) practitioner who came to us complaining of feeling chronically nauseated and dizzy, especially while meditating.

When we began working together, I asked her what would happen if she trusted her body's impulse to move around and around, instead of fighting it. She was surprised but very open and said she was willing to try anything. After taking a few deep breaths to loosen her perception and alter her consciousness a little, Karen began to move in a circular fashion, arms, legs and torso circling rhythmically, responding to an inner compulsion she had resisted, she told us later, for fifteen years. After a few moments, she stood up and began to sway and dance, her arms moving round and round in front of her, looking for all the world like they were stirring a cauldron. This went on for at least ten minutes, after which she collapsed in a heap, her nausea and dizziness totally abated.

It was great to work with someone so open. Karen immediately saw that her mind/body block had been expressed in both a conscious and an unconscious use of her mind to resist her body's impulses and its expression, as if that were the mind's sovereign task in meditation.

This is a common issue with meditators in the West who tend to assume — perhaps because of our culture's inherent biases — that the body is superfluous, inferior and works against achievement in meditation if not rigorously suppressed. (Our understanding is often clouded by what we see, or think we see; and what we think we see in meditation is a static body rigorously controlled by the mind. This is especially unfortunate as meditators and teachers from India to Tibet to Japan have explicitly understood meditation as at least in part a body practice.)

Delighted by her discovery and quite willing to further explore the new whirling meditation she had discovered within her, Karen readily agreed to add a short period of spontaneous movement — a sort of dynamic meditation — to her daily spiritual practice and so open up to her body as a mind.

THE PERSONA AND ITS SHADOW:
JEKYLL AND HYDE AM I

One reason we like to think of our minds and bodies as separate is that it allows us to maintain the illusion that we are guiltless, allowing us to blame something outside ourselves for our ills, to attack that cause with righteous zeal and lament the injustices of life. Such an approach has worked quite well in the case of many infectious diseases, which may be why the germ theory remains so popular today — although Chinese medicine and homeopathy, among many other medical traditions, address infection without reference to it — and why we seem to take antibiotics for every little thing.

The difficulty is that by insisting we are separate from our bodies, we set the stage for an adversarial approach to illness. By maintaining the illusion of a mind/body dualism, we can blame microbes and allergens for attacking us and making us ill, blame our bodies for failing us and our politicians for betraying us, all the while maintaining that what manifests in our bodies and in our lives has nothing to do with us!

This kind of deferral or denial of responsibility leads us to yet another block, one between different parts of the ego itself, between the persona (the little person behind the eyes) and what Carl Jung termed the *shadow*.[1] The ego, needing to assert its own innocence, divides itself into what it approves (the persona) and what it does not approve (the shadow). The shadow material is then either repressed or projected[2] onto someone else.

This mechanism is so common in our society that people are often quite affronted by the suggestion that they might in any way be contributing to what is going on in their bodies. For example, I see many extremely angry people in chronic pain who do not realize how vastly their anger is contributing to their pain. They will frequently deny their anger while blaming everyone around them for their pain, and will quite often look at me incredulous if I so much as hint they might be the source of some of their own tension.

---

1 Jung described the shadow this way in *The Archetypes and the Collective Unconscious*: 'The shadow personifies everything that the subject refuses to acknowledge about himself and yet is always thrusting itself upon him directly or indirectly — for instance, inferior traits of character'; and this way in another text: '. . . the shadow [is] that hidden, repressed, for the most part inferior and guilt-laden personality whose ultimate ramifications reach back into the realm of our animal ancestors . . .'

2 *The Penguin Dictionary of Psychology* describes the term *projection* as 'a symbolic process by which one's own traits, emotions, dispositions, etc. are ascribed to another person. . . . Accompanying this projection of one's own characteristics onto another individual is a denial that one has these feelings or tendencies.'

The hallmark of a persona/shadow block is the deferral of personal responsibility. 'If the universe weren't out to get me, why do you suppose I have been so ill?' seems to pretty well sum things up for those who suffer from this block. They tend to believe that every symptom they have has an external cause (keep in mind that their ego has usually succeeded in externalizing the body itself) and will often expend much energy going after whatever they believe is the cause of their problem. If they cannot identify a cause, they will expect the doctor to find one for them and may get upset if she cannot come up with one — such as an infectious agent or allergen, or in cases of chronic pain, visible damage that might be amenable to surgery — that does not implicate them.

These remarks are not intended to be callous or judgemental. It is only natural for the ego to make a spirited defence of its blamelessness. However, what is often unclear is that it is not a matter of accepting blame. It is a question of taking control. In accepting responsibility for our health, we come to know ourselves as free agents, not victims, and shift control back to the self, where it belongs.

℞ DAVE: SHADOW ENERGIES & TRAUMATIC COMPARTMENTALIZATION

Dave was a thirty-five-year-old man who came to our residential clinic with chronic pain in the left groin. He had had at least five surgeries in the area. The first two were as a small child for an undescended left testicle. Then, as an adult, Dave had strained his groin at work and developed an inguinal hernia. His history included insertion of a protective patch over the hernia site (called a mesh), continuing pain, another operation and, eventually, removal of the mesh. Perhaps predictably, the pain continued. By the time I saw him, he had an attitude, and was hostile toward virtually everyone, including the Workmen's Compensation Board and his various physicians.

Dave's persona/shadow split involved repressed hostility. He had compartmentalized rage in his left leg and dissociated from it in order not to have to deal with his emotion. The energy flow between his upper and lower body was restricted and distorted by a major band of tension in the diaphragm. And he expressed his existential anxiety in his addictive use of cigarettes, anti-depressants and a variety of painkillers.

So, while my attention during our first few bodywork and acupuncture sessions was ostensibly focused on Dave's physical pain, my primary intention was in fact to try to help him connect to his rage. After a few sessions, during which we had achieved a bit of rapport, Dave indicated a readiness to explode. And he did. During his next, memorable session he went into an altered state and began to roar like a large cat, pawing at the floor as if he had claws and even tearing the mattress cover with his teeth.

When he had returned to normal consciousness and lay gasping in delighted amazement at the energies he had expressed, he let us know that it was the energy of a panther he had experienced filling his body and admitted he had always felt a profound affinity with the animal. Almost more remarkable to him was the sensation of his hostility melting into softness and warmth after the reintegration of such primal energies. The fullness and authenticity of his experience and the afterglow of the panther energy in his body made him suddenly intensely curious to know what else could be revealed and released in energy work. Our guy with attitude was now more than eager to plunge into his inner world, his anger and his pain.

To further reintegrate his mind and body and to help him trust the messages coming from his long-denied physical self, we next encouraged Dave to cultivate as rich a relationship as he could with his panther energy by learning about panthers and by looking at panther imagery wherever he could find it. As it turned out, Dave had any number of panther images at home, so he seemed well on his way.

However, impressive as it was, all this work might have been in vain if Dave did nothing to address his existential anxiety. His big release made him feel much better temporarily but he was so used to mistrusting his body, living life from a place of invalidism, that his illness had become his raison d'être, the creative expression of repressed rage and his self-definition. Without his symptoms, it was not long before he was plunged into major anxiety, as he began to contemplate his life.

THE EXISTENTIAL DILEMMA OF RENEWED HEALTH: OR, TO BE . . . THEN WHAT?

One fascinating thing about illness — rarely acknowledged — is that it absorbs our existential anxiety. It is a sad fact that the ever-present and often painful background anxiety, which is the much-ridiculed luxury of the healthy and the wealthy, often resurfaces when the symptoms that have been compelling our attention and our most basic survival instincts begin to wane and we are faced with — life.

Fortunately or unfortunately, improving health can bring this important crisis with it. Because the ego has structured its self-image around the problem of illness, from the ego's perspective health can look very much like annihilation. Here is the secondary gain of illness — a sticky issue if ever there was one. Faced with being well and the necessity of restructuring their identity as healthy and therefore able, rather than ill, many people retreat right back into their symptoms.

If a desire to heal is not bolstered by a willingness to encounter an authentic self and an authentic relationship to the world, we may allow the opportunity to tantalize us then slip between our fingers — often with a perverse sense of relief. Clear intent is crucial throughout what can be a long and arduous, even torturous, process of healing because all the powers of the ego tell us to turn back. Unfortunately, we must sit with our anxiety even though we really have no idea what is going to come out of the chaos. For some, who have built their identities, knowingly or unknowingly, on a different kind of suffering, the road can be too steep, as nothing less than transformation and rebirth is called for.

Dave, who had made dramatic and fulfilling contact with his repressed energies, found himself at just this crossroads. Initially ecstatic, he found his joy quickly giving way to an anxiety so intense that within days he had re-established his symptoms. Helping someone traverse this life crisis calls on a practitioner's greatest skill. Dave needed repeated experiences of free energy flow in a safe and supportive environment where he could revel in it rather than fear it or have to stifle it for fear of terrifying others. He had to dare to stop dissociating from his painful leg and to learn to trust the pain and the rage that it contained. And if he did this, his reward was to have to grapple with his angst, without reaching for pills and cigarettes to block his awareness of it.

Of course, each of these tasks, taken separately, is difficult enough. It is understandable that facing all of them at once can be overwhelming. But, in the long run, we all must climb our particular mountains on our own: resolving our various energy blocks is not something anyone else can do for us. Although others can certainly help by their compassion and presence, the way back from long-term illness or pain may demand of us that we make a spiritual commitment to ourselves that can survive a crisis of identity and a long walk into an unknown territory.

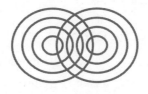

CHAPTER 3

QI AND BLOOD STAGNATION

When there is a severe conflict between the unique spirit of the individual and the ethical and spiritual values of his culture, the ego tends to stand in the way of union between the spirit and the flesh. This is essentially the condition in which modern man finds himself.
— Robert Stein

S tagnation of Qi? Stagnation of Blood? These diagnoses, so fundamental to Chinese medicine, can seem bizarre descriptions of irrelevant conditions to a Western-trained doctor. But, although I admit they struck me as arcane to say the least when I first encountered them, I have since come to appreciate the central importance of energy flows, energy stagnation and Blood stasis.

More than that, I have come to see that these traditional diagnoses are intimately related to the energy blocks we looked at in the last chapter. I now believe that the relationship between the archetypal forces deep in human consciousness, the different ways that energy flows — or does not flow — in our bodies and the way we manage existential anxiety is profound. Appreciation of this relationship may further deepen our understanding of how the body-mind's conscious and unconscious *dis*-ease manifests over time as illness or chronic pain.

WHAT IS STAGNATION?

Traditional definitions of stagnation can be found in any acupuncture text. *Qi stagnation* is generally defined as a situation in which the smooth follow of *qi* is stuck, leading to fluctuating pain, soreness or distension. *Blood stagnation* (sometimes called *Blood stasis*), which may be preceded by stagnant *qi*, is a deeper disharmony characterized by a fixed and stabbing pain. (See table 1.)

Syndrome	Symptoms	Tongue
Qi Stagnation	Pain, soreness, distension, which may come and go. Often changes in intensity and location. Soft lumps, which come and go.	Purplish
Blood Stagnation	Fixed stabbing pain — may be preceded by qi stagnation, cold, trauma or haemorrhage, fixed lumps.	Dark purple with red spots

Table 1: Symptoms and tongue signs of qi and Blood stagnation

To take it further, some authors maintain that *qi* stagnation occurs when our inability to fully process our emotional response to a life situation blocks the flow of our *qi*. Similarly, the more serious condition of Blood stagnation is said to arise when trauma is too painful to assimilate.

These deeper definitions are telling because they reach beyond the purely physical explanation and help us to see that the root of stagnation lies in consciousness itself. Briefly put, stagnation arises when we try to avoid feelings in the body we deem unpleasant. Let us explore why this might be so.

FILTERING AND DIVERSION

The energy field contains a vast range of energy vectors,[1] which are experienced as tendencies, feelings, thoughts and emotions. Of these, some are socially acceptable and some are not.

If we think of our *qi* flowing in rivers (known in Chinese medicine as *channels* or *meridians*), it is possible to imagine how our unacceptable energies are diverted to a kind of back eddy, or even a turgid subterranean *shadow river*. At the same time, if the diversion is sizeable, the main river's flow will lessen significantly — as a river slows and begins to become stagnant when its source is largely diverted or blocked.

Filtering and *diversion* refer to the mind's ability to block or redirect energy by discriminating between one feeling and another. The mind deems some energies appropriate and others inappropriate or unwanted and normally permits the flow of only those that the ego feels are acceptable in the moment. Either function may interfere with the natural flow of original energy, or *qi*, through the body-mind.

What is more, the diverted energy becomes a disposal problem. The mind blocks unacceptable energy by tightening muscles wherever it is felt. For example, we tighten the jaws, shoulders or stomach muscles to control anger we cannot express, tighten the chest to avoid sadness or grief, tighten the lower back to contain fear, and tighten our pelvis to control sexual energy.

To see how the ego's strategies proceed in particular situations, let us look at the energies of anger and fear.

---

1 The word *vector*, borrowed from mathematics, is being used here to denote the triad of movement, force and trajectory, characteristic of our feelings and emotions.

ANGER

Anger is a very powerful emotion and can be destructive, so it is small wonder the ego believes it must be contained. We usually learn when quite young to put a lid on it. To block its expression, we tense our shoulders and our necks and clamp our jaws as if literally biting our tongues. Unfortunately, however much we push the feeling down, the energy of anger remains and contaminates the whole energy field until it can be released.

While violent anger must be restrained, habitual suppression of the upward movement of energy leads to neck and shoulder tension. The increasing tension eventually materializes as discomfort or symptoms like migraine headaches, upper back pain, tempero-mandibular joint (TMJ) pain, asthma and hypertension; and, over a longer term, can be a factor in strokes, heart attacks and depression. In time, the body changes structurally too. Gradually, the chin goes forward and the shoulders become hunched as the upper back and neck stiffen. Occasionally, the suppressed energy will find its way into the stomach to produce an ulcer or gastritis.

FEAR

The movement of fear is very much the opposite. While anger moves up and outward, fear moves down and inward. Fear moves energy into the legs so that we can run from whatever is scaring us. And if we actually run, the energy is discharged and all is well. If we cannot run from a threatening situation, the pent-up energy will make our legs shake, tremble or quake. If we are chronically afraid and chronically unable to distance ourselves from what is fearful to us, we tend to control the flow to the legs by clamping the lower back and buttocks. Unfortunately, the energy of fear remains and contaminates the whole energy field until it is released.

Over the long haul, this can lead to a whole variety of chronic symptoms, including lower back pain, pelvic congestion, hemorrhoids, irritable bowel, constipation, prostate swelling and bladder or uterine and cervical problems.

THE MEANING OF SYMPTOMS

At the most basic level, pain or discomfort will generally indicate that we are holding tension in the area where it has manifested. (In fact, as we shall see in later chapters, much of the pain and discomfort we suffer arises from bracing against this original pain: tension exacerbating tension.) If these symptoms are considered distinct and treated in isolation from the rest of the body-mind — as is usually the case in conventional medicine — this underlying tension will remain and may be exacerbated by the removal of its means of expression. Or worse, the tension and the energy block it creates may be driven even deeper into the body where they will be even more difficult to feel, access and treat. The desensitization of our body-mind to the pain that is being expressed may provide relief in the short term but it is not good medicine.

It may seem simple to understand pain as blocked energy caused by tension but in fact denial of our tensions and blocks is often the biggest hurdle we have to get over during the healing process. Most of us are genuinely unaware of the amount of tension we are holding; our chronic tensions are so familiar to us we often cannot feel them as tension. Unfortunately, as long as we are unable to feel the tension we hold and acknowledge it, we can only look outside ourselves for the meaning of our pain; and can only look outside ourselves for a solution.

Chronic symptoms, then, may be read as whole, complex narratives of our emotional experience and response. As such, the energetic implication called to awareness by each symptom is far more relevant to the overall health of our body-mind than what-ever medical diagnosis the symptom might have attracted.

Once we admit we might be holding tension and that our symptoms are kindly telling us where it might be located, then we can begin the work of learning how to let the tension — and the symptoms — go.

CONTAINMENT AND DISSOCIATION

Containment and *dissociation* are terms that refer to the ways in which the body-mind tries to further manage and dispose of unwanted energy. Energy that has been filtered and diverted from the energy 'rivers' or meridians remains unacceptable and must be contained so that it cannot return to the flow. Then, if it is truly unbearable, it is treated as if it were not only waste but toxic waste. In other words, the existence of the dumpsite is disowned. Containment refers to the process of preventing the *qi* from returning to the flow and dissociation refers to the mechanism of denying the existence of the dumpsite. (To mix our metaphors grossly for the sake of another example, dissociation might be likened to solving a family mental illness by locking the madwoman up in the attic, or like assuaging community outrage by locking the unforgiveable crimi-nal up and throwing away the key).

If the dumpsite happens to be in an extremity such as an arm or a leg — as, for example, in regional pain syndrome — then the entire limb may be dismissed from the ego's sense of self. Such localization and sacrifice is clinically fascinating to witness, but it is a dysfunctional energy management strategy and in the long run, a tragic forfeit of life and feeling. For example, trauma survivors will frequently contain and dissociate from an injured extremity. One such woman I recall had electrocuted her hand in a live socket. She had a functioning arm as far as anyone could tell but she just would not use it and was even loathe to look at it. She explained that she did not like the arm. During dynamic interactive acu-bodywork (DIA), the arm would shake violently but before long she would visibly dissociate from it. It was almost as if someone had flipped a switch in her psyche and she just went off somewhere. A close examination of her arm revealed the telltale signs of Blood stagnation — coolness, prolonged blanching of the skin with pressure and a paradoxical combination of numbness and increased sensitivity to light touch.

It is increasingly evident that chronic pain and many chronic illnesses are based in just this sort of dissociation. And this is not as strange a proposition as it might appear at first, for contrary to popular thought, dissociation is not a rare or unusual phenomenon occurring only in people who have been severely traumatized. In fact, it is a capacity all of us have and with which most of us are familiar.

In acute, dangerous or life-threatening situations, dissociation is available as a built-in strategy our bodies can call on to remove the distraction of pain and enable extraordinary and sometimes heroic actions. But it may also be called upon in much less dramatic circumstances. Many people have had the experience of injuring themselves during vigorous physical activities, such as contact sports, without feeling any immediate pain. During intense physical or mental activity, we dissociate both to focus attention wholly on the task at hand and to permit the body to be pushed beyond its usual limits. If we are injured, we generally feel very little pain; later, consciousness slowly settles back into the body and the pain reveals itself.

In chronic illness, the same strategy works against us. Dissociation often begins with a simple physical or emotional adaptation — such as favouring an injured leg, or breathing less deeply — that stresses other parts of the body. However, when the parts of our system that are compensating for the dissociation become painful in their turn, further adaptation and favouring may occur, and if there is no reintegration of the dissociated part — if the injured leg is not used again; if the emotional situation that caused us to breathe shallowly is not resolved — or if there is no specific sacrifice, dissociation may engulf the whole body by degrees.

I often wonder these days whether total dissociation is not much more widespread than we imagine. If posed the question, many people I work with report feeling that they are never fully in their bodies. Although most have trouble putting words to their feelings, in various ways they let us know that they just never feel fully present. Hands-on work with such people confirms that their minds and bodies are dissociated much of the time. It is not that they are out of their bodies (as in near-death experiences when people can experience being above their bodies looking down, beyond their own pain and suffering). Rather, they are in their bodies, and can feel them, but as if at a slight distance. One woman's description was very apt: *there yet not there; present yet not present.*

COMPARTMENTALIZATION

Containment and dissociation are really two aspects of a strategic continuum that gives rise to various degrees of psychosomatic *compartmentalization*. If we seal off feelings and dissociate from the isolated area, we effectively form what might be called a psychosomatic cyst, an unglamorous kind of pearl intended to neutralize an irritant. The ego is then free to maintain its sense of identity by ignoring this cyst and its forbidden contents.

One fascinating variety of compartmentalization is the multiple personality disorder (MPD, now officially known as Dissociative Identity Disorder). In this disorder, whole personality gestalts become compartmentalized, so that different personalities, containing different blocked energies, exist as separate personas within an individual. These different personas can even have different physiological correlates — for example, different handwriting styles, drug responses, visual acuity and even symptoms.

It has long been recognized that people who are skilled at dissociation are more likely to have suffered severe childhood trauma. Such people may have very little body awareness, unrecognized MPD or other marked psychic disturbance. Because they are not fully present in their bodies, they tend to be accident-prone and/or to develop illnesses that resist conventional intervention. Further, such people have great difficulty with the healing process, which demands that they be present and aware, because that is the last thing they want to be.

Although multiple personalities and regional pain syndrome appear to be very different illnesses, they are both forms of compartmentalization. In MPD, compartmentalization occurs in *time* and in mental space (different personalities appear sequentially), while in regional pain syndrome, the compartmentalization occurs in *space*, in the body. At the end of the day, personality disorders and regional pain syndromes are just different expressions of the same disorder, which might be called *separation from a centre of authentic energy.*

Much more common than either of these extremes is a situation in which various compartmentalizations of mind and body (psyche and soma), or time and space overlap to produce complex psychosomatic cysts and varying degrees of *qi* and Blood stagnation. In practical terms, this means that the exploration of a somatic (bodily) pain compartment with acu-bodywork (DIA) will not uncommonly expose a psychic (mental or emotional) cyst. And this eruption of emotional material can, if it is intense enough, resemble a subpersonality. When such material is brought to consciousness and integrated, bodily pain can vanish, confirming the energetic interplay of psyche and soma.

DRUGS

When symptoms break through the containment/dissociation barriers unannounced and unwanted, people will generally reach for drugs, or worse, consider drastic irreversible interventions such as surgery. In this way, modern medicine gets dragged into the process of containment/dissociation and physicians become unwitting extensions of their patients' primitive ego strategies. Indeed, many drugs are designed to mimic the functions of containment and dissociation, for example, drugs that contain include anti-depressants (such as amitriptyline). Drugs that dissociate include opiates and anxiolytics.

The peculiar fact that anti-depressants are often effective in chronic pain is superficially puzzling. Physicians often assume that chronic pain patients are actually depressed and are manifesting their depression in their bodies. But a much more simple explanation is the energetic one: since breakthrough pain pushes people to look for increased containment, anti-depressants provide exactly that (people on anti-depressants often report that their feelings are better contained, they are less emotionally labile, more balanced or in control). And the increased containment often results in reduced pain perception, so long as people stay on the medication.

The opiates, on the other hand, often allow pain to be registered in the usual way but without the emotional charge. The experience has been described as dissociative bliss. Since Candace Pert discovered the opiate receptor in 1972 research has focused on how to use and improve upon the body's own endogenous morphine. Her research has implied that thoughts create molecules, which are the material equivalent of the thought. In other words, there is a direct correlation between thoughts and neuropeptides, between a particular thought and the creation of a particular neuropeptide. Thus, the endorphins — the body's own morphine-like molecules — are actually the neuropeptides that represent and carry out the thought of dissociation. We can and do *think* our own morphine.

Dissociative bliss has often been seen as a good thing. Researchers are always hoping to find a drug that will produce bliss without dependence and much chronic pain research has focused on endorphin production. But if endorphins produce dissociation, then more endorphins will only exacerbate the problem. For example, in research on Reflex Sympathetic Dystrophy (RSD), using rats, the opiate receptors were found to be maximally utilized. This means that in this particular form of chronic pain, the body's endorphin output may already be maximized — which is to say, the individual is already maximally dissociated. Surely, when pain is breaking through a state of maximum dissociation, it is time to try a different approach!

Anxiolytics help people dissociate from their existential anxiety, which perhaps explains why they are considered so addictive. In this case, the anxiety continues to accumulate even though it is not perceived and any attempt to come off the drug means confronting overwhelming anxiety — an experience that is often misinterpreted as withdrawal. In fact, people are just feeling their own anxiety again, albeit more intensely than before, since they have been dissociated from it for a while. Ironically, anxiolytics have the curious property of inducing a chronically agitated state in long-term users, thus producing precisely the symptoms they are taken to control.

REVERSAL

Any attempt to heal chronic illnesses must clearly involve tackling many kinds of blocks, denials and dissociations. Stagnant *qi* and Blood are markers of underlying ego strategies, and healing must involve bringing such strategies to the surface, examining them, and focusing intent on *de-containment, re-association* and *integration*.

Of the two stagnations, stagnation of *qi* is generally easier to work with, particularly if it is relatively recent. Since the energy is simply held in check, all that is really needed to allow the energy to flow freely again is to take the brakes off. Further, people with *qi* stagnation are not usually significantly dissociated and so tend to improve more quickly. Blood stagnation, however, is quite a different matter. Here, containment and dissociation must be fully appreciated as illness-maintaining ego strategies and flow cannot be re-established without a conscious decision by the individual to confront his or her own pain.

Re-associating can be painful. If you have ever slept on an arm, and woken to find it numb, you will know that allowing the blood to flow back into the arm can be exquisitely painful, and often one waits a minute or two to get psyched up for it. Multiply the intensity a hundredfold and you have some idea of what returning consciousness to a dissociated area of the energy field can be like. Further, skilled dissociators tend to have fragile egos that can easily be overwhelmed by the intensity of the material contained in their psychic cysts. When this happens, everyone gets thoroughly frightened and the sufferer quickly retreats to the safety of dissociation. All this can make for slow and protracted healing for dissociators, rife with fits and starts and setbacks. Often the most they achieve is a kind of stalemate — they are more present than before but that very presence means they are also present to whatever residual pain they hold.

There is no easy way around it. Awakening the sleeping dragon tends to be a scary — and risky — process.

FACING THE PAIN OF REALITY

One way to find the courage to re-enter painful areas is to realize that no matter what we might naïvely hope, there is no running from pain once it has arisen. Containment may allow us to control our pain, and dissociation may decrease awareness of it, but both exact a heavy price — and that price is usually pain in another form. Containment creates physical tension and a sense of being imprisoned while dissociation leads to physical deterioration and disability. After all, if we are a bag of tension, the body's flushing and vivifying energy flows are impeded, and if we are not present in our bodies, the body literally wastes away, as if cut off from its source.

Again, pain is a messenger and shooting the messenger is not a smart way to deal with its message. After all, the progression of an illness is not impeded when we stop listening to its urgent messages; quite the contrary. Why we take such an approach to illness is beyond my understanding these days. Yet the whole culture has colluded in such insanity and our medical system is founded on it.

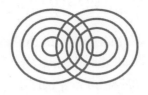

CHAPTER 4

TRANSCENDENCE AND TRANSFORMATION

There are three states only, the waking, dream, and sleep.
Turiya is not a fourth one; it is what underlies these states.
But people do not readily understand it.
Therefore it is said that this is a fourth state.

— Sri Ramana Maharshi

*T*here is a story in the *Mahabharata* about a young archer who trained himself to a high level using only the clay image he made of the renowned master who had turned the boy away as an apprentice because of his low caste. One day, years later, the story tells us, this same master was walking through the woods and chanced to glimpse a young man performing feats of archery the like of which he had never before witnessed.

He recognized the lad as the boy he had refused to mentor and at the same time realized that he was far more skilled than his own protégé. Cruelly, he then demanded the young man's right thumb in payment for the training he claimed the youth had received through the clay image of himself that he noticed the boy had with him. Without protest or hesitation, the boy bowed, severed his thumb and presented it to his guru, his devotion astonishing all who witnessed the act.

If such devotion and such cruelty seem remarkable, the import of the story is more so. Not only did the boy defy his supposed caste destiny to achieve all that the master could have taught him, and more. By simple devotion and hard practice, he was made a truly great archer by the cruelty and cunning of his guru's demand, and by his unhesitating sacrifice of the thumb that held so much hard-won skill.

The story goes on to tell how the lad's willing loss merely served to propel him beyond skill to genius — beyond skill of the body to skill of the spirit. The story ends with the triumph of the young man, who comes to prominence as one of the finest archers in the land, without his thumb. To this day, archers are often portrayed in Indian art with a ring on their thumb in honour of this story of the power of devotion, the transformation of a would-be student into his own teacher and the spirit's transcendence of mental and physical limitations.

In many ways, the story of the boy's determined journey to his heart's desire is also the story of every healing journey. In the end, we, like the young boy, can find no real help from gurus or doctors. Nor are we able to begin our healing journey while focused on what is impossible in our material circumstances (bad genes, or negative diagnoses that leave us with little hope, like an archer without a thumb). Like our young archer, whose birth into a low caste appeared an absolute barrier to the realization of his destiny, we must step around the 'impossible'. Alone in the woods, the story suggests, we, like he, have only to set our intention — embodied for the archer in the little clay image of his teacher — and devote ourselves without doubt to our goal.

Soon, our archer finds what a great teacher would have shown him: that ultimately we must look in our own hearts to find the teaching we seek. Curiously, not much later, the story reveals that the real-life guru whose teaching the boy wanted so badly is in fact a brutal, self-interested and unscrupulous man who, not incidentally, produces students of much less ability. How many of us have experienced something similar in looking to the godlike powers of the Western medical establishment to come to our aid!

In the end, the boy's final breakthrough comes when he understands that neither his archer's thumb nor his guru are truly central to the very high levels of understanding, intention, vision and skill he has cultivated in himself.

TRANSFORMATION AND TRANSCENDENCE

The processes of transformation and transcendence at the core of this story of technical prowess turning to genius are also fundamental to allowing ourselves to heal. Unfortunately, the terms *transformation* and *transcendence* have often been charged with religious or occult significance and so are frequently misunderstood or shied from. As I intend them in the context of this book, however, transcendence and transformation are actually everyday experiences in which there is nothing occult, mysterious or even uncommon — though there can be much that is surprising and even awe-inspiring.

Unfortunately, a lack of awareness will hinder our ability to recognize these occurrences. This is partly because our perception of all experiential phenomena is limited to what we have learned to see, learned to hear and learned to feel. That even our perceptions must be learned is a bit of a surprise to most of us but travellers who visit those very rare parts of the world where photographs are still not part of the everyday culture may find that people do not know how to read them — do not recognize the people, buildings or landscapes we see there as two-dimensional images of three-dimensional objects but instead see exactly what is there: a shiny, square, flat, coloured surface.

Although most of us have forgotten learning to translate two-dimensional colours and forms into three dimensions in order to *see* the information contained in a photo, we certainly do not lack for clues that this is what others are doing with the glossy square of coloured paper they are passing around. And because there was a time when all visual information that came to us was just as unorganized — infants take some time to learn how to interpret that mass of visual stimulus their eyes bring them — we have all the resources necessary to make this further adaptation in order to expand our perceptual abilities to see what we could not see before.

So, assuming that we could all use some increased sensitivity to the processes of transformation and transcendence that are a less tangible part of our lives, let us have a deeper look at these concepts in the hope that we might be able to more easily recognize them.

FRAGMENTATION AND ORIGINAL ENERGY

First, however, let us consider what we call *original energy*. Original energy might be defined as the unrestricted flow of energy we had before we started to limit it during the process of ego construction. Although much can happen *in utero* to compromise a fetus's energy system, we can normally assume that a newborn's movements and behaviours are largely unrestricted, in that babies generally do not consciously control or inhibit the natural flow of their energy.

Growing up changes all that. The process of ego development means containing and dissociating from unacceptable energies — anger, fear, inappropriate sexual urges and so on — and so we fragment and lose touch with much of our original energy. Accumulating outside consciousness, these forgotten energies go unnoticed, with the result that what we consider to be our normal, everyday, rational consciousness is in fact an active and complex state of denial — in that significant portions of our total energies are consistently denied expression. Although such a state may be considered 'normal' by society, it might more accurately be understood as a virtual illness — for at some point, the backed-up energies will almost certainly materialize as pain or disease.

Reintegration of this psychic fragmentation and its reflection in our bodies demands both transcendence and transformation. The journey from fragmentation toward a new integration involves becoming aware of previously unconscious energies (transformation, or shadow work) and bringing those energies into a larger whole (transcending the opposites). These closely related concepts can become confused, so it is important to make the distinction here: transformation refers to the rediscovery of lost energies but does not necessarily mean that these energies have been reintegrated; whereas transcendence refers to the integration of disparate energies but does not necessarily imply that *all* the available energies have been rediscovered and integrated.

LEVELS AND VECTORS:
A LITTLE MORE VOCABULARY

The phrase *body-mind-spirit* is often used to try to render the dimensions of human existence that are often slighted in references to the physical body. Each of the three components, body, mind and spirit, represent increasingly abstract aspects of our being and awareness and have therefore been depicted hierarchically by many philosophers, as if each were a different level in a vertical arrangement. For example, mind is often understood to be somehow above, or encircling the body, while spirit is understood to be higher than, or encircling the mind. However we speak of their supposed distinctions, it is important to remember that ultimately body-mind-spirit is one phenomenon, not three — is, in fact, three-in-one.

In addition, permeating the body-mind-spirit is an emotional (or astral) field that contains all manner of disparate feelings, tendencies and energies. These energies constitute the qi of Chinese medicine, or the prana of Ayurveda. As previously mentioned, to the extent that these energies exhibit movement, force and directionality, they might be called vectors which, in contrast to the body-mind-spirit hierarchy, differentiate themselves in a lateral — rather than vertical — plane.

With that understanding of levels and vectors, we could say that transcendence is a vertical integration of body-mind-spirit, while transformation involves a lateral shift in which new, previously unconscious, energetic vectors are experienced in a way that radically alters our perception of reality and of ourselves.

The two principles constitute a wholeness, a complementarity in which each implies the other just as yin implies yang. We can speak of them as distinct, understanding that our minds need, and enjoy making, these distinctions and that language demands them. But they are ultimately inseparable — because transformation is the foundation of transcendence; and transcendence is the means by which transformation becomes stabilized and integrated in consciousness.

CONTAINMENT/DISSOCIATION: THE SHADOW OF TRANSFORMATION/TRANSCENDENCE

Transcendence and transformation occur throughout our lives but the direction they take depends on whether we consciously accept, or unconsciously resist, them. To consciously embrace them is to increase field integration, which generally means better health. To reject them, on the other hand, means containment and dissociation, which, as we have seen, promotes chronic untreatable illness. In other words, we could say that containment and dissociation are the shadow side of transformation and transcendence.

Transcendence and transformation must work together like a kind of warp and woof. If, for example, we attempt transcendence before the mind/body or persona/shadow schisms have been brought to conscious awareness through transformational experiences, we are in danger of reaching a kind of intellectual pseudo-enlightenment while remaining, in fact, psychically and/or physically dissociated or disembodied, as if we had tried to weave a woof onto a nonexistent warp. People in this state may appear to be integrated, aware and grounded but their physical or psychic impairments speak volumes about how the psyche has dealt with its existential anxiety: in many cases, the ego has split itself from its foundation in the body entirely, sometimes leaving a deceptive appearance of equanimity.

ᘯ *ALICE*: TOO MUCH TRANSCENDENCE

Alice was a long-term meditator who came to us with chronic fatigue and asthma. She could not understand why these physical difficulties should have persisted unaffected through her long years of discipline and discovery as a meditator. She rarely raised her voice, appeared tranquil, even subdued, and said she felt calm. But her breathing was restricted, she was prone to asthma attacks and suffered from chronic fatigue: it seemed that something was being forcefully suppressed.

It gradually became clear to Alice as we worked that she was cut off from her body and lived almost entirely in her head. She had little access to her feelings, often not knowing what she was feeling or even *if* she was feeling. It turned out that during childhood she had learned to suppress her emotions and live from her head as a mechanism of survival. And it occurred to her as we worked that meditation, as she was practising it, was in fact a formalization of this strategy of subduing her feelings and letting her head take charge and so was of limited use in integrating her mind and body.

Alice had to work hard and long to reclaim what she had lost but she had the sincerity and spirit necessary to her task. Through many months of counselling and acupuncture, she slowly learned to feel again and to identify emotions she had not been aware she had. It was almost as if she had to relive her childhood, she said, and restructure her ego from the ground up. During this difficult period, Alice decided to stop meditating because she found that it had a negative impact on her progress, actually taking her away from the direct experience and response to experience she so desperately wanted. As of this writing her work continues.

Difficulties with transformation, on the other hand, may arise when individuals are caught between conflicting energy vectors that they are unable to integrate. People trapped in such conflicts may give the appearance of resolution by containing one or other of the energies. However, tension and stagnation, eventually precipitating as chronic pain, chronic fatigue and/or depression are the likely outcome. Others oscillate between the opposing energy matrixes, giving sequential expression to the various vectors but, again, without ever actually integrating them. This can produce movement disorders, multiple personalities, uncharacteristic behaviour, anxiety, insomnia or manic-depression.

ৡ KEVIN: TOO MUCH TRANSFORMATION
Kevin was a depressed seventy-year-old man with the classic symptoms of Parkinson's syndrome — continuous shaking and

muscular rigidity. He was stiff and tight but unable to stop moving. He fidgeted, his foot vibrated, he paced about, he changed position constantly. When he stopped for a few moments, his anxiety would increase dramatically and sooner or later a foot or a hand would begin to vibrate, or he would get up and begin to move restlessly about.

At first, his depression seemed especially hard to account for as he had done a lot of personal growth work, participated in healing groups, and had had many different kinds of bodywork. But seen in the light of our understanding of the transformation/transcendence dichotomy, his symptoms were very revealing. In Parkinsonism, there is a constant flux, constant oscillation but no centre of calm, no rest, no solid ground from which the movements might derive some meaning.

For some reason, Kevin had never seen much point in meditation. Transformation was what excited him and he had zealously pursued it throughout his life. Mulling this over, he and I wondered whether it could be that he had devoted his life to transformation but had undervalued transcendence so that, in time, the ceaseless transformations became involuntary and manifested themselves as a movement disorder that exactly mirrored his imbalance. At seventy, Kevin's many transforming life experiences remained unintegrated and he therefore felt his life had been a waste. No wonder he was depressed!

Kevin, too, had to work long and hard to find some healing. In contrast to Alice, who needed to get into her body and feel the energies moving in her (transformation), Kevin had to learn how to let go and fall into a place of silence and peace (transcendence). Significantly, this was the one place, in all his explorations, he had never been. As of this writing, he is off most of his medications and much less depressed but his journey continues.

MEDITATION: A VEHICLE FOR TRANSCENDENCE

Ideally, meditation is a practice that clarifies and integrates mind, body and spirit and so is a valuable way of literally practising transcendence. The particular form of meditation matters less than the commitment to regular practice. Like any skill, it must be learned well and practised regularly — which is not so hard if we choose a form we look forward to. It is not something to be learned or practised in a crisis, nor is it useful in achieving a specific result on a specific day. But, if practised day after day, with little or no thought to a particular achievement in the short term, it will build remarkable and unforeseen strengths. And it will heal.

Meditation might be said to be the art of being, the skill of doing nothing, of allowing energy to flow freely in the body, into organs and bones, into the far reaches of the physical self and beyond. Regular practice leads to an experience of inner quiet and abundance in which there are no thoughts — a state akin to deep sleep, except that the mind remains alert. It is the ground state of consciousness, significantly different from waking, dreaming and deep sleep. Indeed, so different is it, that it has been called the *fourth state of consciousness.*[1]

This so-called fourth state transcends and integrates the three more common states of waking, dreaming and deep sleep, as if including them but exceeding them at the same time. One could say that the meditator is in all four states at once — awake, in that she is aware; dreaming, in that she is awake to the inner world; at rest, as if deeply asleep; and beyond individual awareness in that she is aware of the ground of consciousness.

What does this mean? Research into the physiological characteristics of meditation reveals that the more the meditator moves

---

1 This fourth, or ground, state of consciousness is known as *turiya* in the Advaita Vedantic tradition.

into a state of inner peace and quiet, the more electroencephalo-graphic (EEG) brain wave coherence there is. In fact, it is now effectively accepted even in Western scientific circles that such coherence reflects a unique state of consciousness, different from waking, dreaming and sleeping. Although difficult to describe accurately, the inner experience of this state has been described as *relaxed awareness, restful alertness* or *dynamic nothingness.*

Relaxed awareness may not seem particularly extraordinary, yet few people experience it without training. Strange as it may seem, most people are incapable of being relaxed and awake at the same time. In our relaxation classes, we find that people often fall asleep the moment they begin to relax. It seems that for many people, to be alert is to be tense and to be relaxed is to be asleep.

The stress of modern living is such that most people live with chronic sleep deprivation and carry huge amounts of accumulated fatigue in their physiology. So, whenever they relax, sleep takes over as the body tries to catch up. It can take months of meditation before the deep rest it provides begins to stabilize the practitioner sufficiently that it becomes possible to be awake and relaxed simultaneously.

FORMS OF MEDITATION

There are numerous meditation techniques, and each of us must find one that suits our particular physiology and temperament. Some traditions use *mantras* — a specific word repeated rhythmically — to calm the mind and focus the meditation; some suggest following the rhythm of the breath; others focus attention on specific objects, body parts, rhythms or energy centres. Autogenic training teaches the skill of progressive muscular relaxation. Devotional meditations focus on an image, such as Jesus, Buddha, Krishna or the

Virgin Mary. Moving meditations — such as tai chi or qi gong — incorporate body movements.

Whatever style you choose, it is crucial to make a commitment to the practice, and it is generally important to be willing to learn from someone. There is really no substitute for being taught by a certified teacher but if that option is not immediately available to you and you want to try something in the meantime, a short generic breathing meditation is described in the last chapter of this book.

MEDITATION AND THE PSYCHIC SPLITS

As mentioned in the first chapter, meditation can assist in developing a coherent energy field, with all its associated benefits — such as the *Meissner Effect* and so-called super-health. But meditation, especially a quiet sitting meditation, may not be enough to heal the mind/body or persona/shadow splits. It is also rare for sitting meditation alone to be sufficient to break down the compartmentalization associated with regional pain syndromes where tension bands create barriers that retard the spread of coherence across the field.[2]

At first glance, this might seem a bit odd. One might think that because meditation promotes relaxation, regular practice should progressively melt the intra-psychic blocks associated with bands of tension, expose shadow material and allow transformation. And sometimes that happens, but it can take a long time; worse, as we have hinted above, meditation can actually stabilize dissociative tendencies.

In the West, at least, our tendency is to dissociate head and Heart,

2   Many of the meditation traditions take these blocks into account. Unfortunately, because of the way meditation has been incorporated into our society, what people are practising in the West as meditation is often merely a fragment of the whole way. Vajrayana practice, for instance, makes something of a specialty of directly confronting repressed energies.

mind and body, and to attempt to solve our existential anxiety by projecting it outward where it appears as familial, social, political and environmental problems of all kinds. At the same time, and for the same reason, we usually have no idea what it would feel like to fully inhabit our bodies. Maximally contained and dissociated, we have no real intention of dismantling the walls we have established if it means confronting our angst, so, if we meditate, we often do so with the unconscious intention of increasing our dissociation, rather than reducing it. It is for this reason that, in my experience, Eastern meditation techniques, while well suited to investigating the problem of existential suffering, can sometimes exacerbate illness in Westerners.

The difference between the mind/body dissociation and the primary existential split is often not clear to Westerners pursuing Eastern meditation traditions that explore — sometimes in great detail — the existential (Self/self) schism. For example, the yogic traditions describe no fewer than seven states of *samadhi*, all of which refer to the existential level. And unless we are careful, the penultimate state, the state of pure being, could be confused with total mind/body dissociation. (In fact, the state of pure being is fundamentally different from a state of mind/body dissociation. Differentiation is not the same as dissociation. The former is an integrated state while the latter is dis-integrated.)

This is one of the reasons it can be so important to have a teacher. However, the proof is in the pudding, as they say: the limited calmness achieved through meditation by someone with an embedded mind/body separation is nothing like the bliss of beingness. In the first case, anxiety and tension sit in the body like a volcano waiting to explode, while in the second, energy is experienced as free-flowing through an open and unblocked body.

It is crucial to be clear about this because while meditation is trumpeted in the West as the new cure-all, many traditional meditation techniques regard healing the body as a relatively minor issue. Some of the oldest and most venerable practices — in which the goal is nothing less than the achievement of the highest state of union — regard the body-mind as a temporary illusion that will fall away at death and is really rather unimportant. The Westerner wanting to understand and resolve physical and emotional blocks, on the other hand, needs to feel her body before she can transcend it. In other words, we have to be in the body in order to heal it.

TRANSFORMATION: RECLAIMING A FRAGMENTED BODY-MIND

The twelfth card in the major arcana of the tarot deck is the so-called Hanged Man. But this hanged man is hung not by his neck but upside down by one ankle; and is not dead but fully alive, albeit in a state of suspended animation, caught up by a bit of rope around his leg.

The Hanged Man has apparently been rendered helpless by this reversal but is otherwise unharmed. And if we put ourselves in his situation, we will understand that he is seeing life a little differently. In the classic tarot decks, this victim of misfortune wears a remarkably sanguine if not merry look on his face. It is as if he is rather enjoying his new perspective and understands what we may not at first glance — that he can free himself whenever he is ready. Meanwhile, what was ground is now above him, what were the heavens are now beneath his feet. The image speaks eloquently of a situation in which a person's whole world — his values, beliefs and attitudes — has been literally turned on its head.

One way of understanding the image of the hanged man is that it represents the healing crisis called *enantiodromia*. Although a vital part of the healing journey, enantiodromia — fundamental transformation — typically turns lives upside down. As the individual comes face to face with these transformational energies within herself, many of the strategies honed for a lifetime to preserve the status quo fail.

Such transformations can be both extremely positive and very frightening: a man in midlife leaves the secure job he hates to become an artist; or a woman risks censure and economic uncertainty to walk away from an emotionally unsatisfying relationship. Such major changes are typical of the conscious manifestation of transformational energies. However, when transformational forces remain unconscious, or when their manifestation is blocked, they tend to create real, external chaos or give rise to disease. A teenager destroys his creative potential by becoming addicted to drugs; a community leader leads a double life and spreads HIV; a woman gets incapacitating migraines but cannot admit the anger that may be contributing to them; a cheery worker gets ulcers from hidden worry.

A hallmark of the presence of unintegrated psychic conflicts is vacillation between the opposing energy vectors, with the inevitable outcome of depression and underperformance. After all, it is depressing to feel trapped between a rock and a hard place, unable to express oneself wholeheartedly. Such people get sick with containment problems and, in treatment, they may continue to waver between an expressed desire to get better and the desire to suppress or deny symptoms. (The fact that the conflict is based in the unconscious dynamics of transformational energies generally passes unnoticed.)

This kind of fragmentation is so common, I would say it is present in everyone with any illness whatsoever. Latent transformational energy makes its presence known in physical symptoms, which we tend to misinterpret as indicative of a pathology. That is, we assume something is wrong rather than right. If we then suppress the symptoms, we drive the energy deeper into the body, where it can fester for a while before re-emerging as a more ferocious illness. Meanwhile, the mind/body and persona/shadow splits enable us to distance ourselves and pretend we have nothing to do with the disease process.

The sad thing is, it is all so unnecessary! Transformational energy is just raw energy, neither good nor bad. Suppress it and we become sick; embrace it and we become well. So it only makes sense to become aware of whatever repressed energies we might harbour. Then, by deliberately shifting attention into the body, we can start to release the trapped energy. It is really quite simple but can be frightening, precisely because we have to come into the body — which our mind/body split insists is dangerous, possibly even lethal, psychologically.

Still, it is in the body-mind that the energies are located, so we have to *intend* the shift into the body then, once we are committed, allow our process to be facilitated through direct physical exploration of body tissues, where so much energy, intelligence and memory are held. In my experience, dynamic interactive acupuncture and bodywork techniques (DIA), directed to opening areas of pain and discomfort, can bring consciousness to psychic splits much more quickly than meditation.

SYMPTOMS AS TRANSFORMATIONAL POTENTIAL

Because the socialization and individuation processes tend to create a persona, or false self, the presence of suppressed energies the ego has deemed unacceptable is the rule rather than the exception. We can assume that nearly no-one escapes. From a transformational perspective, therefore, *what* the symptom is makes little difference to its ultimate energetic meaning: virtually all symptoms can be assumed to represent a materialization of transformational energy. That being the case, it follows that an experiential exploration of symptoms may access some of those suppressed energies and give rise to transformational experiences.

CONSCIOUS TRANSFORMATION & SACRIFICE

Transformational energies, once contacted, should be brought to consciousness where they can be embraced. If symptom exploration is engaged consciously, the likelihood of being thrown into chaos by the transformational energies released is lessened and the disparate energies can be integrated through transcendence — energetic release being coupled with meditation to integrate the original energy as it is recovered. In this way, the tendency to increasing fragmentation, so prevalent in illness, can be arrested. And, with repeated experience, this process leads to increasing coherence in the body's energy field.

However, it is easier said than done. Anyone taking the path of transformation/transcendence should be prepared for a rough ride. Transformational energies can be intense, painful and fearsome; and the ego uses all its powers to shun them because they are found in symptoms we do not want to acknowledge and feelings we would rather deny.

So, even with the best will in the world, the integration of transformational energies can take time and personal struggle. Sooner or later, we discover that while interactive bodywork (DIA) can effectively de-stress the body, the ego's ingrained patterns are so strong that the original tension patterns have a disconcerting way of restructuring themselves. We slowly come to realize that something fundamental about the way we handle these intense energies has to change. Our habitual strategies no longer work, and the awful truth dawns on us that *we have to give up something* we cannot imagine relinquishing if we wish to become truly free.

This is the act of sacrifice, alluded to in the story that opened this chapter of the young archer who severs his thumb. It is the sacrifice that forms the crux of the transformation/transcendence process. Before transformation, we sacrifice our original energy to satisfy the ego; and now we do the opposite — we sacrifice the ego in order to release original energy so we can live more authentic and integrated lives.

Just as an archer's thumb would seem indispensable to his archery, most of us assume that our ego is indispensable to our lives. So, we generally look for solutions — like symptom suppression — that do not threaten it. When we realize that it is our own precious ego that is largely responsible for our difficulties, a monstrous struggle can ensue as the ego strives to maintain its self-image with every ploy it can muster. Meantime, our original energy becomes increasingly strident in its demands to be heard.

Although the outcome of this struggle in any individual case is unpredictable, sooner or later the ego must find a way to accept the flow of original energy if the healing experience is to become stabilized in consciousness.

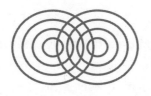

CHAPTER 5

THE FIVE ELEMENTS

The five Elements, Wood, Fire, Earth, Metal and Water
Are the foundation and spirit of all Nature
They are alive both around us and in us;
Through understanding the five Elements
We may begin to understand both Nature and ourselves.
— J.R. Worsley

The *five element* or *five phases* tradition in Chinese medicine proves an extremely useful adjunct to transformational medicine. Sometimes referred to as the *inner* or *hidden tradition*, the five element system is a method of physical, psychological and emotional typing that allows a practitioner to work with the whole individual rather than treating disease or pain as if they were somehow separate from the person experiencing them. Although such an idea — which is the essence of holism — might not seem very startling to the average person, for some reason the concept has gone missing in today's highly technologized conventional medicine and has even been denigrated in some schools of Chinese medicine — where it originated.

The beauty of the five element system is that it shifts our attention from pain or disease as a thing in itself toward an awareness of pain and disease as manifestations of the body, the mind, the emotional nature and even the spirit of the individual who 'has' them. The treatment of acute, temporary and discrete pain and disease through such miracles as organ transplants and broad-spectrum antibiotics has preoccupied Western medicine over the last century. Chronic pain and chronic disease, on the other hand, are the expression of complex processes peculiar to the individual who suffers them, and are often better served by the many thousands of years of empirical observation that inform such Eastern healing practices as Ayurveda and classical Chinese medicine.

ENERGY DIVERSION AND ILLNESS

Yet the distinction between acute and chronic illness is really a chimera. What we call acute illness is in fact only illness we have not paid any attention to as it develops. Before symptoms manifest in a way we can no longer ignore, there is usually a long period of latent, or *virtual*, illness during which our lives and habits, our thoughts (and perhaps especially what we cannot or will not think about) act together to make an illness particular to us inevitable.

In other words, under stress, everyone blocks, diverts or distorts the flow of energy in their body in ways that reflect their attitudes and their thoughts, their fears and their anger, and this energy accumulating in the body-mind eventually materializes as symptoms. Once symptoms arise, moreover, the diversion of energy generally accelerates — as if the body is bent on throwing good money after bad.

But the real magic of the hidden tradition is the way in which it allows the practitioner an understanding of the way an individual manifests his or her illness. Just as particular emotions and habits, fears and thoughts lay the groundwork for symptoms, those symptoms, once manifested, are *direct pointers back to those original energies* that have been diverted or fragmented. Why this is so exciting will become clear as we go forward.

THE DANGER OF STEREOTYPING

I will be referring throughout this book to a person's *constitutional type* but I want to acknowledge immediately that any typology must be used with caution. However subtle and however illuminating, typology is merely a tool and must never be allowed to reduce an infinitely complex organism to a formula — to something we think we can know, when in fact we know almost nothing. As such reductionism has all but destroyed the utility and subtlety of conventional medicine, it would be regrettable indeed to repeat the error here. Constitutional typing should be regarded as simply one more tool to help people interact imaginatively so that healing is part of a free, dynamic and living relationship.

THE FIVE ELEMENT PARADIGM

In the five element tradition, each person is understood to have physical, emotional, psychological and spiritual characteristics

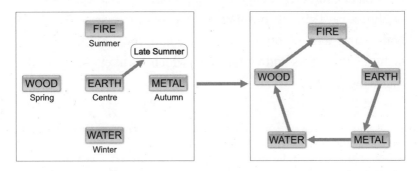

Figure 1: The four seasons and five elements

that resemble the quality of energy inherent in a particular season of the year.[1] In addition to the seasons with which we are familiar in the West, China, with its long agrarian tradition, not surprisingly acknowledges a fifth late-summer harvest season between high summer and autumn. In Chinese medicine, this third of five seasons is considered the central axis around which the other seasons revolve and to which all of them in some way relate (see figure 1).

The seasons, or phases, each relate to a particular element. These are the elements referred to in the name *five elements*. They are: *Wood*, the element of spring; *Fire*, the element of summer; *Earth*, the element of late summer or harvest season; *Metal*, the element of autumn; *Water*, the element of winter.

CHARACTERISTICS OF THE FIVE ELEMENTS

The energetic characteristics of the seasons and the elements are easily grasped since they are everyone's common experience. The elegant and holistic framework that is worked around these perceptions can dramatically alter our understanding of the meaning of disease, helping us fathom how our individual susceptibilities, together with the relationship between our emotional natures, life themes, talents and proclivities, can predispose us to certain kinds of illnesses. Table 1 summarizes the organ relationships, the body-mind and emotional relations and the life themes and qualities, strengths and weaknesses, which I will elaborate in the following pages.

---

1   Of course, such an approach is by no means unique; it is common to many traditional medicines, including Western medieval and esoteric traditions. Some readers will be familiar, for example, with the 'four directions' of native North American culture.

	Wood	Fire	Earth	Metal	Water
Main organs	Liver (yin) Gall Bladder (yang)	Pericardium & Heart (yin), Small Intestine & Triple Heater (yang)	Spleen (yin) Stomach (yang)	Lungs (yin) Large Intestine (yang)	Kidneys (yin) Bladder (yang)
Emotions	Anger	Joy	Worry	Grief	Fear
Tissues	Tendons	Blood vessels	Muscles	Skin	Bones
Season	Spring	Summer	Later Summer	Fall	Winter
Personality associations	Decisive, creative, visionary	Passionate, joyful, loving, excited	Caring, sympathetic	Reverent, inspired, open, ascetic	Self-sufficient, philosophical, solitary
Disease associations	Headaches, hypertension, menstrual pain, eye disease, arthritis	Heart disease, insomnia, manic depression	Digestive disorders, muscle pains, chronic fatigue	Arthritis, skin, lung disease, allergies, asthma	Kidney disease, low back pain, memory loss, deafness
Life theme	Growth, creativity, direction	Harmony, being in tune	Altruism, empowered giving	Death/ transcen- dence	Bringing potential into manifestation

Table 1: The five elements

WOOD

The energy of the Wood element is the energy of the spring, when the sun begins to warm the earth and life bursts forth all around. Imagine a spring day: there is new life everywhere you look and a fresh smell in the air. That is the character of the Wood element. Like spring, Wood energy is about growth, exuberance and upward, outward or expanding movement. Think of the spring flowers as they shoot up from the ground. There is a kind of optimistic urgency, a hurried enthusiasm as the young plants compete — for sunlight, for water and for food. Those that have them in abundance grow fastest; those that are denied tend to do poorly or die.

In much the same way, a person with a Wood constitutional type expresses exuberance, growth, creative expression and direction. They are wonderful people to have around, full of ideas. Every creative company or project needs one. On the other hand, Wood people do not like obstacles much, and tend to ride roughshod over them without considering the consequences — which is to say, they can be a little insensitive. They have little time for rules and regulations or bureaucracies and get easily frustrated when things do not go their way. They generally have a short fuse.

The Wood element is associated with creativity, vigour, animation, bursting forth, explosiveness, youthful strength, aggression, direction and competition. Sight being the most directional of the senses, Wood energy has traditionally been associated with vision and the eyes. Wood people are perceptive and forward-looking, too, which makes them good planners and decision-makers, especially in circumstances where their ideas can be manifested quickly, so that they do not get bogged down. They work best in imaginative and free-thinking environments, where creativity is encouraged and they are rewarded for expressing and actualizing their ideas.

WOOD'S ORGAN RELATIONSHIPS

In Chinese medicine, each of the five elements is divided into its yin and yang aspects. The yin function has more to do with *being*, the yang more with *doing*. Each element is then associated with two organs, one yin and one yang (with the exception of the Fire element, which is associated with four).

Some confusion attends the organ assignments, however, because

Westerners tend to think of an organ as a discrete object in the body — one might even say that conventional medicine's view of organs is a surgical one: organs are removable body parts. In Chinese medicine, on the other hand, organs are considered energy nodes or even energy vectors rather than objects. A literal equation of the Chinese organ-energies to the Western organ-objects is therefore insufficient to an understanding of energy medicine.

Briefly, in the five element tradition, each organ must be regarded primarily as a particular mind-body energy vector only incidentally related to the physical organ that shares its name. Capitalization of the names of the energy vectors is used to make the distinction — e.g. *Liver* stands for liver energy, whereas *liver* denotes the organ itself. Confusing as this may sound at first, it gets us a little closer to a subtle understanding of the body and of the spiritual energies of the very distinct though complexly interrelated nodes or vectors which we in the West have been conditioned to see as organs.

The organs traditionally associated with the Wood element are the *Liver* and the *Gall Bladder*. Both hold energies of successful and directed growth. The Liver is yin and relates to *planning* and *preparation*, while the Gall Bladder is yang and relates to the quality of *decision-making*.

WOOD: BALANCE AND IMBALANCE

When our creative expression is blocked, frustration and anger tend to arise. Consequently, the life theme for people of a Wood constitutional type often has something to do with how they deal with anger. Of course, everyone is familiar with frustration but Wood people tend to make it a central theme. They will get very upset about what they see as an injustice and go out of their way to pick a fight, or go to war over issues other people might walk away from. Their battles are frequently unwinnable but, strangely, that will often only make them more determined. Think again of a bulb pushing its shoot toward the light; if a boulder has rolled over it during the winter, it will push all the harder to succeed in getting to the sun.

Unfortunately, once anger is sparked it can always find fuel. The world is full of injustices, so there is never a shortage of issues to rile a Wood constitutional type. Not that injustices should not be confronted, far from it. But the Wood type seems to use them as self-justification and as a focus for aggression: anger seems to exude from these individuals, either openly through violence or covertly through passive aggression and manipulation.

When in balance, Wood personalities can tackle challenges without losing their cool. They are creative and move forward with openness and excitement. When out of balance, however, the anger — which has to go somewhere — moves toward one of two poles, depending on circumstance and predisposition. On the one hand, it moves outward in an *explosive* gesture; on the other, it *implodes*. Either way, chaos is created in the outer or inner environment.

Exploder	Balanced	Imploder
Angry, belligerent, aggressive	Flexible, creative, clear perception	Depressed, apathetic, passive-aggressive

Table 2: The balance/imbalance of the Wood element

WOOD SYMPTOMS AND TENDENCIES

An imbalance of Wood energy is suggested by hopelessness, inability to compete, problems finding or sustaining direction, a feeling of stuckness or of stored-up resentment. The body begins to clog up. On a physical level, things like blood clots, tumours, cysts, eye problems or cataracts might appear, or the individual might be prone to repetitive sprains and strains of ligaments. Other symptoms traditionally associated with Wood are headaches, spinal disorders, arthritis, infertility or menstrual difficulties. Often, Wood symptoms tend to be one-sided, such as migraines.

On a mental level, there may be an inability to make decisions or plan. Clouded vision, confusion, poor judgement and organization; or the reverse — over-planning and over-organization of everyone and everything. Such people typically have difficulty relaxing, and may have nightmares, particularly of being trapped.

On an emotional level, Wood people may have trouble setting boundaries, or saying *no*. They may express inappropriate anger, rigidity, irritability, self-criticism or criticism of others. Imploded anger often masquerades as depression, giving an impression of apathy. Don't be fooled. The popular drug, Prozac, for example, has been reputed to cause violent behaviour in some people, a phenomenon without a good physiological explanation. An energetic analysis would show us that the drug does not *cause* violence so much as permit the manifestation of a latent anger already resident. Simple enough perhaps, but not obvious unless one is aware of the complex workings of energy vectors in the mind and body.

At the worst, there can be lack of vision, creativity and enthusiasm, and no interest in anything new. This kind of apathy is referred to as a *loss of spirit*, and reflects a profound imbalance. The essential problem is that the individual can see no way to express the totality of who they are. Oftentimes, they are terrified of the rage they feel and see no option other than to contain it and dissociate. In this way, they gradually distance themselves from their deepest nature. From there, compartmentalization proceeds until they have completely lost contact with themselves, and there is nothing left to fire the passion of living.

༇ *DEBBIE*: FROZEN SHOULDER

Debbie came to us with a frozen shoulder that she had developed shortly after a minor strain lifting a heavy pile of linen at work. By the time we met her, three years had gone by and there was little sign of improvement. She held the arm across her chest, refused to use it at all and complained that any movement hurt it. Although only forty-five years old, she seemed strangely resigned, almost as though she had given up — though she had plenty to say when it came to her compensation claim and her resentment toward her physicians for mismanaging her injury. She explained through some grimacing that although she had accepted her disability, she was not about to let those 'idiots down at the Board' off the hook.

One day without warning, however, Debbie entered the void during a bodywork session and began belting a pillow with her injured arm. The attack went on for several minutes; when she had recovered, she revealed that she had imagined dispatching her ex-husband, who she said had been abusive. She was astonished that she had been using her frozen arm and shoulder to do him in.

Afterward, she had several hours of improved mobility and diminished pain. Such experiences — if we are willing to listen to them — can directly inform us of the relationship between contained emotions and chronic pain.

FIRE

Fire is summer's energy, when the year's growth energy reaches the zenith of its expression. Fire energy has to do with actualized potential, expansiveness, joyful spontaneity and full expression of life. Just think of a summer day — hot sun pervading the garden, bees buzzing around the flowers in full bloom. Imagine lying on your back on the grass next to a friend or lover, savouring the richness, and you immediately get the flavour of the Fire element. Just like summer, Fire energy is about action, warmth, excitement and joy. There is an urge to form relationships, to pursue romance, love and sexual desires. The Fire energy is Heart-centred, truthful, spirited, compassionate and represents a full expression of the self. It shows in the aliveness or fire in people's eyes. It is about feeling, touching, about opening the Heart to everything; it manifests as a carefree sense of absorption in the moment — and an equally carefree neglect of the clock. At their finest, Fire people can be so aware, trusting and responsive to life's nudges, they seem just plain lucky to others who plod along carefully plotted avenues in life.

FIRE'S ORGAN ASSOCIATIONS

The Fire element is associated with two organ pairs rather than the usual single pair; they are the *Heart/Small Intestine* and the *Pericardium/Triple Heater*. Of these two pairs, the Heart and the Pericardium are yin; the Small Intestine and Triple Heater are yang. In the five element tradition, the Heart spirit is regarded as the energetic centre of the body-mind-spirit, whilst the energies of the other three organs provide layers of protection to keep this centre from injury by life experiences.

One rather curious organ, the Triple Heater, is regarded as the outermost of these three layers. But this quintessential Chinese organ does not actually exist as an organ at all: it is a function. A function without an organ is no problem for Chinese medicine, of course; but it is a big problem for Western medicine, for surgeons and students of anatomy. The Triple Heater can neither be drawn nor removed because it represents the *space* in and around the body. Take away the body and the space would still be there. It could be said to be the arena in which the body exists.

On the material level, the Triple Heater refers to three sections roughly corresponding to the chest, abdomen and pelvis, known in Chinese medicine as the three *jiaos*, and acts as a homeostatic regulator that controls the distribution of heat between the areas of the body. But its homeostatic function extends beyond the material, beyond the body. As the outermost psychic layer, the Triple Heater acts as a kind of *social thermostat*, an early-warning or surveillance system governing social interaction. Given the prevalence of compartmentalization referred to elsewhere, it is not surprising that imbalances of this function are fairly ubiquitous.

Although there is a material structure called the pericardium, in Chinese medicine it is more important as a function than as a structure. In the hidden tradition, the Pericardium plays the role of *Heart protector*, not in the usual sense of a physical envelope but rather in the sense of protecting us emotionally.

The Small Intestine as an energy vector is also a bit of a stretch for anyone new to the hidden tradition. Anatomically, it has got nothing to do with the Heart at all. Energetically, however, it performs the function of emotional and mental *information sorter* — deciding what is important and what is not, with reference to the Heart's truth. On a material level, of course, the small intestine does sort nutrients, so there is some correlation, but that is about as far as it goes.

Finally, although the heart is a material structure, energetically the Heart is not so much a pump as a frequency modulator which Chinese medicine refers to as the *supreme controller*. In the hidden tradition, the Heart is the place where the spirit resides, the place where we have direct access to our truth — the Heart's truth. More about this in a moment.

FIRE: BALANCE AND IMBALANCE

When in balance, Fire personalities feel totally in tune with life. They seem to glide effortlessly along while everything simply falls into place around them. Unlike Wood people, who tend to get frustrated, nothing seems to bother the healthy Fire constitution; and if an obstruction does arise, they simply move in another direction and interpret the experience in a positive way. Similarly, Fire people are generally incapable of harbouring resentment, and when they get angry, they tend to quick explosions and flare-ups, which disappear as fast as they came.

However, things are not always smooth sailing. When Fire people go off balance, they lose their connection with life and feel out of tune. The flip-side of joy, attunement and excitement — sadness, loneliness and boredom — seem their lot. And although less common, the other extreme is also possible — mania or frank psychosis.

Joyless	Balanced	Overjoyed
Sad, bored lonely & chaotic	Effortless attunement	Manic, controlling and/or delusional

Table 3: The balance/imbalance of the Fire element

FIRE SYMPTOMS AND TENDENCIES

On a physical level, a Fire imbalance may be suggested by circulatory difficulties such as blood pressure problems, varicose veins, or numbness of the extremities; or as disturbances of heat distribution such as heartburn, hot and cold sensations or hot flashes. If the digestive system lacks heat, there can be sluggish digestion, abdominal pain or watery diarrhea. If there is excess heat, it can lead to joint inflammation, hypersexuality, chronic infections, dryness of the lungs, inflamed throat and sinuses, burning diarrhea/urination or constipation.

On a mental level, Fire permits thoughts to flourish, and sorts what is valuable and what is not — a function of the Small Intestine. An imbalance might be suggested by confusion, dullness, disconnectedness, or an inability to complete projects. Sometimes the Fire person cannot distinguish what is good for them from what is not. Too much heat can lead to anxiety or insomnia. Too little can lead to withdrawal, coldness or fear of rejection.

On an emotional level, the Fire element controls the access to the Heart, which means that such people are particularly prone to emotional bruising. Fire people tend to interpret every moment's inattention or thoughtless comment as a betrayal of intimacy. This manner of interpretation lies behind many of their ups and downs. Imbalances of the Heart Protector and Triple Heater functions produce all kinds of difficulties with intimate relationships and generally reflect a fear of intimacy. A few bad experiences can make some people close off their Hearts and become impenetrable. In such a situation, the Pericardium and Triple Heater lose their ability to see clearly what is safe and what is not.

The innermost protector, the Small Intestine, controls Heart-Mind communication and so reflects Heart-Mind congruence. This is a big issue in chronic illness as few people in our culture — especially those who are unwell — have any Heart-Mind congruence at all, or even know what it means to have such congruence. Instead, we have a society in which a Heart/Mind schism is the norm, in which most people run their lives from their heads, disregarding their Heart's truth and suffer anxiety-ridden existences as a result, sensing the psychic division that is cutting them off from an authentic life but having no real idea what it is all about.

At the deepest layer, too, fire can fade to almost nothing or flare too hot. Too little fire can bring sadness, loss of enthusiasm, emotional coldness, or emotional vulnerability; and when the fire goes out there is a loss of spirit — without access to their natural *joie de vivre*, Fire people fall into a joyless slump. Too much fire on the other hand produces manic behaviours: perpetual clowning, inappropriate laughing and joking, or ceaseless chattering.

℞ *LISA*: BACK PAIN

Lisa was an enthusiastic, driven go-getter who had suffered several years of back pain following a motor vehicle accident. Not one to let anything slip her notice, she had gathered every bit of information she could about chronic pain, but had found nothing that had been any help. During our initial meeting she took notes, asked endless and circular questions, talked without stopping, and countered every comment I made as if we were engaged in a debate. She continued taking notes the whole time she was with us — even though we suggested it was not necessary — but no amount of information ever seemed to be enough for her. Nothing was ever quite right, and she seemed quite incapable of stopping, even for a moment, to actually listen to anything other than her own mental chatter.

Lisa's endless quest for more information was likely a strategy to cover her lack of connection to her own inner knowing. She was trying to fill the void with whatever she could lay her hands on, all the while getting increasingly tense and anxious over her inability to understand what was *causing* her pain. Although her extraordinary behaviour was clearly exacerbating her tension, Lisa seemed quite oblivious, never quite understanding the degree to which she herself was the source of many of her problems.

EARTH

Although Earth energy is associated with late summer, it is also the centre around which the other seasons revolve and to which they all relate. Ploughing, planting (spring), fruiting (summer), dying back (fall) and lying fallow (winter) all relate to late summer's harvest. And because the anatomical centre of the body is in the stomach area, Earth energy is correlated not only with centring but also with nourishment in general — of both the self and others. The essence of Earth energy is nourishment, altruism and, by extension, motherliness.

Imagine the characteristics of late summer and you will begin to get a sense of the Earth element. It is harvest time; the days are still warm. It is time to store food, stack wood and prepare for the coming cold. Harvesting, nourishment, tasting and savouring, the capacity to receive what is coming at you instead of wanting something else, thoughtfulness, understanding, selflessness, devotion and groundedness are qualities that span the distance between the earth as *mother* and the human relationship of mother and child, and all that it implies — contentment, fertility, fulfillment, support, impartiality (the earth nourishes all without judgement).

Earth energy also relates to the cycles of the body, such as the menstrual cycle, life rhythms, sleep rhythms and so on. Earth people are capable of entraining others' field frequencies; to be in tune with others in this way makes them good at sympathetic listening.

EARTH'S ORGAN ASSOCIATIONS

The Earth organ associations are the *Spleen* (yin) and *Stomach* (yang), the Stomach being known in Chinese medicine rather colourfully as the *official of rotting and ripening*. Although we can understand the stomach as a receiver, a locus of digestion and nourishment, and can fairly easily extend that concept to include all aspects of process, embodiment, the meeting of the outer world and the inner, at first glance, the spleen, at least in the Western mind, has nothing at all to do with the digestive system. However, we must remember that the Chinese Spleen is not the Western spleen but rather the yin aspect of digestion and assimilation. Chinese medicine considers the task of the Spleen to be that of *transportation* and *transformation*, of appropriately processing and distributing digested material. The Spleen takes the essence of the food we eat — the energetic element that is almost as light as the air we breathe — and mingles it with the energy that is taken from the air in the lungs. Both are processes of nourishment, broadly speaking; and Spleen, like Stomach, is considered to process more than food: it is also responsible for the absorption and processing of anything we take in — ideas, information, sensory experience or any other aspect of the mind-body-spirit continuum.

EARTH: BALANCE AND IMBALANCE

When in balance, people with an Earth constitutional type are centred, thoughtful and altruistic. They like to nurture others and feel fulfilled by being in service. Earth people are attracted to service industries and to helping professions such as nursing or social work, and their skill at tuning in to the needs of others makes them much sought after counsellors and caregivers.

Earth people tend to run into difficulty because their natural desire to serve often overrides their willingness or ability to look after themselves, so sooner or later they get drained to the point of burn-out. Energetically, the problem is a block somewhere in the cycle of giving and receiving. When people are incapable of receiving, even to the point of feeling guilty when looking after their own needs, they may give of themselves until they are exhausted. At the same time, their desire to receive can be expressed indirectly through manipulative, ingratiating or dependent behaviour, which has a sticky or *icky* quality to it.

On the other side of the coin, when people are incapable of giving, they often get so filled up with old undigested material they cannot take in anything new. Fearing there will never be enough, they can clog up with old undigested mental, emotional and physical baggage that they seem incapable of processing, with the result that they appear stubborn and selfish, overweight or phlegmy.

Difficulty giving	Balance	Difficulty receiving
Selfishness, stubbornness	Altruism, groundedness	Ingratiation/martyrdom insecurity/dependence

Table 4: The balance/imbalance of the Earth element

EARTH SYMPTOMS AND TENDENCIES

On a physical level, an Earth imbalance is suggested by any symptom emanating from the epigastric area (the body's anatomical centre), the digestive system or body rhythms. Problems such as indigestion, anorexia, ulcers, diarrhea, gastrointestinal upset, too much or too little weight can be Earth-related. Body rhythm disturbances show up as hormonal or menstrual problems. And finally, problems of *holding the centre*, or *holding things together*, can suggest an Earth disturbance — such as prolapses of the uterus or bladder, weak or fragile body tissues, bleeding disorders or varicose veins.

On a mental level, difficulty centring often shows up as obsessive thinking or worrying. This might manifest as insomnia if the individual is plagued by thoughts that go around and around. Sometimes — just as if the head were in fact spinning — this condition can bring on vertigo or nausea.

On an emotional level, Earth people tend to be inveterate worriers. They have a tendency to chronic anxiety, which can manifest as nervousness, dependence, neediness and an excessive catering to their own or others' perceived needs, or flightiness and panic attacks from a lack of groundedness. On a deeper level, Earth constitutional types can be very rigid in their thinking and unable to consider creative ways to deal with problems.

ꝺ JANE: FOOD ALLERGIES

Jane was a university professor who came to us to explore her food allergies. Although obviously highly intelligent and outwardly sophisticated, when it came to food she behaved like a two-year-old. She would bring food into the treatment rooms, pick at it with her fingers, slop it onto the carpets and make little attempt to clean up. She was adamant that there was something wrong with her digestive system and that she had little choice but to do as she did. Although naturally her strange eating habits put people off, it quickly became clear that her behaviour was designed to get attention. For some reason, although it was fairly obvious to everyone else, Jane had no idea what was going on and was highly resistant to considering other explanations for her symptoms.

METAL

In some ways, Metal can be the most difficult element to grasp, perhaps because the energy has to do with the fall, letting go and death — a collective cultural stumbling block. Think of the autumn — the days are getting shorter and the nights cooler; the leaves are turning colour and beginning to fall. Nature seems to call time to the long halcyon days of summer — time to *let go*.

There is stillness and potency in the autumn air and the early mornings can be misty as though cloaked, contemplative. There is a sense of awe at the dying of the year; and such festivals as All Souls' Day, Hallowe'en (All Hallows Eve) and the Day of the Dead mark the calendar's turn to the underworld, the inner world, to sacred mysteries. At the same time, harvest festivals celebrate the bounty of the summer just past. If the harvest has been abundant and stocks for the winter are ample, it can be a relief to let go into the coming stillness, knowing the fullness of those stores will carry us through to the next year and the next harvest.

Metal energy is downward, subsiding and contracting, the opposite of the expanding, upward movement of Wood. There is a melancholy or pensive quality to it, a sinking or surrendering. The sinking quality resembles the *sinking of qi* in tai chi practice, a pooling and gathering of energies, the taking of deep strength in stillness. The surrender is of the smaller or individual self to the larger, interpersonal and limitless energies of the greater world. We let go in order to bring in something new, something larger, something transcendent.

If we are connected to the transcendent — that space within all things that never perishes — and are willing to move into the unknown, we can allow ourselves to surrender to the death mystery, which is integral to transformation and rebirth. But death is a profound and terrifying proposition — it is the realm of the existential and mind/body dualisms, and the source of our most profound anxieties. Few people face it willingly or even consciously. Those who do are transformed, for to truly embrace the death mystery is to open oneself to transcendent wisdom, grounded in compassion and fearlessness and connected to the divine.

Appreciation for harvest and for the entirety of the life cycle just past gives rise to some of the other attributes of Metal energy, such as valuation, sense of purpose, meaning and communication of that meaning — which might be through words, reverence, ritual or action. Metal people are born priests or teachers. The *compassionate sage* is an archetypal image of Metal, an image that has traditionally been associated with fatherhood and the communication of wisdom. The sage or spiritual father, *inspires*, both figuratively and literally, giving rise to two apparently disparate concepts both associated with Metal — that of physical inspiration and expiration, and the inspiration associated with a deep connection to the transcendent. Metal types often radiate an awareness of spirit and show a respect for the sanctity of life.

METAL'S ORGAN ASSOCIATIONS

At a physical level, Metal governs the functions of *purification* through excretion or exhalation, and *inspiration* or subtle nourishment. The *Large Intestine* (yang) lets go of the old and the *Lungs* (yin) take in the new. These organ associations make immediate physiological sense but one should remember that such associations are always related to the whole body-mind-spirit continuum. Letting go is as much about the experience of surrender in our lives as it is about the release of the spirit in death; as much about the letting go of ego in transformative experiences as it is a reference to bowel movements. Similarly, the Lungs refer as much to inspiration (inspiration/expiration) and the transpersonal (we all breathe the same air) as to the simple act of inhaling. The physical meanings remain implicit in the larger context of the body-mind-spirit continuum.

METAL: BALANCE AND IMBALANCE

The compassionate sage is the embodiment of wisdom and

Heart-centred understanding that is the highest achievement of the Metal individual. Having embraced the death mystery, the sage embodies a transcendent joy, a deep appreciation for life, an acceptance of the impermanence of things and an abiding sense of self-worth and connection to the divine — whatever that may mean to a particular individual.

Unbalanced Metal people, on the other hand, may either become morally rigid, making absurd rules for others, or physically rigid. Or they may become formless and depressed, despondent or physically or mentally incapacitated. Behind these imbalances is a sense of disconnection and a desperate need for meaning that cannot be answered.

Unfortunately, a culture that has an intense collective fear of death blocks transcendent wisdom, producing a paucity of sages and an abundance of false wise men promising varieties of eternal life and freedom from pain. Conventional priests, doctors, teachers and other traditional leaders tend in this context to be the blind leading the blind.

Too Formless	Balanced	Too rigid
Low self-esteem, depressed, empty	Warm, flexible, connected, non-attached wisdom	Cold, brittle, cut off, moralizing

Table 5: The balance/imbalance of the Metal element

The acknowledgement, appreciation and approval that characterize the deep digestion phase of a cycle we have lived through from first growth to harvest are especially important when it comes to illness and the transformational process. Regardless of an individual's personal constitutional type, everyone faces a letting-go process if they wish to heal; and this is never more true than in chronic illness, when it becomes nothing less than essential.

But such letting go can be nearly impossible if illness is seen to be of no value, if there is nothing to be harvested from it, if its character as a culmination of a life process cannot be acknowledged. Taking the time to explore symptoms and to find their value is crucial to transformation (and it is precisely those with balanced Metal energy who have the kind of wisdom needed to help others let go into the transformational process, since they have travelled the road themselves).

METAL SYMPTOMS AND TENDENCIES

At a physical level, Metal problems can manifest in the lungs, which take in the new, and in the large intestine, which lets go the old. Typical complaints might include asthma, shortness of breath, coughs, allergic rhinitis, nasal congestion, chronic bronchitis, sleep apnea and emphysema. Typical intestinal symptoms might include constipation, diarrhea, irritable bowel syndrome and abdominal pain. The inability to let go combined with intra-body communication problems can manifest as rigidity of the spine, rheumatic pains or neurological degeneration (such as Parkinson's syndrome or multiple sclerosis), muscular atrophy, tremors or frank paralysis.

On a mental level, there can be obsessive or rigid thinking of the kind sometimes aptly described as mental constipation. Such people are dictatorial, argumentative, proud or just plain stubborn — in other words, unable to let go intellectually. That their illness suggests a need for change is generally lost on them, and they will often cling to some theory that both supports their entrenched ideas and absolves them of any personal responsibility for their discomforts. Such a situation can be vexing to caregivers, who can often see the obvious but find themselves caught in the web of co-dependency.

On an emotional level, Metal types are often holding unresolved grief and are using a great deal of energy to fight awareness of their pain. Unable to face transformation, or change their thinking, they can get mired in a bleak depression that turns their emotional surroundings into a barren moonscape. Unfortunately, because they are unwilling to change in any way, they have nowhere to go but deeper into illness to prove that they are right. Sometimes such people would rather die — and often they do — than face the psychic death of transformation, which would take them inward on a journey to rebirth.

At the deepest level, Metal people suffer from depression, alienation and low self-esteem. They feel disconnected and sense something is missing but hesitate to explore the emptiness they feel. They want to connect with the sacred but feel abandoned, alienated and useless. Instead of exploring their inner emptiness, which might lead them to the transcendent, they often seek to fill it instead with something tangible, like *stuff* — papers, possessions, information, whatever. Or else, go the other way and become ascetic, shunning possessions altogether in the hope that denying their desires might lead them to the sacred. Unfortunately, the self-loathing concealed in such asceticism only spirals them downward into deeper depression.

℞ *MYRNA*: CHRONIC CONSTIPATION & DIVERTICULOSIS

Myrna had suffered a long while from constipation and diverticular disease. A fifty-five-year-old minister, she reported that she had a bowel movement only every three to four days and that the stools were usually thin and spindly. Every now and again, when she got really constipated, she would go and have an enema or a colon cleanse. Although she clearly had a problem, Myrna's concern for her bowels seemed excessive and she seemed morbid and a bit depressed. At the same time, she was very suspicious of our methods and was not keen to try anything new.

Myrna was definitely hard to get close to and was initially hostile to the acupuncture we offered her. However, she did eventually give it a try. In one particular session, she entered the void without warning and afterward got up hurriedly and rushed from the room. It later transpired that she had had the biggest bowel movement she could remember. After that, she lightened up considerably.

Myrna just could not let go, even physically, but when she eventually managed to do so, it was an almost spiritual experience that altered her personality radically. Would that every bowel movement could be so enlightening!

WATER

Water energy is reflected in the winter season. It has to do with deep personal resources and unmanifested potential. Imagine the winter: it is cold and still, the ground is frozen and perhaps covered with snow. The trees are bare and the leaves are gone. The light in the sky seems empty, pure and fragile. The birds and animals are fewer. It is as if the energy that animated life during the rest of the year has been pulled inwards. But although it appears relatively inert, there is potential in the ground: seeds wait for the right moment to spring to life. That image gives us the essential feature of the Water element, *unknowable potential*. A seed so small you can hardly see it may, with warmth, grow into a plant, a bush, a tree.

Another aspect of water can be found in the image of the ocean or a lake — the unknown, the darkness, the chaos of the deep. When we look into deep water, it is usually with an edge of fear, or wonder: what lurks in those depths? Fear, or lack of fear, of the unknown is a big feature of the Water element. Some of the language associated with Water includes reflection, wisdom, potency, foundation, courage, silence, the unknowable (often referred to as chaos), ancestors, hidden, deep, profound and mysterious. With Water, there is a sense of total connection to the void, and acceptance of the possibility of not knowing. Chinese medicine considers that the Water element, which governs the Kidneys and the Bladder, is the repository of our constitutional strength (Essence, or *Jing*) and is the source of our will.

Winter is the time of death and of gestation, potential rebirth. Water types bring a sense of essential self, of listening to the silence, and of depth. So deep and still is their life connection, they can seem to need to be on the edge of death or chaos in order to feel alive. Such people are often aware of the huge energies that sit inside them and do not dare to express them; there can be a terror of manifesting. At the same time, unlike Fire types who seem to be able to do nearly anything they put their hand to, Water constitutional types often only get one crack at life.

WATER'S ORGAN ASSOCIATIONS

The organs associated with the Water element are the *Kidneys* (yin) and *Bladder* (yang). Although these are certainly our watery organs, the energetics associated with the Kidneys especially has more to do with stored or potential energy. Energetically, the Kidneys are the storehouse, having to do with potential energy, while the Bladder is more involved in the actualization of that potential. It is said that Kidney energy relates to constitutional strength, the strength of our *being*, our given strength or Essence, while the Bladder energy reflects our willpower and how we use it to dispense those resources, or the strength of our *doing*.

WATER: BALANCE AND IMBALANCE

When in balance, Water people are quiet, thoughtful types who avoid idle chit-chat but make good listeners. They are powerful and self-sufficient, philosophical about the uncertainties of life and relatively comfortable with not knowing. However, the power inherent in such a position is not actualized without some spiritual work, so the problem for Water people is manifesting their potential. Water people usually thrive on working with their relationship with fear, their willingness to be present with the unknown and their ability to utilize and express that energy.

The difficulty of bringing something big into manifestation can be likened to the difficulty surfers have of finding the right wave. Surfers like to be sure of a good wave before making a commitment because catching the wrong wave can waste effort or spell disaster. Like experienced surfers, Water people have the ability to see trouble coming a long way off, which gives them an uncanny ability to stay out of it. But the downside is that they may have difficulty making a commitment to anything at all, for fear of making the wrong choice. Like a big wave forming in the ocean, it can take a long time for a Water person to gather momentum; but, once up and moving forward, it can take an equally long while for them to stop.

Water people can veer one way or the other on the fear issue. The fearless live on the edge, always challenging their fears in order to feel the thrill. These people tend to take up inherently dangerous occupations like racing car driving or mountain climbing. The opposite tendency produces people who cannot motivate themselves and, paralyzed with fear, never seem to get going in life.

Too much fear	Balance	Too little fear
Conservative, fearful, anxious	Potency, power, deep wisdom	Recklessness and/or bravado

Table 6: The balance/imbalance of the Water element

WATER: SYMPTOMS AND TENDENCIES

On a physical level, the *sine qua non* of the Water type is low back pain and weak knees. However, any problem involving the lower abdomen and bladder can be a clue to a Water imbalance. Frequent urination, getting up at night several times, prostate problems, weak legs, joint brittleness — especially in the low back, hips and knees. If there is a weakness of Essence, it can manifest as excessive fatigue, excess or deficient perspiration or lower abdominal discomfort and bloating.

On a mental level, there can be anxiety or a lack of flow in the thought process. On an emotional level, the Water person can be distrustful. Or she can feel constantly overwhelmed. The deepest level of imbalance is suggested by overt fearfulness, or fearfulness masked by a variety of rationalizations (those people who can talk themselves out of any adventure whatever by focusing on every conceivable danger). On the other hand, apparent fear*less*ness or bravado may be a defence mechanism signalling that a normal fear response and sensitivity have been suppressed. Such people may be physically reckless or take other kinds of unnecessary risks.

Others use willpower to drive themselves beyond their limits at work, workaholism being just one more way to numb the unbearable existential anxiety that is just under the surface. Unfortunately, such behaviour drains and scatters essential energy, depleting it prematurely and can lead to chronic exhaustion. Such people also risk losing track of themselves altogether and/or encountering their anxiety full force, and may be so overwhelmed that a panic similar to the panic of drowning takes hold of them.

Such people may appear chaotic, fragmented or even paralyzed, unable to mobilize their energy at all. Occasionally, their paralyzing fear will manifest as extreme conservativeness but such a cover-up tends to produce a rigidity that makes them prone to crack under pressure. It only takes a couple of unexpected stressors to shift such people from a functional existence into complete shutdown. Either way, fear prevents access to their inner resources and the individual carries on unaware of his own potential.

When the energy of anxiety comes to the surface, it can produce a tremor in the physical body like the surface wobbling one sees when water is vibrated. Curiously, allowing such vibrations to occur unimpeded can be exactly what is required to convert the fear into a creative energetic experience.

☿ ANDREW: DISSOCIATION

Andrew was an alcohol and substance abuse counsellor who came to us after a motor vehicle accident. Apparently not one to hurry at the best of times, Andrew had slowed down so much after the accident, it took several minutes to get him to answer a simple question. It was almost as if he had to go off somewhere outside of himself and search around in order to find the answer. His unusual symptoms were a complete mystery to both himself and his physicians, and although there was little physical evidence, everyone concluded he must have sustained a brain injury.

Andrew had also long been troubled by an obscure abdominal and back pain that defied diagnosis. It interested me right away that most of his symptoms occurred in the area of the solar plexus, the area of the power chakra, and that although he had been examined repeatedly, nothing of great significance had ever been found. The investigations he had undergone had not been harmless either. In his quest for an explanation, Andrew had no less than three exploratory laparotomies and — perhaps because nothing was found — had been offered a variety of obscure diagnoses ranging from chronic relapsing pancreatitis to porphyria.

In my experience, Andrew simply exuded spiritual power. I could not sit near him without feeling something awesome. But he had not brought whatever huge potential lay dormant in him to consciousness, nor learned to channel his energy creatively. Instead, he had manifested symptoms around the power chakra, then contained and dissociated from those symptoms. Then, crudely put, he had asked *others* to open him and find the source of his discomfort rather than searching for the source himself.

To choose the quick fix — such as surgery or pills — over the exploration of symptoms can sometimes be tragic. Few people realize the cost until it is too late. When Andrew allowed himself to go into the void and decided to be fully present with his pain, that pain disappeared. He shook and shook and when the shaking stopped, the pain was gone. This seemed to confirm that his slowness was in fact a block originating in his contained and dissociated energy, and that the accident had increased the dissociation to such an extent that his consciousness was almost severed from his body. Briefly, Andrew had been using so much energy to distance himself from both his power and his pain that he had been made nearly catatonic, as if by strong medication.

SPIRALS WITHIN CIRCLES

I hope this thumbnail sketch of the five element system has been sufficient to hint at its enormous scope. A cyclical system, more-over, permits layers within layers. There are as many ways to look at the elements as there are interpreters of them; and each of these has its uses. At one level, the five elements describe psychosomatic constitutional typing. At another level, the system can be applied to cycles and transitions or phases that take place naturally over a lifetime as well as cycling continually through our lives (spring/ Wood as the growing years of childhood and adolescence; sum-mer as the productive years; late summer as the harvest of life in late middle age; autumn as the letting go of worldly preoccupa-tions and the turning toward the spiritual life, which is a cultural norm in some older societies; and the death/rebirth and gestation times of deep winter). Some prefer to call the system as a whole the *five phases*, as the cyclical dynamic character of the seasonal phases seems to them more significant than the more static quali-ties of the elements.

In addition, several layers of influence from various elements may be recognized in each of us. Many practitioners schematize three kinds or levels of influence, often from two or three differ-ent elements. For example, an individual could be 'Fire without, Metal within and Earth behind' or 'Wood without, Metal within and Earth behind'. Or less schematically, 'Fire, Fire and Water'. Practitioners consider that only rarely is anyone largely defined by a single element or phase. 'Earth, Earth and Earth', for in-stance, is an exceptional assessment.

At yet another level, the system can be applied to whole cultures (perhaps many of us would agree that the culture of the United States betrays a dominant influence from the Wood element with aspects of Fire and of Water). And between the elements, there can be interactions that give rise to pathological processes. I will return to this theme later.

Despite the huge potential of the five elements as a system, the process of integrating transformational experiences remains a task we generally have to undertake through meditation and introspection. Without integration, transformation can go around in circles and become a frustrating and repetitive process. If that happens, it can become a trap. In the next couple of chapters, I will present additional perspectives that can both simplify and integrate the five elements.

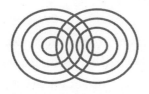

CHAPTER 6

THE SIX TEMPERAMENTS

*All emotions are modifications of one primordial, undifferentiated
emotion that has its origin in the loss of awareness of who you are
beyond name and form.*

— Eckhart Tolle

*S*imilar in many ways to the classic five element
system, the so-called *six temperaments* and *eight character types*
classification, developed in France by Yves Requena and Gaston
Berger, groups the five elements in a simple yet elegant way I have
found very useful in locating and releasing blocked original
energy through acupuncture.

The five element system's depth and its insightful description of
the interactions between the elements' energies and its understanding of the way in which disease arises in individuals are its great
strengths. In contrast, the French system, though perhaps less
richly textured, recommends itself by the ease with which it can be
applied. Pairing the two systems can be a particularly powerful and
simple way to access original energy without getting lost in
abstractions.

Although acupuncturists often talk of elemental constitutional
types — Wood, Earth, Water, Metal or Fire — as we have in the
preceding chapter, they will often intermingle a strange language
that has to do with energy zones, circuits, axes and vectors of the

body. The French system makes much use of this language so, without getting too bogged down in acupuncture theory, let us have a quick look at what this vocabulary refers to.

Briefly, the body surface can be divided into three zones of influence, disarming in their simplicity, namely the back, the sides and the front of the body. There are three yang axes and three yin axes. The back zone is referred to as the *Tai Yang* (Greater Yang) axis, the side zone as *Shao Yang* (Lesser Yang) and the front zone as *Yang Ming* (Yang Brightness).

Each of these yang zones of influence has a yin counterpart and together they make a complete circuit. Specifically, the *Tai Yang* axis is paired with *Shao Yin* (Lesser Yin) to complete the circuit known as Tai Yang–Shao Yin; *Shao Yang* is paired in turn with *Jue Yin* (Least Yin) to make the Shao Yang–Jue Yin circuit; and *Yang Ming* is paired with *Tai Yin* (Greater Yin) to form the Yang Ming–Tai Yin circuit. Each of these circuits governs certain organ vectors or functions, and each is associated with particular elements we met in the last chapter (see table 1).

Zone	Elements	Energy Circuits
Back Zone	Water / Fire	Tai Yang–Shao Yin
Side Zone	Wood / Fire	Shao Yang–Jue Yin
Front Zone	Earth / Metal	Yang Ming–Tai Yin

Table 1: The three zones and their circuits

These three energy circuits double the Fire element as it represents — as you may recall from the last chapter — four rather than two organs, as with the other four elements (see figure 1).

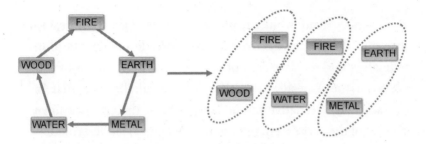

Figure 1: Deriving three circuits from the five elements

Now, one more thing to remember is that each one of these axes embraces two energy vectors — an organ pair previously described in the five element model, so that a relationship now becomes apparent between two otherwise disparate organs (see table 2).

ENERGY AXIS	ORGAN ASSOCIATIONS
TAI YANG	Bladder (BL) — Small Intestine (SI)
SHAO YANG	Gall Bladder (GB) — Triple Heater (TH)
YANG MING	Stomach (ST) — Large Intestine (LI)
TAI YIN	Spleen (SP) — Lung (LU)
SHAO YIN	Kidney (KI) — Heart (HT)
JUE YIN	Liver (LV) — Pericardium (PC)

Table 2: Energy axes and corresponding organs

CONSTITUTIONAL TYPING ACCORDING TO FRENCH ENERGETICS

Although Requena described the process by which he has derived eight character types arising out of his six temperaments, it is fairly complex.[1] And, while the process may be of great interest to acupuncture professionals, to explore those derivations here in any detail would — if we are not careful — shift the focus of this book from the experiential to the theoretical. Bearing that in mind, a useful alternative might be to look at the constitutional attributes of the various energy vectors we have so far described.

As we go through this exercise, it is worth remembering that yang temperament types tend to mobilize their energy more easily, being more active and outgoing, while the yin types tend to be quieter and stiller.

THE TAI YANG AXIS: WATER–BLADDER / FIRE–SMALL INTESTINE

The Tai Yang axis has a Fire pole and a Water pole and relates to the organs of the Small Intestine and the Bladder. Although a circuit of Water and Fire might seem unlikely, there are energetic similarities between these polar opposites. For example, both the Fire and Water aspects of Tai Yang are characteristically active in the world, willful, intense and accomplished. They often devote their lives to an ideal that engages their passion, sometimes to the detriment of other aspects of their lives. And both are prone to neck or back stiffness and bladder problems. It is their styles that differ. Those at the Fire end of the spectrum tend to be excessively present — loud and self-assured — like a blazing fire. They are more 'in your face'. At the other end of the spectrum, the more Watery types are cooler and more analytical, pushing themselves through life, using willpower rather than instinct to overcome doubts and fears. Like a stream wearing through rock, they persist quietly through the years. In other words, the circuit spans the terrain between

1   Those who are interested in learning about this system in greater depth may refer to Appendix 3, French Energetics: The Eight Character Types.

Mind and Heart, between rational analysis and the more flamboyant style of going with gut feelings.

Within the Tai Yang axis, it is predictable that someone with a temperament more toward the Fire end of the spectrum will benefit from a little cooling down, while the cooler types could use a little firing up. This is precisely what makes it so effective to pair them. Both poles reflect the same original energy — the Fire end needing to cool down, the Water end needing to lighten up.

THE SHAO YANG AXIS:
WOOD–GALL BLADDER / FIRE–TRIPLE HEATER

The Shao Yang axis runs between the poles of Wood and Fire, through the organs of the Gall Bladder and the Triple Heater. Again, Wood and Fire might seem an unlikely combination. However, they pair up very well. Fire shares the creativity, spiritedness and competitiveness of Wood, as well as its tendency toward anger. However, they differ in the way they manage that anger — the Wood end of the spectrum tending toward implosion, the Fire toward explosion. As a result, those at the Wood end of the spectrum are more prone to depression, apathy, indecisiveness and lack of self-confidence, while the Fire types, though they can be passionate and Heart-centred, tend to be more overtly resentful and aggressive.

Thus, the Shao Yang encompasses what the five element perspective might classify simply as Wood, spanning the territory from repression-stagnation when the creative flow is blocked, to decisive, bold and Heart-centred action when the energy is effectively channelled. And both have a tendency to develop lateral symptoms based on muscular tension arising out of constant frustration — such as migraine headaches, neck and shoulder stiffness, lumbosacral pain or hip problems.

THE YANG MING AXIS: EARTH–STOMACH / METAL–LARGE INTESTINE

Yang Ming is concerned with the anterior of the body and the digestive system, spanning the region between entry and exit, between the oral and the anal. Earth and Metal share an energy circuit with a gastrointestinal focus: the Earth element rules the middle to upper digestive system — the esophagus, stomach and duodenum; the Metal element the two extremes of that system — the bowels, the teeth and the sinuses. The Earthier types generally have a warmer disposition and tend to be more cheerful, benevolent, outgoing and confident. They like their food, enjoy good wine and pleasant company. When out of sorts, they lose their centre, get irritable and resentful, and tend toward gastritis, food sensitivities, gastro-esophageal reflux, and the like.

The more Metal types share the active and outgoing nature of Yang Ming-Earth but tend to have a cooler disposition. Their coolness is both somatic and psychic, so they can appear detached, impassive, composed. When in balance, they are both elegant and forthright, full of wisdom and transcendent joy; when out of balance they tend toward depression and can become a bit anal, in the sense of being obsessive or mentally constipated, sometimes becoming fixated on what they see as right action — such as orderliness, duty and responsibility. They also often have a tendency to chronic sinusitis or dental caries.

Whether Earth or Metal, Yang Ming types when out of balance often have problems with digestion — again, either somatic or psychic — with the process of taking in the new and letting go the old. If Earth, the difficulty is more likely to be something to do with taking in, while if Metal, the difficulty is more likely to be with letting go.

THE TAI YIN AXIS:
EARTH–SPLEEN / METAL–LUNG

The Tai Yin axis spans the dichotomy between separateness and closeness, Earth types preferring closeness, and Metal types preferring to be separate. Tai Yin–Earth types tend to be mellow, calm, soft and often plump people who enjoy feeling connected and loved, and who like to be the centre of attention. They like their creature comforts, often have sugar cravings, tend to gain weight easily and get varicose veins. They have little worldly ambition and do not care much for schedules or punctuality. When in balance, they find fulfillment by being in service, giving solace to others and being maternal. When out of balance their energy becomes insufficient to altruism, so they become either couch potatoes, or dutiful drudges — growing resentful and needy in the process. They can become a bit *icky* in their unusual need for reassurance, comforting and closeness.

On the other hand, Tai Yin–Metal types prefer to be alone and separate and tend to need a lot of space. In contrast to the plump Earth, they are often asthenic (thin), and tend to be quiet, reserved, introverted and meticulous. They like order and solitude, dislike chaos and crowds. When in balance they appear quiet, serene and low-key. When out of balance they tend to get run down, fatigued and depressed, and suffer from frequent coughs and colds, asthma or eczema. On a mental level, they can become morally rigid and intolerant — illnesses that corroborate their desire for greater distance from others. So the Tai Yin axis is very much concerned with appropriate boundaries — not in terms of intimate relationships but rather in terms of personal space. The Earth end of the spectrum likes to get close, the Metal end wants a lot of space. A balancing of the boundaries toward a healthy centre can be helpful for both temperament types.

THE JUE YIN AXIS:
WOOD–LIVER / FIRE–PERICARDIUM

Jue Yin is another Wood and Fire axis but, whereas Shao Yang (above) represents the yang aspect, Jue Yin is the yin aspect. The cardinal feature of Jue Yin people is mood variability or anxiety. Rather than getting frustrated and angry like their Shao Yang cousins, they tend to experience their angst as raw anxiety and get fidgety instead. Those at the Wood end of the spectrum tend to be more inhibited, sensitive and withdrawn, sometimes appearing shy because of an inability to express their feelings. In contrast, the Jue Yin–Fire type is more blatantly nervous and agitated, unable to relax and constantly on high alert. But whether Wood or Fire, their chronic tension makes them prone to muscular aches and pains, migraine headaches and insomnia.

As with the Shao Yang, this seems to be in slight contradistinction to the five element perspective, in which the Pericardium imbalance moves more around the joy/sadness dichotomy and less around anger. This is an example of the differences between the two systems, which at first can be a bit confusing. But rather than attempt to resolve the apparent differences it can be more useful to realize that both points of view are valid. After all, the Pericardium is more an energetic function than a physical structure. Looked at from the point of view of five element theory, the Heart Protector (Pericardium) has to do with the regulation of intimacy and the Heart's boundaries. The Jue Yin axis confirms our intuition that someone with a Heart bruised by betrayal is quite capable of chronic worry or resentment. By holding both ideas simultaneously, we can get a larger picture of the Heart Protector's function.

When in balance, the Jue Yin personality is creative and optimistic, tending to use their creative imagination to pursue realistic goals. When out of balance, they tend to become dominated by their emotions, neurotic and escapist, taking refuge from life in fantasy, a place of escape from their incessant anxiety.

THE SHAO YIN AXIS:
WATER–KIDNEY / FIRE–HEART

Of all the polar opposites, this Water/Fire axis is probably the most extreme. Shao Yin–Water people are introverted and timid, unable to get going because of a fear of life, while the Shao Yin–Fire people are always on high and exude heat. Their common ground is that both are sentimental, feeling types. At the Water end are people who exhibit the deep hidden quality of the Water element, whose life theme revolves around how they deal with fear and how much they have to overcome to face life. Such people are often secretive and a bit paranoid, like to wear dark clothing and always feel cold. They tend to be reticent, self-reproaching, depressed and defeatist. Frequently, they suffer from low back or knee pain. By contrast, Shao Yin–Fire people are bubbly, expansive and impulsive and like to wear brightly coloured clothing; they exude heat and like to be the life of the party. They may also tend to be hypersexual and manic. Although it is difficult to find commonality between these two extremes, the same energy circuit is involved. While the spectrum is unusually broad, simply put, the Fire type could use some cooling down, while the Water type could use some passion and excitement.

All in all, the value of the French energetic system is that it gives us a simple way into the often complex realm of symptom exploration — especially in chronic conditions — using best-guess typology and broad zones of involvement (back, front, side). It saves a lot of time and energy and encourages a greater emphasis on direct bodily responses to guide interactions, instead of relying on the mental gymnastics of complex acupuncture theory.

I will try to show how important this is as we go along. For the time being, suffice it to say that the classic five element approach entails a fairly skilled form of history-taking that involves— among other things — emotion testing, which can take a long time to master and is often never fully understood, leading to erroneous categorizations and less useful treatments. The French system, on the other hand, does not require so difficult an inquiry. By locating the most likely energy circuit involved in a symptom, it can give a helpful pointer to someone's overall constitution. In a later chapter, I will show how this works in practice. For now, I want to explore one more dualism — the Heart/Mind split — before turning to the Ayurvedic understanding of psychosomatic and spiritual energy, the chakras, and integrating them into the developing picture.

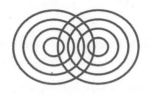

CHAPTER 7

THE HEART/MIND SPLIT

The heart has its reasons of which reason knows nothing:
We know this in countless ways.
— Blaise Pascal (1623–62)

*O*ne of the most important of all the blocks to bodily and spiritual wholeness, or health, is that between Heart and Mind — a schism that has particular relevance to Western collective consciousness, which tends to consider the functions of feeling and thinking polar opposites, if not frank antagonists.

In Chinese medicine, conversely, Heart and Mind are so closely associated and their unity so vital to health that there is one word for them both, *xin*, and any separation or distinction between them is considered a precursor to illness. This *xin*, or Heart-Mind, is said to be the residence of memory, thinking, consciousness, mental activity (including emotions) and sleep, and is considered to be the home of spirit, or what Chinese medicine calls *shen*. If Mind and Heart are divided, the effect on the *shen* can be catastrophic. Unfortunately, as some degree of schism is so common in the West as to be considered the norm, its role in illness can be missed.

Happily, the moment we become aware of the omnipresence of this split and reckon its real cost to ourselves and our societies can be life-altering. In his autobiography, *Memories, Dreams, Reflections,*

Carl Jung recounts that moment of awareness in his own life. His own blind acquiescence in our civilization's denial of the Heart became startlingly clear to him during the course of a conversation with Chief Ochwiay Biano of the Taos Pueblo Indians of New Mexico in 1932. The chief was quite candid in his perception of the white man's Heart/Mind split:

> 'See . . . how cruel the whites look. Their lips are thin, their noses sharp, their faces furrowed and distorted by folds. Their eyes have a staring expression; they are always seeking something. What are they seeking? The whites always want something; they are always uneasy and restless. We do not know what they want. We do not understand them. We think that they are mad.'

When Jung asks why he thinks they are all mad, Ochwiay Biano replies, 'They say that they think with their heads.'

> 'Why, of course,' Jung reports was his surprised reply. 'What do you think with?' 'We think here,' the chief told him, indicating his heart.

Jung did not miss the chief's point. 'I fell into a long meditation,' he wrote later. 'For the first time in my life, so it seemed to me, someone had drawn for me a picture of the real white man. . . . This Indian had struck our vulnerable spot, unveiled a truth to which we are blind.' Jung felt himself led to a profound insight into the imbalance in Western civilization's understanding of the human psyche, and a realization that 'we' have become so habituated to the split between thinking and feeling that even he — a pioneer of psychoanalysis with a significant early interest in what we now call schizophrenia — was taken by surprise when it was so graphically pointed out.

'I felt rising within me like a shapeless mist something unknown and yet deeply familiar', he writes as he reflects on European history's wilful, avaricious — or, in other words, *heart*less and seeking — depredations and the stark limitations of the consciousness that was marked by those staring eyes, by contrast with the enviable serenity of the Pueblo, whom he had observed in his sojourn there, profoundly at home in the centre of his cosmos.

It is difficult to accept the possibility that something fundamental in consciousness might have been lost, that collectively, we may all be slightly mad. Although many people will readily admit that they use their heads to chart all aspects of their daily lives and that they suffer a lot of anxiety as they do so, few seem to recognize that their endemic angst is in fact generated by a loss of connection to their Heart centre.

But as a cultural phenomenon, the shift from Heart to head is nothing new. One need only recall René Descartes' assertion — *I think, therefore I am* — splashed boldly across the smooth darkness of his existential *tabula rasa*. It is the perfect expression of our continuing conviction in the West that reason is somehow synonymous with human existence. Everyone knows the sentence. What is more, we all behave as though we believe it. The rational mind continues to assert its superiority, taking it upon itself to dismiss other modes of perception and awareness as irrational and therefore faulty. Such circular, self-serving thinking — the very essence of denial — is a typical emanation of the Heart/Mind split.

Regrettably, however, the rational mind as reflected by the brain — which leading ethnographer Joseph Campbell emphatically referred to as a secondary organ — is not really up to the task of being our spiritual or energetic centre. It is there to make day-to-day decisions — to add up the grocery bill, build our homes and cities, or put a human being on the moon, depending on our requirements. But it cannot comprehend emotion or spirit other than as theories. It just does not have the capacity.

THE LANGUAGE OF HEART AND MIND

Although Chinese medicine acknowledges no fewer than five *souls* or spirits and nearly as many qualities of energies in the body, the English language is currently peculiarly bereft of comparable vocabulary to describe inner states and realms. So before going any further, I want to go over some of the distinctions I have made in this book and to emphasize that these distinctions are provisional. In providing these definitions, I acknowledge that readers may have other ways of understanding some of this language: I only ask for acceptance of these definitions for the purposes of this book.

As I hinted above, that the Chinese word *xin* has no counterpart in English is telling. It means that in the very act of speaking of it as Heart-Mind, we must enact the split by clumsily cobbling the two words into one. Alternatively, we could try to avoid a schism by translating it simply as Heart, or as Mind — either one of which is misleading — or more accurately but rather technically rendering it as *Heart-Yin* (for Heart) and *Heart-Yang* (for Mind). All of this, however, makes any integrated understanding of Heart and Mind hard to grasp through language.

All things considered, I consider the term *ego-mind* or *mind* (with a small *m*) are most useful when referring to the individual, analytical, thinking mind, separated from the body by the mind/body split and will use *Mind* (with a capital *M*) to refer to the larger consciousness that transcends or integrates the mind/body split. Equally, the word *heart* (with a small *h*) will refer to the physical heart, while *Heart* will refer to the metaphoric Heart or Heart energy. Finally, I will use the phrase *Heart-Mind* to imply the integrated think-ing-feeling unity, roughly corresponding to the Chinese word *xin*.

ASSUMPTIONS OF MIND

Mind exists in linear time, in a world of past and future, and under-stands that world in terms of cause and effect. Such thinking has been equated with the biblical concept of *logos* or the *Word*. As a re-flection of our culture's mind-based thinking, Western medicine has been characterized by reductionism, linearity and causality.

Linearity	past, present and future
Cause and effect	an effect implies a prior cause
Coolness	detachment
Reductionism	the whole is equal to the sum of the parts
Determinism	the universe is mechanistic
Problem-oriented	actively seeks out problems
Rational	looks for reasons
Absence	projects into past and/or future

Table 1 : Attributes of Mind (Heart-Yang)

Mind tends to be rational and detached and energetically *cool*.[1] Because it always looks to the past or the future, it is *absent* from the present moment. Such absence is a characteristic feature of

---

1 The paradox of a yang function being cool is expressed in the familiar yin/yang symbol as a little bit of yin inside yang, and similarly, the paradox of a yin function being warm is expressed as a little yang inside yin.

people who live in their heads — familiar examples being the archetypal absent-minded professor, or perhaps the heady and driven businessman or businesswoman. Briefly, it could be said that the key assumption of mind is the existence of linear time.

In contrast to the linearity of mind, the characteristic of a Heart-centred awareness is an attention focused completely in the present moment — a state which some say is the condition of divine or creative inspiration. In this state, past and future merge into an eternal *now*. The Heart cannot exist outside of the now because, unlike the mind, it does not imagine a past and a future. It can only acknowledge the truth of *what is* in the moment.

Non-linearity	acausal interconnectedness
Acausality	there is no *specific* cause for any phenomenon
Holism	the whole is more than the sum of the parts
Indeterminism	the universe cannot be fully understood mechanistically
Problem-free	problem and solution are the same
Non-rational	truth is quite often unreasonable
Presence	the present is all there is
Warmth/radiance	compassion

Table 2: Attributes of Heart (Heart-Yin)

With awareness focused in the present moment, the Heart exhibits the capacity to be present with whatever experience is occurring in the moment. Thus the Heart reflects *what is* while the mind reflects *what is not* — that is, *what was* and *what might be*. And, in contrast to the detachment and coolness of mind, the compassion of the Heart comes across as energetically *warm*.

THE DIFFERENTIATION OF HEART AND MIND

Prior to the existential split, Heart and Mind exist as an undifferentiated whole, a fusion of Heart-Yin and Heart-Yang. It is with the dawning of self-awareness that the active principle of Mind arises out of the Heart centre to form a differentiated axis that plans, decides and projects into the past and future. However, the emergence of Mind does not alter the fundamental attributes of the Heart centre, which remains whole and unchanged, compassionate, silent and intensely present.

Integration of a warm Heart with a cool mind gives us the familiar yin/yang symbol with its areas of fluid exchange, dependent co-arising and interdependence; areas of yin darkness in yang brightness, and vice versa (see figure 1).

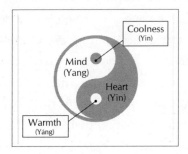

Figure 1: Heart-Mind and the yin/yang symbol

Of course, differentiation of these two principles is no problem, as long as they remain connected. It is *dissociation* that leads to difficulties. Dissociation between Heart and Mind is marked by the kind of ungrounded activity that is characteristic of modern Western society. It is that busy, busy, frenetic rushing around that increasingly seems to be the norm.

RELATIONAL HOLISM
AND WHOLE-SYSTEM PERCEPTION

One way to better understand the relationship between the Heart and Mind is to consider the body-mind-spirit as an ecosystem. An ecosystem is a complex, interdependent system in which every component is related to every other component. Remove, damage, increase or decrease one component, or add a new one, and you affect all the others. The cause-and-effect principle that the linear mind uses to understand the world allows us to see one component's direct effect on another but misses systemic, relational interactions (which, in linear scientific or medical contexts, are dismissed as mysterious and irrelevant side effects). The Heart, on the other hand, is a whole-system function that is both immanent and transcendent. It sees everything as a part of a system that is more than the sum of its parts.

Struggling with the paucity of language for such whole-system concepts, modern science has come up with complicated explanatory phrases. For example, the principle of *relational holism* acknowledges the overall effect of instantaneous non-linear interconnections between system components. Similarly, modern medicine is slowly coming to grips with the notion that human beings can be better understood as *complex adaptive systems* — the biological equivalent of relational holism. A Heart-centred awareness can intuit such interconnections without necessarily bringing them to rational consciousness as we must do to put them into language.

THE MIND/BODY SPLIT:
MIND IMPOVERISHED AS EGO-MIND

Integrated functioning of the Heart-Mind requires that the Mind remain fully cognizant of its origin — which it can do by acting in concert with the vibrational rhythm generated by the Heart centre. Practically speaking, this means developing Heart-centred awareness, and paying heed to feelings and intuitive hunches rather than ignoring them and relying totally on reason. Without this Mind-Heart connection, the Mind's assumption of linear time, and its inability to be present and quiet in the moment, gives rise to the dual tetherings of *desire* and *aversion* (or what in Buddhism are identified as various forms of *attachment*), as it fantasizes about the past and the future. Desire might be defined as the memory of past pleasure projected into the future; aversion as the memory of past pain similarly projected.

Inevitably, the ego-mind develops strategies designed to fulfill desires and avoid any encounter with projected pain. The foremost strategy, arising from a deep suspicion and fear of the body and its pain, is a retreat into an imaginary mental hideout located somewhere behind the eyes. From this safely encapsulated cerebral locus, the ego looks out at a menacing world and tries to figure out how to stay safe. With this retreat into the mental realm, the mind/body split is established and Mind is reduced to mind. And this ego-mind tends to view the body as a threat. After this, every little ache or pain is viewed as a pathology.

Once ego-mind takes over, illness becomes pretty much inevitable as every physical symptom becomes a problem requiring rational explanation and treatment. However, ego-based strategies by their very nature tend to defer healing to some future moment that never arrives, while illness continues to fill the present. This is one reason why chronic illnesses often stubbornly resist treatment — they cannot yield to mind-based interventions, because mind itself is the source of the difficulty.

By contrast, a Heart-centred view sees past and future simultaneously so that problem and solution exist together in an eternal now. Experiencing this understanding in the body-mind is one of the keys to healing.

CHINESE MEDICINE
AND THE HEART/MIND SPLIT

In Chinese medicine, the Heart is said to be the home of the spirit or *shen* of the individual. And this Heart is likened to the Emperor, a semi-divine being who resides in the Imperial palace and functions as the kingdom's spiritual leader. This Emperor does not actually do much. His *wu wei* — or effortless mastery — means nothing is done yet the kingdom's body-mind-spirit functions harmoniously by its very nature. It is the picture of optimal health.

When Heart and Mind dissociate, however, sooner or later the ego-mind takes over as self-proclaimed monarch of the realm, and the Heart centre is increasingly forgotten. As the mind relies on reason, our feelings, intuition and hunches — including calls of distress from the body — are ignored, viewed with suspicion, pathologized or confronted antagonistically.

Such a situation leads to anxiety and depression, or as Chinese medicine puts it, *deficient Heart Yin* and *deficient Heart Spirit*. Of course, in Western culture, anxiety and depression are common diagnoses but they are usually treated mechanistically — in other words, treatment is usually directed at supporting the split-off ego-mind and the brain rather than the whole self. The loss of Heart Spirit is rarely appreciated; and, while anti-depressants can certainly change brain chemistry to help people function better in their daily lives, their use does nothing to address the loss of Heart-Mind integrity, which may become even more entrenched under their sway.

In the body, loss of Heart Spirit is often reflected by the presence of tension bands, the specific location of which is predicated on our underlying constitutional type. For example, yang constitutional types — Wood and Fire — will often have a tension band in the upper chest and/or neck area, that may give rise to headaches, neck and shoulder pain. The more yin constitutional types — Water and Metal — may well have more tension in the diaphragm and pelvis, and wall off the Heart by suppressing the movement of *kundalini energy* (to be discussed further in chapters 8, 13 and 16), which otherwise would rise upward from the pelvis to open the Heart. While Earth types, being energetically at the centre, often have maximum tension in the diaphragm.

THE ORGANS OF THE HEART-MIND

In Chinese medicine theory, the Heart function encompasses an integrated relationship between itself and other yin organs: specifically, Heart, Liver and Kidneys rule the treasures of the *shen* (spirit), *qi* (energy) and *jing* (essence), respectively. The Heart stores the *shen*, the Liver regulates the flow of *qi* and the Kidneys store the *jing*. In contrast, the Mind is mediated by the yang organs of Small Intestine (which sorts or discerns), the Gall Bladder (which decides) and the Bladder (which acts). Meanwhile, as we have seen, the integrity of the Heart is preserved through the Pericardium and Triple Heater energies, which form layers of defence against insults directed at the Heart.

THE MISTAKE OF THE INTELLECT

When ego-mind takes over, the Mind's organ functions are compromised to the point of becoming self-destructive — a situation which Ayurvedic medicine calls *pragyaparadh*, or the mistake of the intellect. In the parlance of Chinese medicine, firstly, the Small Intestine begins to incorrectly sort experience and distorts the messages coming from the body. For example, anxiety and pain are framed as *bad* instead of being understood as useful information emanating from the body's energy field. Secondly, the Gall Bladder makes poor decisions with regard to energy management, either aggressively attacking the symptoms or containing and then retreating from them by dissociation, instead of softening and letting the energy move. And finally the Bladder — using the will — institutes fear-based self-destructive actions, such as inappropriate acting-out behaviours, drug-taking or even surgical procedures to eradicate unwanted symptoms, instead of redirecting the will internally to facilitate body-mind-spirit integration.

RE-AWAKENING THE HEART

Since loss of the Heart centre is such a universal phenomenon, the goal of re-awakening it is a common theme in the healing journey. Paradoxically, one way to help re-awaken the Heart is to go back to the beginning and redifferentiate Mind and Heart so that the ego-mind becomes more aware of its dissociated state. After all, the ego cannot reintegrate something it does not know is missing. In his book, *Nourishing Destiny*, Lonny Jarrett explains the importance of this differentiation process. He points out that if we are labouring to justify a particular course of action, then we are almost certainly in our heads. The Heart, he says, needs no reasons or justifications to feel what it feels, while the ego-mind is always seeking rationalizations for its behaviour, which usually amounts to chasing after various addictions that briefly alleviate our existential angst.

One useful technique to awaken the Heart, then, might involve making a point of closely observing our rationalizations and, whenever the opportunity arises, cutting them off at the pass and deliberately becoming fully present.

During DIA, subtle energetic shifts will often signal that we are approaching the Heart centre. They include a deepening of emotional affect, chest or epigastric discomfort and/or an exacerbation of symptoms. Once through this formidable barrier, a deep sense of calmness and peace will often arise, together with the emergence of understanding or insight. Frequently, this shift will follow an agonizing pain to which we have intentionally surrendered. There may be the extraordinary sensation that the mind has stopped. The first time this occurs, the qualitative change in inner experience can quite literally blow the mind.

Reframing our negative interpretation of painful or uncomfortable body experience is fundamental to allowing the emergence of a more integrated worldview centred in the Heart's truth. For this, it is often best to go directly to the information-sorting Small Intestine. After all, decisions made and actions taken are by necessity based on information received, and if that information is distorted, the other Mind functions will be correspondingly compromised.

For example, to reframe pain as a teacher rather than an enemy, or anxiety as excited anticipation rather than doom and gloom, is to reframe our body as a repository of energetic wisdom, rather than a fearful machine that keeps going awry. And mental justifications can be exposed for what they are — rationalizations rather than core truths.

๐ *JULIA*: THE BLACK HOLE OF GRIEF

Julia was a forty-five-year-old woman who had developed a bizarre condition that was making both her arms increasingly weak. She had shown great promise as a freelance artist but her condition was robbing her of the ability to fulfill her ambitions. Julia had numbness and shooting sensations in her hands and fingers, which were also becoming increasingly stiff. Conventional treatment with anti-depressants and counselling had so far done little and Julia was understandably frightened and depressed. MRI scanning of the discs of the neck showed minor bulging at several levels but nothing remotely suggesting the need for surgery.

The true location of her distress, however, was revealed during our first meeting when she described a sensation of a *black hole* in the centre of her chest.

As is quite typical of chronic illness, Julia's condition was multi-faceted, one energetic factor overlapping another. First, I guessed her to be a Shao Yin–Water, a constitution that has great difficulty mobilizing original energy, which tends to get contained in the root chakra and pelvis. Her tight diaphragm perhaps spoke of a need to please that had resulted in a loss of personal power and the anger that follows such a loss. Her Heart Protector, the Pericardium, was still on overdrive protecting her from the pain of her father's premature death many years previously, which had led to tension in her upper chest and shoulders. Overall, her mind/body split prevented her from trusting the signals coming from her body. As a result, she had tension bands in the pelvis, diaphragm, shoulders and neck, a significant mind/body split and a Heart/Mind split to boot. In short, she was a great reservoir waiting to spill its dikes.

During early sessions, Julia swam in grief and terror that seemed to have no shore. Gradually, her shoulders started to loosen and shake and her arms and hands started to vibrate. Eventually, her hands grew warm. After a session, the black hole in her chest would often radiate heat. Session after session, we worked to reframe her feelings and thoughts as they arose, emphasizing the positive nature of her grief and rage and that recovery lay in going through the feelings rather than around them.

Julia's story is not over. But a few months after she left us, she wrote and expressed excitement over an insight she had gained while writing poetry. In her words:

> . . . this was a significant moment (writing the poem, that is), because it was in doing so that I became sharply aware of my head/heart split and the effect it has on creating. I started writing it after doing some meditation, breathing and shaking, and the first two verses sort of wrote themselves. Then it stopped, although I knew it wasn't finished. I struggled with it for ages, until I decided to go back to the point from which it started . . . and then I realized that what I was actually doing was going back to the *feeling* that had triggered it. When it had 'stopped' was the point at which I had gone into my head (intellectual, words, ideas) and lost the feeling. Of course I needed the words and ideas too but as soon as I saw that, it was easy to finish it, and I felt like going out for a bottle of champagne, as it seemed like such a significant discovery. Nothing I didn't know in my head, but I'd never realized it so fully before. It's hard to describe, but it was a bit like knowing it in the body, the physical reality of it.

As of this writing, Julia's shoulder and arm symptoms have subsided, her depression is much improved, her hands are warm and her creativity is beginning to return.

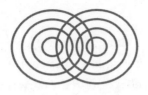

CHAPTER 8

THE CHAKRAS

Meditate deeply and faithfully and one day you will wake up in ecstasy with God and see how foolish it is that people think they are suffering. You and I and they are all pure Spirit.

— Paramahansa Yogananda

$\mathcal{T}$he traditional Ayurvedic system of the chakras is another useful way of mapping the body-mind's subtle energies. My purpose here is not to elaborate on the complexities of this ancient system but only to present the seven main energy centres and to show how these centres might correspond with the five element constitutional typing we have been looking at. Although some have argued that such cross-referencing is untenable, since the Chinese and South Asian medical perspectives are quite different (readers will note that the Ayurvedic and Chinese elements do not correspond in the table below), I have found it so useful in my practice to hold both systems in mind, I now consider doing so an opportunity to embrace genuine complexity rather than a test of the superiority of one or another system, or an anxious negotiation of their differences.

THE CHAKRAS

The chakras are energy centres. Although different sources describe varying numbers and locations of these centres — and they are certainly numerous — there is general agreement about the primacy of the seven that run down the centre of the body. Table 1 lists these seven main chakras and the correspondences that can be made with Chinese acupuncture and the five elements.[1]

Chakra	Sanskrit name	Ayurvedic element	Acu-points	Chinese name	Chinese element
Root [1]	Muladhara	Earth	CV-1	Huiyin, 'Meeting of Yin'	Water
Sexual [2]	Svadhisthana	Water	CV-4	Guanyuan, 'Origin Pass'	Earth
			CV-5	Shimen, 'Stone Gate'	
			CV-6	Qihai, 'Sea of Qi'	
Solar plexus [3]	Manipura	Fire	CV-12	Zhongwan, 'Central Cavity'	Wood
Heart [4]	Anahata	Air	CV-17	Shangzhong, 'Chest Centre'	Fire
Throat [5]	Vishuddha	Space	CV-22	Tiantu, 'Heaven's Prominence'	Metal
			ST-9	Renying, 'Man Welcome'	
Third eye [6]	Ajna	[No element]	GV-24.5	Yintang, 'Seal Hall'	[No element]
Crown [7]	Sahasrara	[No element]	GV-20	Baihui, 'Hundred Meetings'	[No element]

Table 1: Chakras and correspondences

The seven main chakras tabled above can be usefully grouped into lower, middle and upper; and these have been considered to be the physiological, personal and spiritual levels, respectively. However, I

---

1 The letter-number codes (e.g. CV-1) refer to acupuncture points and can be found in any acupuncture text. The acu-points are not direct correspondences but only best-guess approximations.

find it more useful to think of the seven chakras in two groups of three upper and three lower with the Heart chakra as a central integrator (see figure 1). Conceived of this way, a very interesting symmetry becomes apparent: chakras in the upper and the lower grouping mirror each other, reflecting the void, (the root and crown chakras), individuation or agency (the solar plexus and the throat) and connection (the sexual and forehead chakras) respectively.

The void refers to the unknown, the no-place out of which everything arises, which some have called the Tao; individuation refers to the principle of agency, or yang; connection refers to the principle of communion, or yin. The lower three chakras reflect these themes as they relate to the ego-identified individual; the upper three chakras reflect the same themes as they relate to the transpersonal. A central principle assists in the integration of the personal and the transpersonal and this integrating principle turns out to be Heart — prime energetic generator and, as *xin* or Heart-Mind, our real centre.

Many people live their lives out of the lower three chakras, never accessing the transcendent resources of the upper energy centres. A collective bottleneck seems to exist between the third (power), fourth (Heart) and fifth (throat) chakras, which can be reflected in physical symptoms, with the result that many people with chronic pain and/or other chronic illness are manifesting difficulties at these levels. And it is here (at the fourth and fifth chakras) that the five element tradition has great relevance — it just seems to lend itself to the kinds of difficulties that arise at these two levels.

Although both transformation and transcendence are involved at all levels, at the lower chakra levels, transformation seems to dominate. However, when we move through the Heart centre to the upper chakras, it is vertical integration and transcendence that appear to be the main work of the local energies. Beyond the throat, accessing the forehead and crown chakras requires other aspects of Chinese medicine because at these levels the elements themselves are transcended (you will notice in table 1 that there are no elements associated with these chakras) and the aspirant increasingly requires direct insight to proceed. That is not to say that acupuncture is not pertinent in this phase of the quest, only that the five element model and the interactions between the elements become less relevant.

If we are able to open the Heart, we begin to gain access to the transcendent energies of the upper three centres; and the development of these upper centres, balanced and integrated by the Heart, *is* transformational healing.

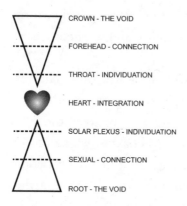

CROWN - THE VOID

FOREHEAD - CONNECTION

THROAT - INDIVIDUATION

HEART - INTEGRATION

SOLAR PLEXUS - INDIVIDUATION

SEXUAL - CONNECTION

ROOT - THE VOID

Figure 1: The Heart and the chakras   *Figure 2: Symbol for the Heart*

Interestingly, the symbol for the Heart chakra (see figure 2) is a condensed form of this same image (imagine pushing the bases of the triangles in figure 1 together to engulf the Heart). Looked at in this way, the symbol seems to imply that a stable, active and even brilliant wholeness is achieved through an integration of the personal and transpersonal, the individual and the transcendent, through the mediating faculties of the Heart. And although the symbol comes from South Asian traditions, in Chinese culture, the *three upon three* can be traced back to the *I Ching* (or, in pinyin, *Yi Jing*, usually translated as the *Book of Changes*) written around 700 BCE, and its divinatory hexagrams. Then again, it appears in Egyptian mythology, and in Western traditions it shows up in the Star of David, so it is very much a transcultural, perhaps archetypal, image.

THE ROOT CHAKRA: ROOT SUPPORT

The first, or root, chakra (*muladhara*, meaning *root support*) is located at the base of the spine just below the coccyx, behind the anus. Chinese medicine, which calls the energy centre here *sea bottom*, also describes two points in the same area: one (GV-1) is located at the base of the spine; the other (CV-1) is a little further forward, at the perineum (between the anus and the scrotum in men, or the anus and the vaginal opening in women). CV-1 — which will be familiar to tai chi and qi gong practitioners as *huiyin* (*meeting of yin*) — is the first point on the pathway called the Conception Vessel (CV) and is the place of *ultimate yin*. Meantime, GV-1 (*changqiang*, or *long strength*) is the first point on the pathway called the Governing Vessel — which runs up the spine — and has a name that reflects its energetic function of strengthening the back (by tonifying yang at the root).

Traditionally, the root chakra is associated with groundedness, connection to the Earth and the instinct for survival. In Chinese medicine, CV-1 is regarded as the most yin place on the body and therefore a source of primal yin energy (the corresponding *ultimate yang* point is at the seventh chakra or *baihui*, at the top of the head). Similarly, Ayurvedic medicine conceives the root area to be the source of *kundalini*, which we will touch on in a moment.

MANIFESTED AND UNMANIFESTED ENERGIES

The idea of a deep potential out of which things arise and manifest gives the root chakra a correspondence with the Water element, which also represents unmanifested potential.[2] Unfortunately, in many people the energy remains unmanifested. Such people, who cannot mobilize their root energy, often find life a constant struggle and live in a state of overwhelm, never able to get going in a fundamental sense. They risk gradually stagnating all their life energy in the first chakra, which may eventually spiral them downward into chronic illness.

Water constitutional types tend to have to deal with fear — the emotion most closely associated with our basic survival — as their life theme. When they get stuck, the root chakra's domain is often where the stagnation will manifest in symptoms. Common problems for Water constitutional types, for example, include sacral and anal pain, erectile dysfunction, vaginal infections, hemorrhoids and prostate difficulties. Related symptoms may overlap into the second chakra, manifesting as low back and pelvic pain, cystitis, and other bladder problems. When someone consistently produces problems in this area, and/or seems unusually immobilized and unable to get on with life, then it is a good bet their energy is blocked in the root chakra, and that *fear* is a theme in their life.

---

2 Some people associate the root chakra with the Earth element of Chinese medicine. To be sure, the sense of grounding/centring of the root chakra relates to Earth but, in my view, the Water element makes more overall sense. Both Water and root are concerned with deep personal resources and unmanifest potential.

℞ *ALAN*: THE LANGUAGE OF ACCIDENTS

Alan was thirty-five years old when he came to our clinic to explore an injury he had sustained in falling off a ladder. He had landed straddling a two-by-four and had suffered pain in the area of the root chakra ever since, including excruciating pain with an erection. Years had passed, his self-esteem was shaken, his marriage was strained and Alan was extremely unhappy.

There was little doubt that Alan was a Water type, who ironically had injured himself in the very spot that would trigger his deepest fears. It was pretty obvious his pain frightened him but, perhaps understandably, he was also very motivated to find a way out of it. So when we gained enough trust from him, he was able to accept the insertion of a needle into the root chakra, while he breathed deeply and stayed present — something he had never been able to do before while receiving acupuncture.

Meanwhile, we set up a circuit of acu-points that targeted his primal energetic diversion — that of raw, existential fear. Within moments, Alan entered the void and started to shake uncontrollably, his pelvis moving in ways he would not normally have permitted. After the session, he reported that he was able to get an erection without pain for the first time in years.

Although every injury is unique, this story is by no means unusual. In fact, it is fascinating to me how frequently people injure themselves in the very place their energy is stuck. Indeed, it is hard not to wonder, after seeing this kind of thing over and over again, whether there isn't something pushing people to call attention to their energetic imbalances through pain.

THE SEXUAL CHAKRA:
YOUR OWN DWELLING OR ORIGIN

The second chakra (*svadhisthana*, meaning *your own dwelling or origin*) is located just above the pubic bone and is the centre of both sexual energy and creative inspiration. Like the root chakra, this chakra shares some common ground with the Chinese conceptions of both the Earth and Water elements. The Earth element seems to me to be the best match for the second chakra as both sexuality and creativity are so central to our being and such a deep source of nourishment to all levels of the body-mind-spirit. Furthermore, svadhisthana is also clearly concerned with interpersonal connection, which is very much an Earth theme.

THE GATE OF LIFE AND THE SEA OF QI

Chinese medicine calls the area a couple of finger-widths below the belly button and almost halfway to the back of the body, the *dantian*, and considers this area the storehouse of the body's energy. Points with names such as *qihai* (CV-6, sea of qi) and *mingmen* (GV-4, gate of life) are illustrative of the enormous power attributed to this region of the body.

Tapping this energy source is central to a number of disciplines known collectively as qi gong. Through qi gong meditation and exercises, the energy of *mingmen* can be gathered and diffused throughout the body and, in doing so, can unlock pelvic energy and channel it through the central energy pathways known as the Du Mai (the Governing Vessel [GV], which runs up the back) and the Chong Mai (the Thrusting Channel, which runs through the centre of the body) and the Ren Mai (the Conception Vessel [CV], which runs up the front of the body).

In the South Asian tradition, kundalini energy is the basic energy or creative force and is said to lie dormant at the base of the spine until mobilized through special meditation and breathing techniques. The classic image is of a sleeping serpent, coiled around the base of the spine, near the coccyx. When the serpent is awakened, energy begins to flow up the spinal column through three energy channels, or nadis, to open the higher chakras in succession.

The first of these channels, Sushumna, is the central column and probably corresponds to the Chong Mai of Chinese medicine. The other two, Ida and Pingala, are depicted by the two coiled serpents around a central staff (the Sushumna) and probably represent Chinese medicine's Du Mai and the Ren Mai. Although the correspondences are not exact, Ida is said to carry cool, lunar, yin energy and might be said to correspond to the Ren Mai. Conversely, Pingala is said to carry warm, solar, yang energy and could be said to correspond to the Du Mai. (The image of two coiled snakes around a Caduceus is still used today as the symbol of medicine).

Whatever the details of the ancient systems, it is clear that both are aware of the tremendous power that lies in our lower bellies and understand that it requires training to nourish and protect and draw on this energy.

THE LOVE/SEX SPLIT

Because all chronically ill people are by definition exhausted, it seems tragic that most are not able to tap this freely available energy source that lies hidden beyond the sight of the ego. One thing barring access to *mingmen* energy is a deep-rooted block that seems to plague Western civilization, arising from a collective fear and shame of sexuality — a block that psychologists have called a love/sex split.

Ideally, in making love, the heart chakra and the sexual chakra act together, so that intercourse is a coherent expression of sexual and emotional energies. The Chong Mai is the energy pathway that connects (among other things) the pelvis and Heart energy, and unrestricted flow in this central column is necessary to a balanced expression of love and sex. The love/sex split can be seen as a fracturing or sundering of the flow of energy in the Chong Mai, with associated blocking in the Du Mai and Ren Mai, leaving an energetic disengagement that separates the creative pelvic energies from the rest of the Heart-Mind.

The blocking of the Chong Mai is very common and is the clearest example of physical compartmentalization, mirroring — and exacerbating — our persona's wish to deny its shadow material. Although it goes unrecognized by modern medicine, it remains in the collective unconscious and lies at the root of much disease and social maladjustment. The most obvious consequence is the great difficulty we have fully expressing our sexual natures in our love relationships: for many people, it is impossible to do so.

And, as if that were not enough, containment and dissociation of pelvic energies further embody our denial and unease. Although containment and dissociation co-exist in the body, they can manifest in different areas depending on which strategy is dominant. When containment is the dominant response, it tends to create energy congestion and tension in the pelvic area, whereas dissociation gives rise to energy congestion in the upper chest and head, with energy deficiency in the pelvis. Either way, the sexual and creative energies of the second chakra are off limits and the individual's life force is walled off internally.

Healing this block, or any other energetic fragmentation, for that matter, does not occur on the level at which the problem manifests. The opening of higher centres — particularly the Heart chakra — is essential, as compassion is vital to any integration of the sense of betrayal that accompanies wounded sexuality. More about this topic in a later chapter (see chapter 16, Sexual Healing).

THE SOLAR-PLEXUS CHAKRA:
THE CITY OF THE SHINING JEWEL

Although some sources connect *manipura* or *the city of the shining jewel* with the *mingmen* and locate it at the level of the navel, I like to think of it as the solar plexus or power chakra, located between the navel and the xiphisternum (where the ribs come together at the lower end of the sternum). This energy centre has to do with establishing ourselves as separate and autonomous beings, capable of making our own decisions and defining our own values. The centre often comes into play when there is a need to set boundaries, draw the line against other people's behaviour, or otherwise make a statement of personal power.

SELF, ANGER, EXPRESSION, POWER

We commonly feel tension in the solar plexus area when faced with a situation in which pleasing everyone is not possible. Being pulled in a number of different directions at once leaves us feeling helpless and demands that we take a stand. Of course, for the person who is a people pleaser or harmonizer, this can be very difficult.

From an acupuncture perspective, the power chakra seems to be enmeshed with the dynamics of the Wood element, which the reader may recall generates explosive upward, outward and expanding energies. The natural desire to connect and harmonize with others, arising from the second chakra energies, can produce challenging situations when external demands become unreasonable, excessive or manipulative. After all, no-one likes to be controlled. When this happens there is an energetic pull on the solar plexus area, which is experienced as discomfort and strain or can actually feel like the tug or pull from a tether.

Such psychic tetherings have been called *Aka cords*. These kinds of situations generally call for effective boundary setting, that is, finding a way to say no to someone or something, which requires the conscious use of the Wood energies. Another option, of course, is to let go of the situation and move on — a skill which requires conscious use of Metal energies and which is perhaps more the purview of the higher chakras, particularly the throat chakra. Either (or both) of these may be unavailable to people who haven't brought such energies to consciousness. Without access to these energies, we often try to give the appearance of equanimity in difficult situations by remaining quiet and holding on, or containing the resentment that ensues when someone tramples on our space.

If someone has difficulty expressing, or letting go of, anger, then Wood energy will often gather and produce tension and discomfort in the upper abdomen. This tension sits in the diaphragm as tightness and restriction, which can bring a range of symptoms from epigastric pain to asthma. Surrounding structures are also affected by tension which, if it goes on for any length of time, can materialize as organic pathology. Gastritis, ulcers, food sensitivities, gastro-esophageal reflux and pancreatitis can all stem from this kind of energetic dynamic.

Unfortunately, habitually suppressed rage may also get pushed right down into the pelvic compartment where it meets and mixes with the contained sexual energies, creating a veritable powder keg of frightening energies that can destroy — or heal — whoever dares to explore the area. The well-known story of Dr. Jekyll and Mr. Hyde illustrates this dynamic: readers may recall that Mr. Hyde's lust was coloured by a wicked temper. Despite our rational repugnance, sex and violence often erupt together and will likely continue to do so until we stop denying and dissociating from these energies. The cross-contamination of sexuality with aggression and aggression with sexuality is a cultural legacy with implications for us all.

Epigastric pain is often diagnosed as gastritis or reflux when in fact the difficulty is primarily energetic. This is a very common situation in general practice. People come to the doctor with some tension emanating from the power chakra. Not uncommonly, the energetic situation is obvious from the history — as, for example, when the individual says he or she is under some stress and is in a no-win situation. Unfortunately, because of our pathological orientation, the diagnosis of gastritis comes with a prescription for antacids, or worse, drugs that block stomach acid secretion, or even antibiotics, which while effectively relieving symptoms, can lead to alteration in gut function and digestion. Meantime, the no-win situation remains because the symptoms that were speaking to the problem have been obliterated. Such treatment is clearly not a cure for the energetic difficulty and while at first there is no obvious consequence to the use of such drugs, over time alteration of digestive function can lead to all kinds of vague complaints — from chronic fatigue to frank neurological degeneration.

It is not surprising that a lot of modern stress-related illnesses originate in a compromised power centre. Many people feel powerless in a globalized society dominated by huge corporations. In such a society, a relatively small number of powerful people seem to run things while the average person has become faceless and voiceless. The strain on individuals has been considerable and many are suffering digestive breakdown. Meanwhile, prescriptions for stomach acid medicines have skyrocketed, making them some of the most commonly prescribed medications in general practice.

THE HEART CHAKRA:
THAT WHICH IS EVER NEW

The fourth, Heart chakra, *anahata*, meaning *that which is ever new*, is the energy centre around which all else revolves, and which, in my view, harmonizes all the other centres. Located in the middle of the chest, it is traditionally described as an orange-crimson lotus with twelve petals. The essential feature of the Heart energy is its capacity to acknowledge and be present with *what is*.

Unlike the mind, the Heart can only be known in the moment. If the mind rejects the Heart's truth, then the Heart chakra closes. But when the Mind listens to and respects the Heart then the Heart chakra opens and Heart and Mind become united. This is not just mystical rhetoric, either; it is true for every one of us in an everyday sense. Intuition and compassion gain in strength as they are honoured and allowed to express in our day-to-day lives.

The Heart chakra, located between the three upper and the three lower chakras, is anatomically as well as energetically the centre and font of our being. Since being fully present with *what is* is a very good way to centre oneself, many meditations are specifically designed to strengthen Heart-centredness. Heart centring brings our awareness to a deeper place than rational mind and opens the awareness to the qualities of compassion and feeling that are so important to the healing journey.

The Heart chakra begins to open as we stop trying to escape from pain and betrayal and instead realize that pain is in the nature of existence. It is neither fearful nor foreign nor does it, of itself, threaten our psychological or physical survival. In fact, it is often a message or a question from our deepest selves. When we accept that pain is a part of human existence and not some dreadful aberration, we begin to realize that to engage our pain, to focus our awareness in the moment and to be increasingly present with *what is* enlarges our lives and our experience — and, paradoxically, lessens our fear and our pain.

When we find ourselves no longer driven to shut pain out, or divert the fire of intimacy, we begin to remain present when things are difficult and to really live.

COMPASSION

When the Heart chakra opens, compassion arises. Compassion allows us to be present with our own and others' pain without trying to fix or change anything. We can open to our pain, realizing that the emotional pain that is so intimately related to our physical pain arises from the dynamics of the first three chakras and can never be resolved without transformation.

The realization that pain cannot be resolved either destroys us, or it opens our Heart chakra, or both (the Heart chakra often opens when death is imminent). But it is precisely this opening of the Heart that begins the healing of that deep-rooted pain we had only just understood could never be resolved! And this cognitive dissonance — which strikes at the core of our being — bursts the bounds of the ego and its delusions. This is the moment that begins to turn our life upside down; this is the realization that catches us up by the ankle and suspends us, like the Hanged Man of the tarot deck, in a world where everything is the same but everything is different. The way is paved for the opening of the higher, transpersonal centres.

In Ayurvedic philosophy, the root, heart and forehead chakras are said to contain knots, or *granthis*, representing the aspects Brahma, Vishnu and Rudra respectively. It is these knots that are pierced by arising *kundalini* energy as the aspirant breaks the bonds of ignorance that tie us to duality. The knot of Vishnu — which might be understood to represent the peculiar difficulty of opening the Heart — is said to be located in a *trikona*, or inverted triangle, right in the centre of the Heart lotus. Vishnu, the Preserver, is that aspect that presides over and guides our life transitions. In this respect, the knot of Vishnu parallels Chinese medicine's *Golden Gate (Jin Men)*, which we will discuss in chapter 10, Intention.

THE FIRE ELEMENT AND HEART

The Heart's capacity to be present with *what is* precisely reflects the qualities of the Fire element as described in the hidden tradition of Chinese medicine. Those people with a balanced Fire constitution seem to have little difficulty acknowledging *what is*. For the Fire constitutional type, being in tune with life is being in tune with the cosmos. The gift of manifesting exactly what is necessary in the moment is the birthright of a Fire constitution. The rest of us can achieve it too if we do the work to open the Heart.

Those people with a Fire constitution frequently manifest symptoms in the chest area, which are usually energetic — at least to begin with. Often, such energetic Heart-ache is mistaken for organic pathology and investigations will be initiated to rule out angina, while the energetic message of the symptoms is lost. Unfortunately, while the Heart's message goes unheard we, as a society, will continue to understand the phrase *opening the heart* as a description of a surgical procedure, and a multimillion dollar industry will continue to pathologize the heart and demand astronomical amounts of public money to assess every ache or pain in the chest for organic disease.

THE THROAT CHAKRA: PURIFICATION

Located just above the notch at the top of the sternum, the throat chakra (*vishuddha*, meaning *purification*) is the energy centre related to renunciation and detachment, which is perhaps why it has been associated with the Metal element in Chinese medicine. Metal is about letting go and our awareness of the transcendent begins with letting go.

The throat chakra is said to be a lotus of sixteen petals, mauve in colour and oval in shape. To speak from the Heart is to speak through an open throat chakra. However, there is a big difference between expression from the Heart through the throat chakra and expression from the solar plexus. Whereas the solar plexus is concerned with the expression of personal power, an open throat chakra begins to tap into transpersonal and transcendent energies not limited to the individual.

LETTING GO

Letting go at the ego level may temporarily dissipate pent-up energy in the power centre but sooner or later another similar situation will arise. Letting go with an open Heart in a conscious and open expression of one's personal truth through a clear throat chakra, on the other hand, not only confirms our agency and prevents a build-up of tension in the diaphragm but also transcends the ego. In other words, there is a difference between venting and consciously speaking one's truth. Once we begin to let go of our desires and projections and turn our attention inward to develop a relationship with our core truth and with the transcendent, we find ourselves increasingly unruffled by fear, suffering and death, and beginning to speak our truth as only the Heart knows it.

Herein lies the power of the throat chakra. The power to express is in itself neither good nor bad. The quality of expression is what counts and this depends on the state of the other chakras, most particularly the Heart centre. If the Heart is open, the energetic expression will be compassionate and life supporting; if it is closed, the energetic expression can be negative, although still powerful.

Suppose an individual with terminal cancer consults two physicians. Both physicians believe that the patient is likely to die within the next three months but each delivers that opinion in an entirely different way. The first physician hides behind statistics and remains cold and distant. The second physician acknowledges his pain and helplessness in the face of the inevitable, then finds a way to help the patient discover some meaning in his experience. The first physician delivers the information; the second physician speaks from an open and fearless Heart. The second is likely to be somehow able, through acknowledging his own pain, to see — and to show — something quite different.

An open throat chakra can mitigate much negativity arising from the ego level. If, however, the Heart remains closed, then fragmentation, compartmentalization and dissociation can distort what emerges. Often, despite our attempts to hide it, our manner of speech will betray an inner energetic disharmony. For example, if a speaker has a significant amount of unintegrated energetic material (pain, grief, anger, e.g.), then her speech — the verbal expression of energy through the throat chakra — will project the unconscious material through opinions, judgements, mannerisms and emotional affect.

Beyond influencing the style of verbal expression, energy blocks in the area of the throat chakra can occasionally give rise to sufficient local tension to produce symptoms such as stuttering, choking or even asthma.

ॐ *GEORGE*: STUTTERING & MYOPIA

George was thirty-five years old when he came to our clinic. He had begun to stutter after a car accident in which he had suffered a mild whiplash. By the time he came to see us, he had been stuttering for two years, with no appreciable change over many months. During one particular acupuncture session, during which needles had been placed in the upper chest and lower neck, he felt a surge of heat up to his face. Immediately after the session his stuttering disappeared, as did the short-sightedness for which he had worn glasses for a number of years.

This immediate and rather astonishing change in George's speech and sight became the focus of his (and everyone else's) attention during the rest of the program and completely dwarfed his concern over his back and neck pain, which had coincidentally improved at the same time. Furthermore, the improvement was lasting, as he is still speaking and seeing clearly to this day.

THE FOREHEAD CHAKRA: COMMAND

The sixth chakra, *ajna* (meaning *command*) is described as a lotus divided in two, one half chiefly rose-coloured with yellow, the other chiefly purplish-blue, each half having forty-eight petals. Intuition — that inner vision that sees the truth directly, without analysis — is related to this many-petalled *third eye*, located between and just a little higher than the eyebrows in the centre of the forehead. Such inner vision is quite different from regular vision. Because the physical sense of sight is outer-directed, it is constrained to the duality of observer and observed. Intuition, on the other hand, is an inner-directed vision, a direct knowing in which knower and known are somehow connected or even united. In Chinese medicine, this point (GV-24.5 or *Yintang*) is sometimes referred to as *unnamed* because by naming we re-create the very duality that the third eye transcends.

Third-eye intuition is a whole-brain function in which the frequency of brain waves range below the normal waking state.[3] Given that coherent brain functioning is also a feature of the fourth state of consciousness known as *turiya*, accessed through meditation, we can guess that practices that facilitate total brain functioning and coherence will also help develop intuition.

WHOLE-BRAIN FUNCTIONING

Practices such as tai chi, meditation, pranayama and qi gong can all facilitate total brain coherence. And since the fourth state of consciousness both transcends and *includes* the states of waking, dreaming and sleeping, one could infer that intuition is also a transcendent function. It is not really a sense like the other senses. Being a product of holistic functioning, it depends on the other senses but is not limited to them. It uses all the senses and yet it remains unique to itself and cannot be reduced or accounted for by any of the other senses.

As intuition develops, we become increasingly able to directly sense the root of things and situations without having to analyze or filter information through our reasoning faculties. And the more we can trust our intuition, the better it functions; and the better it functions, the more we can trust it. Moreover, though I claim no personal experience of this, I've been told that at some point along

3　These frequencies are: alpha (7–14 Hz), theta (4–7 Hz) and delta (0.5–4 Hz). In contrast, normal waking consciousness generally produces frequencies in the beta range (14–35 Hz).

the way as this intuitive capacity develops, the mists can clear and we become able to literally *see* the truth with the inner eye.

Optimal functioning of the throat and Heart centres are crucial to such *seeing*, which is compassionate and nonjudgemental. Insight that gives rise to judgement is superficial; moreover, it is a short circuit. In brief, it will destroy itself. To see truth whole *is* to see it lovingly. Judgement closes the mind, whereas an open throat chakra supported by the Heart, through the intuitive opening of the third eye, speaks truth and sees truth and in this alone brings wholeness and healing. It cannot do otherwise.

Intuition is so natural yet is so absent from most of our lives, one has to reason that it has been deliberately repressed. In our society, the right-brained, sensing, feeling, intuitive way of relating has been collectively denigrated in favour of the left-brained, rational thought processes of our highly developed analytical mind. That alone has been enough to shut down our intuition, usually from early childhood. The process has gone so far that for many people, the very idea of intuition can be threatening. Some people only feel safe when they have calculated something minutely and understand how it works, instead of just acting on hunches.

The denigration of intuition is a big factor in illness, if not as a specific block to the flow of energy, certainly as a block to understanding of our illness. Without intuition, we seek to blame our symptoms on bacteria, or carcinogens or trauma. Our quest to understand illness has so distanced us from the experience of our symptoms, we have forgotten that the experience itself — would we only give it our attention — is often all the explanation we could want, or need.

THE CROWN CHAKRA:
UNIVERSAL SELFHOOD

The seventh, or crown, chakra (*atma*, or *universal selfhood*) is the gate to the ultimate state of consciousness — union with the divine. Called *sahasrara* by yogis, it is sometimes known as the *lotus of a thousand petals* (or, to be more precise, 972 petals) and is predominantly violet. Chinese medicine refers to this point as *baihui (hundred meetings)* — an interesting echo of the yogic thousand petals. People who can see energy say there is a vortex of energy surrounding the body and that one big source of that energy is at the top of the head (for those who cannot see energy, the SQUID magnetometer can now affirm this phenomenon).

Located at the vertex (or, in some traditions, an inch or two above the head), the crown chakra connects the individual to *absolute reality* — the ultimate void — which both permeates and transcends duality. It is perhaps the hardest thing to put into words because to describe it is to assume an observer and an observed. Because it *is* everything, including ourselves as observers, and is the source of everything, the absolute is not observable in the same way as discrete objects may be. If we are it, we cannot observe, let alone describe, it. But we can perhaps intuit it.

BEING, NOT DOING

By intuiting it, we do not attempt to know it in the usual sense but enter a kind of expanded awareness where we can experience knowing as being. Many books have been written on this subject and, again, I pretend no personal or intimate knowledge of the transcendent. But I know that the most miraculous things that have happened around me have occurred when I have not actually been doing anything in particular. Indeed, I have learned through long experience that the most effective thing to do (both professionally and personally) is often nothing. *Being* rather than *doing*, offering my presence and refraining from interfering with whatever is going on has often been far more useful than anything I might technically *do*. Perhaps in doing nothing but staying present and refraining from judgement, I have unconsciously opened my crown chakra and aligned myself with my highest potential.

I confess it came as a great shock to me to discover this *doing nothing*. Trained as a physician, I am armed to the teeth with all kinds of detailed knowledge about drugs, aids, procedures, diagnostics, regimens, therapies, remedies and on and on. But again and again I have been confronted with the fact that this knowledge is ultimately empty. Something else is in charge when real healing occurs and the best I can do is to stand aside, stay present and let that something do whatever it is going to do.

This is not as giddy as it sounds. Since no one will ever entirely understand what they are confronting in another's illness, *not acting* is at least as sensible as acting and quite often leads to more favourable outcomes. This principle of inaction is at the core of the hidden tradition and when understood is said to lead to spiritual potency (what Chinese medicine calls *ling*), a state in which things occur without our doing anything in particular.

This inaction, however, is not the inaction of a Saturday afternoon couch potato! Quite the reverse. Potency, or *ling*, arises when the principle of intention is activated in a person whose chakras — and most particularly the Heart and crown chakras — are open and harmonized. In a state of consciousness that is aligned with the Absolute, external material changes such as healing can be facilitated. We simply intend, without any particular effort, then rest in the void and observe what happens.

Such intention and such observation is incredibly powerful,

much more powerful than our little egos can imagine, and will carry on all by itself, with little more than slight course corrections along the way — a bit like coasting downstream in a canoe. One need only be present and alert and use the paddle once in a while. It should be stressed that such interactions (if they can be called that) are not a way of controlling others' destinies, or a means of naïvely getting something one wants, no matter how laudable or selfless that desire. Even when one's intent is another's health, there is no way of knowing what might be around the next bend in the river.

SUDDEN HEALING THROUGH THE CROWN CHAKRA

On occasions, and under the right conditions, the crown chakra can open right up with almost unbelievable results. I recall a case from my early years of practice, a woman who had SLE (systemic lupus erythematosus)[4] and who had contracted tuberculosis while on high doses of steroids as treatment for the lupus. She was in a wheelchair for many years with flexion contractures of her elbows, hips and knees. After five years of this, she bounced into my office one day looking totally normal, springing up and down on her perfectly normal legs.

I was incredulous. It simply was not possible. But after I settled down a bit, she told me about the prayer meeting she had attended the previous weekend. During the meeting, which had attracted thousands of people, she felt a bolt of energy enter through the top of her head and in the next moment she got out of her chair and walked.

---

4 Systemic lupus erythematosus (SLE) is an auto-immune disorder that affects many different body tissues, including the joints, skin, kidneys and other endocrine glands. The disease can be fatal and is therefore often treated aggressively with immuno-suppressant drugs.

I have now witnessed several remarkable openings, in which the people involved experienced an enormous flow of energy, originating from the crown and pouring through the body, followed by a miraculous improvement in symptoms.[5] Few people can expect this kind of healing. And that may be for the best, as the cognitive dissonance can be so great that some people may develop a dependence on the organization that sponsored the miracle that restored their health. A more deliberate opening of the crown centre and a more conscious invitation to health is probably the wiser course.

5   It may be worth noting that some of these people had been diagnosed with a seizure disorder and had been taking anti-epileptic medications to prevent future occurrences. Such pathologizing of spontaneous energetic discharges at all levels seems to be the rule rather than the exception in our society, yet in other cultures such people are treasured as showing strong signs of future shamanic ability. And, plainly, their *disorder* was, in these cases, a dramatic instance of the body clearing energy and moving with extraordinary rapidity toward healing.

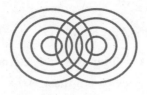

CHAPTER 9

ENERGY DIVERSION

Eventually, a major event occurs in a child's life which knocks his energy off balance. . . . At that instant the primordial yin and yang divide and the five elements become aberrant. . . . The child learns that it is painful and not safe to express, or be in the presence of, a given quality of energy and its related emotion. He begins closing the doors to full self-expression and his spontaneity dwindles.
— Lonny Jarrett

*A*s flexible and as extensive as the five element system is in assessing individuals and allowing them to work with their particular constitutional type, it does not stop there. Based in a philosophy that understands interrelation as the foundation of the universe, the five element system looks beyond the individual to recognize and assess a variety of personal, interpersonal and even suprapersonal energetic interactions.

After all, illness is not merely an individual issue. We are all embedded in familial, societal and environmental matrices and all of these influence our health. The interrelational nature of the five elements can be seen as a metaphorical reflection of the many energy vectors that flow in us and beyond us and that intersect and interact over our lifetimes and that, in doing so, produce good health or ill.

CREATION AND DESTRUCTION CYCLES

What we have been calling the five elements are sometimes known as the five phases to emphasize their cyclical movement from deep winter through the year's budding, growth and harvest seasons to the cooling and subsiding of late fall. Now I want to look at some of the wheels within wheels that chart the more complex relationships and interrelationships.

Five element creation and destruction (or controlling) cycles provide a remarkably perceptive framework for understanding our lives as cycles of creation and destruction; and for further acknowledging that within any one lifetime smaller creation/destruction cycles occur ceaselessly in every aspect of our being. At any one moment, then, we may be generally in an Earth or late summer phase but be experiencing Water energies in relation to a particular life situation. These influences can be huge. To give a more concrete example, if someone we love dies, we will likely manifest the downward, sinking, contracting vector of the Metal element, the emotional expression of which is grief, even though we might be a Wood constitutional type and would normally express quite different energies.

If these various forces are integrated, then good health is the rule. If they are not, manifestation of the self can be very difficult and this difficulty promotes an energetic diversion that is the precursor of illness.

THE CREATION CYCLE

In the context of a lifetime, the Water element, or Water phase, might be seen as the essence or innate potential that comes from the parents and flows into the foetus. After birth, the Water nourishes the Wood element as ego is formed in the child and the young adult. Then, when the ego is established, Wood nourishes the Fire that represents our expression in life. Later, through the years of mature expression and for some time afterward, Fire nourishes Earth — the harvest we reap from our endeavours — spiritually, materially and emotionally. And finally, this Earth nourishes Metal, the final phase of the energetic cycle, which in turn gives way to Water, which will initiate the next round of existence.

The energy moving from Water to Wood to Fire to Earth to Metal and back to Water again has been called the *creation* (or *sheng*) cycle. It is quite easy to see the cycle in the context of a lifetime. Less easy to grasp is the fact that the whole cycle is present in us simultaneously. In other words, ideally all elements or energy vectors are available, with one or another perhaps being dominant in the moment. Difficulty arises if we cannot access the energy of one or another element when it is needed — usually because, for whatever reason, it has been considered unacceptable by the ego.

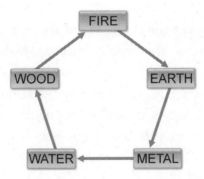

Figure 1: The creation, or sheng, cycle

THE DESTRUCTION CYCLE

A destructive or pathological diversion of energy occurs when a specific energy vector is deemed unacceptable to the ego: in other words, when we decide we do not want to feel a particular feeling.

Figure 2 : The destruction, or ke, cycle

In such cases, the energy — which should flow naturally through the creation cycle into the next element or phase in the cycle — instead gets diverted, usually into the next available phase in the cycle. In time, the blocked energy materializes, first as chronic anxiety and subsequently as organic pathology.

WATER DIVERTED TOWARD FIRE: UNBOUNDED CHAOS

Under normal circumstances, the Wood element supports development of the ego toward its healthy expression in the Fire stage. In other words, our potential (Water) should move through the Wood phase toward Fire. Of course, ego development is rarely smooth. Everyone knows the difficulties of the teens and early twenties. At that stage, the crucial question is whether we will develop adequate skills and resources to get through the chaos and become mature adults.

If, for whatever reason, the Wood or ego-building stage is blocked, the expression of Fire can become severely distorted. Without a healthy ego, everyday life — let alone spiritual and emotional growth — is difficult and natural expression becomes impossible. In terms of the five elements, we might say that the energy of Water has been diverted and is now pathologically affecting Fire. The result is likely to be under-expression of Wood energy, with some distortion of Fire — a situation that might be termed *unbounded chaos*.

Unfortunately, this pattern is quite common in our contemporary world. So many children grow up without the example and nurture of their parents. More than a few reach adulthood without an adequate education or social skills and are unable to make a decent living. In such circumstances, ego development can get pushed aside by the natural and urgent desire to feel the flow and ecstasy promised by the Fire experience — often through drugs, risky sexual relations or other behaviours — before there is sufficient maturity to handle the responsibility. In such circumstances, we witness the distorted and pathological expression of Fire.

Another possibility in the Water/Fire dynamic is the kind of dampening that fear (Water) can have on expression (Fire). In a balanced state, the enthusiasm of Fire should be grounded in the reality and restraints of circumstances. Too much fear (Water) can put the Fire out and the spark of life can be lost. Individuals succumb to apathy or depression, avoiding relationships and challenges of all kinds. Conversely, too little Water and Fire goes raging out of control and manic, explosive or ungrounded states are the result. If the Wood element is unable to channel the Water energy

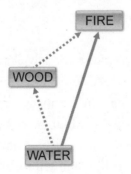

Figure 3: Water diverts toward Fire

appropriately, the Fire phase can be extinguished with a deluge, or blaze unchecked like a firestorm.

LONG-TERM SEQUELAE

If the Water energy diverts toward Fire over a long period of time, we can predict some fairly catastrophic consequences. Habitual drug use can lead to liver, kidney and/or brain damage. Promiscuity, besides its emotional impact, puts people at greater risk of contracting AIDS or other STDs. Manic and depressive states can be painful and waste talents and skills, energy and ambition and can result in long-term drug interventions. (Treatment of the result does not usually achieve very much but it is unfortunately the only thing our society seems to be capable of.)

☈ *DENNIS*: RISKY BEHAVIOUR

Dennis was a Wood constitutional type. A rebel at heart, he had experimented with drugs, tattooed his whole body with dark images and wore unusual haircuts designed to shock his parents' generation. Obviously both creative and intelligent, he had been in a car accident at the age of seventeen that had left him in considerable pain. Unfortunately, he had chosen to put his life and education on hold while waiting for what he thought would be a large cash settlement. In the meantime, in his mind, there was no way he could get on with his life.

On the surface, Dennis seemed physically fit and it was hard to see why he was unable to pull out of a downward spiral of drugs and risky behaviours in spite of being warned many times of the possible consequences. By the time we saw him, he was twenty-one and his life was in chaos. He now had a partner and two children yet seemed quite incapable of pulling himself together.

WOOD DIVERTED TOWARD EARTH: JOYLESS LABOUR

The diversion of Wood energy toward Earth without going through Fire is probably the most common and well-described energetic disturbance in Chinese medicine. In the usual picture, the aggressive, outward energy of Wood ends up instead in the body's centre, upsetting the stomach and interfering with the digestion. It is experienced as chronic epigastric tension, which may eventually materialize as a peptic ulcer, hiatus hernia or gastro-esophageal reflux. On the mental level, it manifests as anxiety and, on the spirit level, as depression or irritability. Most of these syndromes have been discussed elsewhere.

It is quite common to find apparently mature people who have failed to find a fulfilling career and are stuck, putting their energy into a job they dislike. Here the creative Wood energy, which should be moving toward fulfilling expression in Fire, is diverted into mere survival. In fact, this situation is often considered the norm in Western society. Many people seem to expect that they will work to earn basic needs — food and shelter — rather than for the gratification of it. Life itself becomes a struggle as a *joyless labour* is substituted for the expression of mature talents and abilities. In Ayurveda it would be said to be a failure to find one's *dharma*. Joseph Campbell might call it a failure to follow one's bliss.

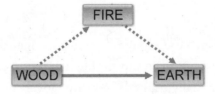

Figure 4: Wood diverts toward Earth

Conventional medicine treats the result of this problem with drugs, some of which have become the most popular drugs of all time. For example, drugs such as cimetidine, which block acid secretion, are used for ulcers, while anti-depressants are used for the concomitant depression. But successful as they are, all they can do is block our awareness of the underlying energetics and that, clearly, is at best a short-term solution. Interference with the mechanism of production of symptoms may get rid of an upset stomach but it does nothing to help anyone find a more satisfying path in life — which is the underlying energetic aberration.

WOOD DIVERTED TOWARD EARTH: LONG-TERM SEQUELAE

The long-term sequelae of being chronically stressed, or not finding one's *dharma*, can be ruinous. On a physical level alone, chronic stomach problems can lead to more severe gut disturbances, such as gallstones, liver disease, pancreatitis or colitis, which in turn can eventually lead to surgical intervention. Alternatively, the tension can end up in the cardiovascular system as hypertension, with all its associated risks. On a mental level, unprocessed anger can leave people looking for injustices on which to lavish their rage. On a spirit level, one simply gets depressed and cynical. And psychological studies have confirmed that chronic anger and cynicism carry a greater risk for heart disease, cancer and stroke.

ༀ *FRED*: DEPRESSION

Fred was a fifty-four-year-old man who was brilliantly creative at almost anything he put his mind to. He was musical, intelligent, well read, professionally trained, had three lovely children and a loving wife. Indeed, he was so good at everything he could not decide what to do with his life. Over the years, he had tried first one thing, then another, and another, never settling on anything for long and missing whatever he had put aside to take up the current project. Meanwhile, his debts continued to grow. After a number of years, he reached a point where nothing was working for him and he was broke.

Fred suffered from never having found his *dharma* — something that would light the fire in his eyes and integrate his various talents. Predictably, he suffered from a depression that resisted all therapy. In many ways, he was too smart for his own good.

FIRE DIVERTED TOWARD METAL: STARVATION IN THE MIDST OF PLENTY

When Fire energy is diverted toward Metal, the natural movement from ripening maturity to the harvest of our accomplishments (Earth) gets distorted and the Fire energy, which should move toward mature growth, gets diverted into the Metal phase, where it agitates and creates anxiety as the incompatible energies of blooming and dying back — to use a simple analogy from the garden — conflict.

On a physical level, when Fire is deflected toward Metal, its heat moves into the lungs (Metal's yin organ), leaving them

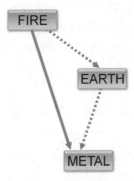

Figure 5: Fire diverts toward Metal

vulnerable to infectious diseases such as pneumonia, or even tuberculosis, instead of into the Earth sector where the energy should be used to help with digestion. When Fire heats the large intestine (Metal's yang organ), we see ulcerative colitis, diverticular infections and/or colon cancer.

Meantime, the diversion of Fire energy away from Earth leaves Earth in a state of deficiency, unable to receive nourishment, psychically as well as physically. In this state, the individual moves toward breakdown and dissolution — often in spite of the fact that sufficient energy is available — because the energy cannot be utilized. This situation, which can manifest as diabetes, food allergies, chronic fatigue syndrome, fibromyalgia or nutritional sensitivities, might be called *starvation in the midst of plenty*.

When the same diversion occurs on a mental/spiritual level, a confusion of the rightful place of human and transcendent relationships can result — sometimes alarmingly. For example, people who have been successful in the eyes of the world but who feel unfulfilled sometimes appear to try to move backwards into the Fire phase of high summer to recapture the feeling of their earlier years instead of digesting the experience of their achievements in Earth's late summer, harvest phase. They remain unfulfilled because the Earth — where the harvest of their life is — has been rejected or denied. After all, to admit Earth, to admit harvest and digestion, is to acknowledge that death is real, and for some that is a significant difficulty.

FIRE DIVERTED TOWARD METAL: LONG-TERM SEQUELAE

The long-term sequelae of this diversion can be calamitous. Difficulty receiving can lead to total allergy syndrome in which people feel there is nothing safe to ingest. Long-term nutritional deprivation can lead to energy deficits that spiral down into chronic pain, neuropathies, multiple sclerosis or other neuro-degenerative syndromes. Diabetes, as many people know, carries increased risk of cardiovascular disease, strokes, kidney and eye deterioration. Meanwhile, the inability to process what is taken in leads to the accumulation of toxic material (what Chinese medicine calls *Phlegm*), which can manifest as cysts, abscesses and even malignancies.

On a mental and spiritual level, chronic anxiety, insomnia and depression can be constant, and the neediness that Earth constitutional types exhibit can drive everybody away so that the sufferer ends up ill and alone.

☙ *COLIN*: TURNING BACK TO THE FIRE

Colin was a financial consultant who, in addition to a successful business, ran a summer camp for kids and a hobby farm on the side. Needless to say, he lived a busy, varied, often hectic life. Nonetheless, as he turned sixty, he started to feel restless and unfulfilled and, at the high point of his career and success, suddenly ran off with a much younger woman, leaving a marriage of thirty years.

After an initial high, Colin fell into a depression as he came to terms with what he had thrown away. Without the greater happiness he had hoped for, he began to find himself chronically fatigued as his new relationship soaked up all his creative energy and complicated his daily life. At sixty, Colin had tried to resist the cycle that offered wholeness through transcendence and integration and instead attempted to reverse the process and move backwards to the excitement of Fire. By confusing romantic love (Fire) with the transcendent (Metal), he rejected the harvest he had prepared with his life (Earth) and instead created a fatiguing and chaotic diversion of his core energies, leaving him prey to exhaustion and depression.

Lest this sound like a very familiar moral tale, we should remember that it is a statement of energy dynamics: the particulars of the story are simply symptomatic of those dynamics. Earth energy is about the cycle of giving and receiving. Whenever there is some difficulty with receiving whatever happens to be coming at us for whatever reason, the cycle of giving and receiving is blocked and energy is diverted into the Metal sector. If Colin had stayed in his marriage, for example, but could not receive whatever was there, the energy diversion and its consequences would likely have been the same.

EARTH DIVERTED TOWARD WATER: ENFORCED HELPLESSNESS

When Earth is diverted toward Water, the centred and abundant energy of the Earth element bypasses the letting go of Metal and moves directly into the formlessness or chaos of Water. Earth — protecting, nurturing and supportive — provides abundant deep energy and a firm ground from which we can move toward *letting go*. Earth might also be seen as the beginning of our learning to *be* rather than *do* and, when this learning is achieved, letting go is no longer a threatening idea. If this letting go is resisted, however, the energy of Earth is diverted to the Water sector, where it becomes a regressive force, inhibiting transformation, and instead giving rise

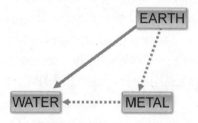

Figure 6: Earth diverts to Water

to mind-body disintegration. This is a very common problem in our culture where fear of the death mystery and of letting go reign supreme.

Surrender in any form is antithetical to ego. Illness, seen as an incursion from outside ourselves, is vigorously resisted and symptom suppression is considered desirable whenever possible. So a self-destructive struggle ensues, which often entrenches the very illness we are trying to avoid. Such a situation might be called *enforced helplessness*. This is tragic not only for the patient but also for the others — often whole families — who are caught up in the dynamics, because an illness, by enforcing a degree of helplessness on us, forces others to be our caregivers. In the end, paradoxically, the ego loses its battle by fighting too hard.

On a physical level, the inability to let go can lead to asthma, chronic constipation, diverticular disease, joint stiffness, arthritis, or Parkinsonism. On a mental and spiritual level, the imbalance can be quite tragic. First, the deficiency in the Metal sector leads to a deep and prolonged depression, even despair. Meanwhile, the concomitant excess energy in the Water sector manifests as increased fear and anxiety, which can be so intense that it completely overwhelms the personality.

The refusal to consider that symptoms have a personal meaning has fuelled our medical industry over the past several decades, and encouraged it to come up with increasingly sophisticated symptom-suppressing techniques. Unfortunately, by trying to avoid pain, we create more and more of it while digging ourselves deeper into denial and negativity, whereas Earth energy, used appropriately, draws the energy of letting go, as anyone who has lain in soft loamy earth will perhaps appreciate. It is a misuse of the energy to try to prevent the inevitable.

EARTH DIVERTED TOWARD WATER: LONG-TERM SEQUELAE

The inability to let go, if it continues for any length of time, will produce escalating rigidity and disarray. Without the ability to relax, the body becomes increasingly tense. As tension increases, the energy consumed to maintain the tension leads to mounting strain on the digestive system to supply energy needs. Since this is rarely enough, innate constitutional energies begin to be sapped and essential essence (*jing*) is depleted. The combination of increasing tension, digestive strain, and declining robustness leads to multiple system failure, which often manifests as strange and untreatable neurological conditions. This is truly chaos — not the chaos of creative transformation but rather its obverse and hellish counterpart, the *chaos of resisted surrender*, which has no end until individuals open to their pain.

༚ *JOHN*: PARKINSON'S SYNDOME

John was seventy years old when he came to our clinic complaining of unremitting pain in his legs. For years, he had seemed vague and indecisive, deferring to his wife who loved to make decisions for all around her. John took no responsibility for his difficulties and as his illness — which was eventually diagnosed as Parkinson's syndrome — progressed, his demands on his wife's time and attention grew. Eventually, he complained so much that he was put on narcotics which, added to his existing condition, put him in what his wife referred to as a permanent morphine haze.

Meanwhile, John took little interest in his condition and continued to deny any responsibility for his drug intake or his behaviour, contenting himself with the idea that he had a disease over which he had no control. It was beginning to become apparent, however, that he was rapidly acquiring a different kind of control: his helplessness had those around him jumping up and down at his every whim. And although this tyranny had not gone unnoticed, no-one confronted him because everyone bought the idea that his disease was somehow responsible. In our society it is just not socially acceptable to point out that disease and person are one, not two, entities.

As John sank deeper into physical helplessness, his wife found herself drawn into twenty-four-hour caregiving. It was a role she disliked intensely but guilt prevented her from expressing her anger directly or passing on the caregiving role to others. It may also be that she intuited that the dynamics of her relationship with her husband — her control and his withdrawal, over decades — were being expressed in his illness, that in fact it was *their* illness. Unfortunately, neither could admit to their part, though each looked to the other for a solution.

METAL DIVERTED TOWARD WOOD: VIOLENT TRANSFORMATION

When Metal energy is diverted away from Water toward Wood, the energy that should be directed toward transformation is diverted instead into new growth.

Metal is a downward, contracting and sinking energy and should flow on through surrender into transformation. Such surrender always involves a confrontation with the death mystery,

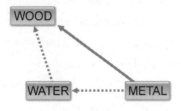

Figure 7: Metal diverts to Wood

which, though difficult, would occur quite naturally in the absence of any resistances. Of course, a confrontation with the psychic void represented by the death mystery is not necessarily the same as physical death. However, of all the movements of energy, the sinking into the formlessness of Water is perhaps the most difficult because it involves complete psychic transformation. It can only occur if the individual has mastered the art of letting go, has connected to the transcendent and is willing to pass through the portal of psychic death into the unknown. In every transformation there is a sacrifice and in this case it is a sacrifice of the ego itself.

If transformation is resisted, the energy of Metal gets diverted into the Wood sector, where it is used to bolster the existing ego structure rather than facilitate the process of ego transcendence. Too little energy in Water disrupts the transformational process while too much energy in Wood results in increasingly desperate attempts to control the rising chaos. The situation might be likened to King Canute's famous attempt to stop the movement of the tide by shouting orders at the water. It did not work, of course, nor ultimately does the control strategy hamper the transpersonal forces pushing for transformation.

Such a diversion and its results can be seen in things like body-part replacements, cryogenics and in various states of ego inflation; but the disease that really characterizes this particular energetic diversion is cancer. Indeed, uncontrolled growth in the presence of resistance to change is almost a definition of the disease. One might call such an experience *violent transformation*.

At a mental and spiritual level, the same dynamic occurs: the diversion of Metal energy leads to incursions from the ego and manifests as various strategies of control as a way of coping with the premature onset of psychic uncertainty. We control the chaos in our bodies by suppressing symptoms, the chaos in our minds by rigid and fearful ways of thinking and the threat of chaos in society by authoritarian rule.

It is easy to see Metal diverted into Wood by looking at other cultures whose political or religious orthodoxy we do not identify with. It is a bit harder to see the rigidity in ourselves and our own society but the forces of transformation and resistance are very much alive and active at home. Change is frightening and our collective resistance to it is reflected in the increasing number of absurd regulations made by authorities who are facing impossibly conflicting demands and are out of control. The irony is that overregulation tends to make people angry (Wood), which leads to the very chaos the regulations sought to control. Either way, transformation still occurs.

METAL DIVERTED TOWARD WOOD: LONG-TERM SEQUELAE

In the same way, attempts to control the spread of malignant disease can lead to violent assaults on the body that may do more harm than good. The ravages of chemotherapy, radiotherapy and mutilating surgery — our violent and warlike approach to cancer — speak eloquently of our anxious sacrifice to our fear of change. We are so scared of transformation that we often opt for self-destruction rather than face the unknown. But since the person and the illness are actually one entity, not two, the war on cancer is essentially a war against the self.

℞ EUNICE: BREAST CANCER

Eunice was a thirty-one-year-old woman who espoused an idealism that included, amongst other things, advanced theories of self-realization and personal responsibility. She exercised, ate no meat, practised positive thinking and kept a stress-free routine. But one day she felt a lump in her breast and her attitude changed.

When she was told she had a particularly virulent tumour with a low five-year survival rate, she abandoned her holistic philosophy and took the road of conventional cancer management with equal zeal. Eunice had a radical mastectomy and lymph-node dissection, had her ovaries removed, underwent chemotherapy and radio-therapy, then went all over the world in search of new and often risky forms of treatment.

In spite of her efforts, after about four years Eunice succumbed to her disease. Only about a month before her death did she abandon her search for a cure and begin to work on coming to a place of acceptance. Of course, when death intervenes, there is no way of knowing whether another course might have produced a different outcome. But perhaps that is not the point. When it comes to trans-formation, we all stand helpless before the mystery. Who knows what ingredients are necessary, what preparations should be made, whether this or that approach would be better, or whether a psychic transformation could have precluded a physical one? There is really no way of knowing. But then, to not-know is the essence of Water, and transformation occurs anyway. Probably the best we can do is to be fully and compassionately present. And perhaps Eunice experi-enced her own transformation in the best possible way for her.

THE BIG PICTURE

I hope this short analysis has given the reader a glimpse of the enormous scope of the five element system. Its ability to throw light on some of the forces impacting on the illness that particular individuals encounter is nothing short of astounding. By explor-ing the various personal and transpersonal dynamics, it is possible to come to a deep understanding of the experiential meaning of our symptoms and such an understanding can promote the trans-formation and transcendence so necessary to healing.

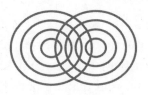

CHAPTER 10

INTENTION

When you shipwreck in the shallow waters of your intellectual notion of what your life is about, wherever you shipwreck is where your depth is. Then you go down into your own abyss to find the forgotten, omitted energy which should have been informing your life but which was being excluded by your conscious posture.

— Joseph Campbell

*T*he idea that illness and pain carry messages that call us to expand our awareness is not generally acknowledged in the West. We assume that relief of symptoms is the duty of our physicians and our goal as patients. Our impulse to move away from our symptoms seems to be based on our understanding that they are foreign to our well-being and, what is more, can only be addressed by professionals. However, if our symptoms are carrying an important message, it might be wiser to *move toward* those symptoms, to explore, rather than turn away from, whatever is calling our attention.

MOVING TOWARD SYMPTOMS

The wisdom of moving our attention toward symptoms is implicit in the fact that, however strong our aversion to them might be, our symptoms are part of us. The idea that cause and effect are distinguishable, and can therefore be treated as separate entities, has its roots in our existential anxiety and our sense of alienation — our own deep conviction that we ourselves are somehow an effect of some distant external cause and vulnerable to meaningless and random dangers from outside, instead of a vital and integrated part of our own creation at every moment.

This alienated view tends, in turn, to make us see our symptoms as separate and therefore removable and our life processes as problems that need fixing. The advent of medicine's magic bullets (antibiotics, organ transplants, chemotherapy, etc.) in recent years has only reinforced such thinking by making it appear that something may be introduced from the outside that will target and remove what we choose to consider an intrusion.

Unfortunately, this idea of the separation of cause and effect, of problems and cures, is not only false, it is the seed thought from which much chronic illness arises. Chinese medicine notes this core truth in its description of illness as being due to separation from the Tao. (The same texts caution that the feeling of separation is a misapprehension because we cannot be separated from the Tao.) In Ayurvedic medicine, as mentioned earlier, this same alienated stance is called the mistake of the intellect, or *Pragyaparadh*.

Both these holistic systems are very clear on the essential point that our illnesses are not separate from ourselves and that behaving as if they are — that is, viewing them as conditions we have, rather than something we are and then asking others to fix the problem — is a serious mistake. By attempting to eradicate symptoms we are, unfortunately, only inhibiting real healing. Such an approach is at best short-sighted; at worst, it is disastrous, as it can push disease further into the body.

But turning away, instead of moving toward, is deeply ingrained in all of us. Most of us grow up considering it — if we are even aware of it — a survival skill. In the process of creating a persona (the self with which we negotiate everyday life), for instance, we learn to turn away from, or inhibit, our deepest impulses to a greater or lesser degree. We do this very naturally in order to fit into our communities but the effort of maintaining this constructed self can make us tired and tense at a deep level. After all, we are struggling against our very selves, alienating ourselves from our true natures in order not to feel alienated from our society.

At some point, our mental, physical or emotional health will begin to show the strain. Pain, disease, distress or other symptoms will arise as a materialization of those primal energies in us that have not been permitted expression. Or, to put it another way, *disease represents aspects of the Self that we have lost or buried.*

Fortunately, by the same token, an illness, if heeded, can become a signpost on the journey back to wholeness. Knowing this, we can learn to struggle less against our symptoms and begin to learn to listen with great care instead, allowing them to help us identify and retrieve our energies, and integrating them into a more authentic self. To do this is to understand to what extent our habitual interference suppresses natural functions, including our body-mind's ability to heal what ails us, and robs us of precious knowledge about our hearts, our minds and our lives.

REGRESSION / INTEGRATION

Although we are not encouraged to recognize the fact, it is worth remembering — especially during the spiritual crisis that a chronic illness can represent — that the adult ego we prize so highly is merely a stage of development between the infant's pre-consciousness and the expanded consciousness of the sage. In other words, a return to wholeness is not a return to an earlier egoic state, nor to the infant's pre-egoic Garden of Eden but rather a move toward a new state, one beyond ego in some sense.

Regression in energy medicine is a purposeful inner journey something akin to the shamanic practice of soul retrieval, a return to the place where our energy was split off, to find what was lost, re-engage it, then begin the task of integrating the retrieved energies into a larger, more expansive sense of self. Many adults, of course, never reach this stage. But chronic or serious illness, perhaps paradoxically, gives us access to the extraordinary transformational energies often otherwise only available at the moment of our death, or through long commitment to meditative disciplines. In fact, when we become stuck in pain or illness, it is usually because we are defending the small — and ultimately false — egoic self against the changes transformation is demanding of us.

THE INTEGRATION
OF TREATMENT AND HEALING

The decision to move toward our symptoms rather strikingly blurs the distinctions between what we would ordinarily consider opposites. Treatment and healing, disease and health, objectivity and subjectivity, even allopathic and holistic medicines — are not fundamentally contrary but rather different ways of perceiving the complex energy system that exists around and through us. The principle of complementarity and dependent co-origination expressed in the familiar yin-yang symbol and in the fundamental understandings of Chinese medicine, suggests that when we are ill, a broadening of perspective is often more helpful than denying one view and insisting on the other.

To move beyond our current limited perspectives to find the positionless position that embraces all perspectives is to achieve what Shunryu Suzuki, legendary twentieth-century Zen teacher, called beginner's mind, the always fresh mind of unmediated perception, new each moment, as opposed to the dense and resistant expert's mind, where pattern recognition and learned assumptions mediate and prejudice perception, blocking new understandings with old ones.

INTENTION AND THE VOID

It is difficult, as well as inadvisable, to try to force a move toward symptoms while in normal consciousness. The ego simply refuses the challenge, no matter how compelling the argument might be. So successful experiential work relies on achieving an altered state of consciousness, in which rational mind is temporarily in abeyance. This is the magic of the void, in which we are aware of inner and outer, subjective and objective simultaneously. In this state of mind, moving toward pain and discomfort becomes very much easier, so by consciously invoking it at every opportunity — and especially during dynamic interactive acu-bodywork (DIA) — we set the stage for fruitful exploration.

As DIA involves two (or more) participants, all present must access this open and unfettered state of mind. Then with mutual, clear and congruent intent, the explorer/witness dyad enters the void together as a whole greater than the sum of its parts. What happens next is really quite fascinating: we enter a previously unknown place, a Pandora's box whose contents are unknowable ahead of time yet profoundly life-altering to anyone who dares open the box. The void is a place of transformation, a cauldron of collective intent and quantum uncertainty, in which various forces interact to produce an unforeseeable outcome.

To further map the profound nature of this transformational zone, I want to return briefly to the beauty of the five element model.

FIVE ELEMENTS AND THE VOID:
THE GOLDEN GATE

Allying the stages of growth, maturity and ego-transcendence to the five element model (figure 1) allows us to understand our life process as spiral rather than linear. In the spiral, a person's individual five element constitutional type manifests within the larger context of the cycle of ego construction, maturation, ripeness, disintegration and transcendence/renewal.

This spiral model can help us understand how certain illnesses may affect certain people at certain times of their lives. Going around the circle with particular reference to illness, we could say that during the yang maturational phase, illnesses tend to be associated with rising energies, and with ego relations (conflict and power struggles, the arena of the lower chakras), while during the yin phase they tend to be associated with sinking energy, with letting go and transformation difficulties. And such an understanding can, in turn, affect intent. For example, such a model can help us see that it is often more appropriate, especially in complex illnesses, to intend transformation and reintegration of buried energies during the yin phase than it would be during the yang phase — when many people are quite properly engaged in building their egos rather than letting them go.

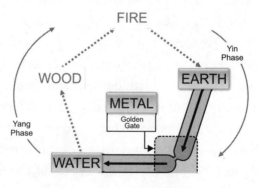

Figure 1: The Golden Gate

But wherever we find ourselves in our cycle or spiral of growth, chronic untreatable illness always demands that a letting go precedes transformation and reintegration. If we cannot relinquish an outmoded way of being and move through the cycle of change that is life, we are, from a five element perspective, stuck on the brink of the disintegrative yin phase, in the region of the Metal element (or Metal phase). From there, the move forward into the transformational chaos of the Water element can be so frightening that many people become paralyzed, or try to reconstruct an ego that has outlived its usefulness and has begun to disintegrate in preparation for the ego-transcendence phase.

But if we want to find healing, we must move through this resistance. To do so can feel like pushing through a kind of tunnel or psychic narrowing. This narrowing has been likened to the waist of an hourglass or to the birth canal; readers familiar with the Bible may be reminded of the striking image of letting go, which notes that a rich man will find himself as unable to enter heaven as a camel would be to fit through the eye of a needle. In other words, unless we go psychically naked and undefended, the passage will prove impassable. In Chinese medicine, this entryway to radical transformation has been called the Golden (or, Metal) Gate (*Jin Men*), the Mysterious Pass, the Door of Death and the Gate of Birth.

Ultimately, we cannot avoid this passage to a more authentic self, though we can delay it until the very moment of death. The great challenge is to pass through the Gate while still fully alive and to emerge clarified physically and psychically. The difficulty is that in order to pass through we must intend the passage without reservation, as if we really were going to die. When we have achieved this intention and this degree of resolution, psychic death is not difficult; in fact, it is essentially automatic.

INTENTION AND PRESENCE

The expanded state of mind that facilitates what I have been calling a moving-toward intent might be called *presence* — that unblocked, integral, engaged and direct mode of experiencing, in which everything is witnessed and nothing is resisted or rejected. It is a way of being in the now rather than fantasizing — as we so often do, minute by minute and hour by hour throughout our lives without really being aware of it — about the past or the future. If the healing response seems blocked, it is usually because our intention is not clear: there are conflicting forces at work and, one way or another, we are not present. So let us look at some factors we have found are significant in creating and maintaining the quality of presence necessary to healing chronic illness.

CENTRING / FIRE

Heart-centring is one vitally important way of expanding awareness beyond our rational minds and is probably best achieved through meditation. As mentioned in chapter 1, The Field of Energy, meditations that open the heart chakra have been shown to produce field coherence, promote intuition, and facilitate the coupling or entrainment of various body rhythms. And because our energy field extends beyond the confines of the physical body, entrainment means that it will influence all nearby energy fields. I therefore make a practice of starting every day with a Heart-centring meditation to prepare myself for whatever may come during the day. And the more successful I am at Heart-centring, the easier my day becomes and the more I find the people I work with accessing the deeper recesses of the void.

Indeed, it continues to astonish me how during DIA people will often enter the void with little or no effort on my part, provided context and intention are congruent, and provided I am in a Heart-centred state. Such seems to be the profound effect of energetic coupling.

HONOURING / METAL

Honouring or validating is an aspect of the Metal element. Metal honours the harvest that is the fruit of one cycle of our lives. If our harvest happens to be a chronic illness, such honouring can seem difficult, even absurd. But without first understanding that our illness is made of the stuff of our minds and hearts, and without some embrace of it as being *of* us rather than alien, some respect for it as a repository of essentially all we have left to learn (in that it is in some measure our Shadow), we will find it impossible to turn to face the chaos of transformation (Water) that will permit us to move forward to new life. Unfortunately, such validation can be very difficult to find in the conventional medicine establishment: we must do the exploration necessary to find meaning for ourselves.

CONTEXT / EARTH

Earth represents security. We all yearn for a sense of security, and a descent into the chaos of a transformation we have yet to glimpse the shape of seems an unthinkable risk without some assurance. Earth represents a safe container or crucible. After all, most of the energies we are searching to reintegrate have been put away for the very good reason that we judged them dangerous. When we attempt to re-connect, fears and anxieties surface. They are often more than enough to halt us in our tracks, particularly if we sense that the energies are not acceptable or respectable, and therefore will not be accepted or respected. (A residential setting can provide a supportive and non-judgemental environment for such transformational energies to emerge but it is most often our own judgements that are most deeply inhibiting.)

TRUST / WATER

If we listen to and act on our body's wisdom, healing often unfolds quite naturally. The ability to listen and to trust in the wisdom of the unknown is an aspect of the Water element. Trusting the body's wisdom, however, understanding that the body knows exactly what it needs to do to heal itself seems a remarkable notion to those of us who have grown up feeling alienated from our bodies.

Trust is also needed when we ask ourselves to consciously have faith in the outcome, even though that outcome is unpredictable. Such a stance can lessen our fear of the unknown, freeing energy to move where it wants. (The current fascination with outcome studies and evidence-based medicine points to a collective misunderstanding of the healing process. Simply put, to anticipate outcome is to compromise results because anticipation — which is a kind of intention — destabilizes and interrupts and even directs the movement of energy.)

SILENCE AND DYNAMISM / WOOD

The transformational dynamics in the void are essentially automatic, in that our body and Mind will take us where they need to go once we stop resisting. But where there are others involved, these dynamics rely on a re-conceiving of the customary roles: the one supposedly giving treatment becomes a witness while the one receiving treatment becomes an explorer. As the session develops, the witness increasingly takes a silent, non-judgemental position and acts mostly to maintain the safety of the crucible. In this way, she serves to ground the transformation (the yin aspect of the void). At the same time, the explorer's intention becomes more active (the yang aspect of the void), allowing the inner healer to be activated and giving expression to as much original energy as possible — in sound, emotion and physical movement.

Day to day, however, the involvement of a second person as witness to our journeying is often an impractical luxury. When we are on our own, the yin and yang of silence and dynamism, grounding and willingness, witness and exploration, must be rolled into one. In dynamic meditation, for example, we must learn to ground our own void experience in a silent internal witness while at the same time allowing any dynamism to manifest.

TRANSFORMATION

Transformation describes the turning point in which the conflicting energies present in the void re-equilibrate themselves into a new configuration. It is almost like making a stew — put in some ingredients, let them simmer for a while and without any particular effort the whole becomes greater than the sum of the parts and it tastes wonderful. Were we to put in the wrong ingredients, however, our stew will not taste so good.

The subjective reality that emerges from the void is unpredictable and often surprising. About all that can be said about it is that however it appears, it represents a more coherent and balanced energetic system. We often feel intensely present and calm after negotiating the chaos, as if we have come home; and the ego rests in a timeless experience of the now, a state of dynamic nothingness meditators sometimes call bliss, and which others have called our original face — which is sometimes further described as the face we had before we were born.

THE ENERGIES OF THE VOID:
MAINTAINING INTENT

Maintaining intent while in the void can be challenging, particularly if difficult, long-buried energies erupt. Take, for example, sexuality and anger, which are frequently suppressed and frequently become mingled. Unconsciously contained in a stiff and tight pelvis, these energies can suddenly look quite frightening — especially as those with significant tension in the area often have a history of sexual abuse — and if the crucible is not sturdy or flexible enough, there is the possibility it could crack under pressure. In such situations, the explorer needs a lot of trust to stay present and keep going, and the witness needs a lot of trust to remain calm and compassionate.

Moreover, in these days of zero tolerance, the legal implications of exploring pelvic energies at all can be worrisome. But as allowing these blocked energies to move can be tremendously healing, a safe distance only serves to limit and even distort healing intent. A good approach, in these circumstances, then, is to make anxiety about such energies emerging explicit ahead of time and then to rest in the Heart-centred space, fully present and open-hearted, yet detached from the specifics of what is going on in the void. With such an approach, there is rarely any problem and a moving-toward intent can be maintained without too much difficulty.

WOOD — ANGER

Anger is a difficult energy to work with. Professionals often try to protect themselves from it with objectivity, technology and limited physical contact. Unfortunately, distance and objectivity (and their physical manifestation as technology), though apparently safer, are the exact opposite of the Heart-centred context required to honour the intention to integrate original energies.

Establishing a safe container as mentioned above — perhaps the setting of mutually acceptable boundaries for the expression of violent emotions — can provide sufficient assurance that anger can be allowed to erupt as a rich energetic experience rather than an exercise in dissociation (for which we all have far too many opportunities in daily life), and so supports rather than detracts from its expression.

WATER — FEAR

Because the fundamental existential issue for the Water constitutional type lies in his or her relationship to fear, those with this disposition may suffer a double dose of fear as they enter the void. Often when the Water energy begins to move, it does so as a fine shivering that can be misinterpreted as a response to cold. We should resist the temptation to attend to the shivering with warm blankets or hot drinks and rather use the opportunity to create a new mental referent for this particular experience of energy movement: not fear but excitement, not cold but deep energies stirring. Such relearning can powerfully affect an individual's experience.

FIRE — JOY AND SADNESS

Although we rarely understand it as a problem, Chinese medicine considers that joy in excess is as harmful as any other unbalanced energy in the body. Mania, false gaiety (picture the salesperson or entrepreneur who mimics cheerfulness to appear likeable and successful to clients and colleagues) and inappropriate levity (of the kind we experience as children in churches and at funerals) are as socially unacceptable as many other emotions and can be hard on the heart and other systems as well.

Sadness — the flip side of joy's coin — is more likely to be the place where the typical Fire person is reluctant to go. However, if laughter is deeply engaged, it will often spontaneously morph into weeping, just as crying will sometimes transform into laughter. When this happens in the void, the two emotions will often flip back and forth until a moment comes when both poles (laughter and crying) are experienced simultaneously. The cognitive dissonance and the direct experience of the energy that is common to joy and to sadness create an invaluable mind-body understanding of this particular continuum.

EARTH — SYMPATHY

The existential issue for Earth constitutional types is worry, combined with a craving for reassurance and companionship. Earth people sometimes suffer from panic attacks and tend to call for help in the absence of real danger. Once again, the way out is through. If, in a safe environment, we can let go into an anxiety attack and feel the terror of it, we will often come out the other side calmed. And once we are capable of providing ourselves with adequate reassurance and safety, this kind of going-through can be repeated as a daily dynamic meditation until the charge on the experience comes down to an acceptable level.

METAL — GRIEF

While everyone must grieve loss, letting go of even the trivia of the mental, emotional and physical realms can be very difficult for those with a Metal constitutional type. They tend to be obsessive and depressive, hanging on long past reason, making loss a central theme and grief a way of life rather than a process.

For these people, it can be helpful to realize that letting go is not necessarily a calm and accepting, serious or quiet endeavour. In fact, it can be extremely dynamic, involving a lot of railing and shouting at everyone and everything, as the ego negotiates a whitewater river to annihilation. As the dynamism begins to relax lifelong tensions, letting go can sometimes lead to uncontrollable, cleansing laughter, which can be just what those who take life very seriously most deeply need.

I once worked with a man who was doing just this sort of railing and wailing so loudly it hurt my ears. The only thing within reach that resembled earplugs was a box of tissues. Without thinking, I rolled a couple up and stuffed them into my ears. A moment later, he opened his eyes to see me looking like something out of a cartoon, and began howling with laughter and could not stop for half an hour — merriment that, not incidentally, heralded the beginning of a significant change in his condition.

INTENT AND RELATIONSHIP

Intent being what it is — one of the most powerful of all energies, however passive it may seem — the source of most real and lasting healing will always lie in the intangibles of relationship, whether that relationship be person-disease, doctor-patient, teacher-student or explorer-witness, or a newfound relationship with oneself, or with one's pain. This means that specific therapies or physical interventions have little value in themselves. Rather, they might be better understood as rituals through which a particular relationship expresses its intent.

It is the intent behind the ritual, not the ritual itself, that carries the power of healing.

If we can grasp this point, we will begin to understand how sadly scientific medicine has lost its way. How with its complex procedures, objective measurements and outcome studies, it somehow misses the boat. How, based on a less than optimal intent — that of moving away (symptom suppression) rather than moving toward (exploration of repressed energies) — it is fated to miss the essence of healing, which is transformation.

As we go forward now, I want to show how these fundamental principles can be applied to expand and transform our relationship to illness.

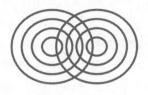

CHAPTER 11

DYNAMIC INTERACTIVE
ACU-BODYWORK

Emotion is the chief source of all becoming-conscious.
There can be no transforming of the darkness into light
and of apathy into movement without emotion.

— Carl Gustav Jung

$\mathcal{N}$ow that we have explored some basic concepts —
interference patterns, fields, ego development, compartmentalization, dissociation and intention, among others — we can start to
look at ways to facilitate *reintegration* through the dual processes
of transformation and transcendence.

Working with the body's energy field rather than its physical
structure means that we must adjust much of our learned understanding of the body and the mind. For example, as we hinted in the
last chapter, to accept that symptoms are not separate from us and
therefore that simply getting rid of them is not possible is a profound
and often difficult shift in understanding — especially for those who
are in pain. But if we are to achieve wholeness (that is, health), we
must find our way to a more body-centred state of consciousness.

Such a shift will enable us to free ourselves of our habitual (or,
some would say, instinctive) avoidance strategies and instead form a
clear intention to move toward, instead of away from, our
symptoms. As we noted in the last chapter, trying to move toward

symptoms in normal rational consciousness is generally difficult, if not impossible. If, on the other hand, we enter a body-centred state, moving toward symptoms can be difficult to resist.

The simple act of moving toward pain integrates mind/body, persona/shadow and existential blocks. In the past, various psycho-therapies and somatics have approached these blocks individually and in their own ways. For instance, 'the talking cure' (a popular nickname for psychoanalysis) addressed itself to the persona/shadow split, whereas the so-called body-centred psychotherapies and somatics aimed at the mind/body split. Meditation seeks to transcend the life/death and existential splits but, as we have mentioned elsewhere, can often simply move practitioners' attention from existing mental, emotional and spiritual blocks. The simple, bold move toward pain in all its forms, with curiosity and with trust in whatever outcome, on the other hand, allows integration on several levels simultaneously. (Ideally, of course, reintegration occurs on its own but, as most of us are unconsciously blocking our heal-ing, assistance with the process is often welcome.)

EXPERIENTIAL VERSUS INTELLECTUAL UNDERSTANDING

It may be that we are so entranced by the power of our minds and so untrusting of our bodies in Western society that this radically simple idea has been such a long time coming (or, to be precise, coming back). Whatever the reason, there is no way around the fact that integration of our energy fields is an *experience* and not something that occurs through talking or reading or thinking, any of which can only prepare the ground. Nor can we achieve much by force of will — in fact, in doing so we can unwittingly accentuate the split and delay the integration. We have to find a way to get out of our heads and into our bodies, to stop thinking about our symptoms and instead explore them first hand. We must live our exploration and our integration.

One practice we have found very effective in our centre is the use of altered states and gentle accentuation of symptoms. We call it dynamic interactive acu-bodywork (DIA) because it uses a variety of somatic approaches as well as acupuncture and aims to release energy or emotion in the interactive context of explorer and witness, or witnesses. The combination of an expanded state of consciousness, a collective intention to move toward pain or symptoms and dynamic participation, provides an extraordinarily open framework within which all parties can help to facilitate *that which needs to happen*. Shadow energies can emerge and be recognized if we allow free expression of emotion; mind and body can become one if we trust the body's wisdom; and the existential split may be transcended — temporarily — when energy flows freely in us.

WHAT IS DYNAMIC INTERACTIVE ACU-BODYWORK (DIA)?

If there ever could be a definition of DIA, it would allude to wholeness, non-action and compassionate presence, and to experiential symptom exploration. Its goal is to discover the original face, or nature, of our symptoms and to let us discover what we can about their meaning in our lives. When we choose to listen to our symptoms by physically, mentally and emotionally immersing ourselves in them, we signal our body that we trust it to reveal its secrets in its own way and in its own time. This is the core relation in energy work: the questing ego/mind meets itself in the body and learns what no outside intelligence could ever teach it.

Needless to say, this is not a relation familiar to us from conventional medicine, where the body is handed over to a kind of technician in much the same way we might drop a car off to be fixed. What is more, whereas conventional medical techniques can be administered by nearly anyone given sufficient training, energy principles must be embodied by those who would make use of them in healing; and, as this embodiment comes only with lived personal experience, practitioners must have made their own exploratory journeys in search of their bodies' deep messages before they will be able to be effective in working with others.

DIA is therefore not — and could never be — a prescribed treatment for any condition. The moment we begin to think that way we have fallen back into acting against, which is the opposite of integration. (In fact, the very idea of a disease implies there is a problem to be fixed and this mindset inclines us to moving away rather than moving toward, which compromises the whole interaction and stands in the way of deep healing.)

It is easy to see from this why the principles of energetic healing are rarely fully understood — even by some exponents of energy therapies. This is no small issue, because many purportedly new energy therapies are currently being integrated into the medical mainstream as if they were simply alternative treatment protocols for diseases diagnosed in a conventional manner. But conventional diagnoses are meaningless descriptions at the level of the energy field because that field is profoundly individual as well as transpersonal and symptoms are themselves descriptions of particular individuals' energy fields. To treat on the basis of conventional diagnosis is therefore always to be led away from wholeness rather than toward it.

THE INTERACTIVE RELATIONSHIP

In other words, although most people come to DIA expecting a kind of treatment, the implicit dualities — that is, a problem and its treatment, or a practitioner and a patient — nested in this expectation are antithetical to healing at the deepest levels, diverting intention away from wholeness. Therefore it is important to understand that DIA's interactive relationship is neither therapeutic nor procedural.

If I had to describe the nature of the relationship that DIA creates in just one sentence, I might say that DIA is *a non-hierarchical relationship grounded in the mutual intent to experientially explore symptoms, without expectations of any specific outcome.* This relationship grows out of the understanding that when two (or more) people come together in a healing context, any interaction which gives one person the role of giving and another the role of receiving health simply reinforces the existential split. Indeed, any therapy entered into with the thought, 'You're the doctor — fix me!' can spiral into textbook co-dependency and begin to actively block healing instead of promoting it. Therefore, to facilitate the best possible DIA dive into the unknown, both parties must be clear of unhelpful notions of disease and cure and understand that DIA is experiential learning, not treatment.

That this is difficult to convey in the context of contemporary Western society is evidenced by the unusual vocabulary you may have noticed in the preceding few pages. My resistance to using the conventional terms — like doctor, therapist, patient or client — leaves me with few recognizable alternatives to describe the relationship of people in a room where experiential exploration is taking place. Explorer and witness — or even, as others have suggested, traveller and guide — are simply the best language I have been able to come up with that answers to the actual context and experience of DIA. In the next section, for the sake of readability and easy comprehension, however, I have chosen to use the more familiar and quite neutral term, *practitioner*.

PRINCIPLES OF EXPLORATION[1]

DIA is founded on the principles of Heart-centring, intention, breathing and the often indistinguishable sound/emotion/movement of the body's free expression, each of which I will explore in some detail below. All parties must work with sincerity and trust and an acceptance of whatever happens, and must strive to put aside all judgements in order to give each other real emotional safety for the journey.

HEART-CENTRING

I mentioned Heart-centring meditation in an earlier chapter but let me elaborate a little here because it is so important. A practitioner's consciousness has a profound influence on the outcome of any energetic exploration. The degree to which she works from a Heart-centred place is the degree to which she will be able to work with compassion and empathy and without judgement. And in the presence of compassion and acceptance, we are generally more able to explore difficult or contained emotions.

Conversely, if a practitioner cannot accept and honour whatever happens in a session, access to deeper material is often blocked. It is no exaggeration to say that Heart-centredness is more important to DIA than any specific technical skill. Mastering it requires a daily meditation practice. (You can use any meditation that works for you. I currently use the Twin Hearts Meditation from the Pranic Healing organization.)

But Heart-centring is even more important in that it is the energetic foundation for every interactive experience. And it is

1 Please see Appendix 1, Void Exploration / DIA, for practical instructions on how to prepare for a DIA session.

these experiences, not her theoretical knowledge, that comprise the practitioner's embodied energetic understanding and cultivate her ability. There are no secrets and no substitute for personal and interpersonal exploration and experience. The body, mind and spirit of the practitioner can only be educated by her sincere, compassionate engagement with other bodies, minds and spirits and by personal questing and discovery.

However, although skill cannot be gained except by this hands-on practice, the collective experience of other practitioners can provide a guide to that practice. With that in mind, I want to try to pass on a little of my own experience of working interactively.

INTENTION AND THE VOID

The void, that place of exploration and healing I have written about in my earlier books, can be found in the gaps between things. One way I have learned to find it in the physical body is to search the ego boundary — that boundary which can be found at the edge between pain and no pain, between what is acceptable and what is not. It is usually embodied in our muscular armouring and can be felt but I have come across some people whose edge is off the body altogether. (Which is not as surprising as it may sound, given that the energy field extends beyond the body's physical limits.)

In fact, the location of the void is always shifting depending on what is going on, so that the practitioner must constantly shift her attention in order to feel her way into the unknown. By palpating the edge and adjusting pressure according to the body's response, we can develop a feel for the infinitesimal gap that is the entrance to the void, and by tuning in to the explorer's vibrational rhythm, find a way in.

I have found that there is a very fine edge between too little and too much, a place between pain and no pain, between what is acceptable and what is unacceptable. Too much pressure produces resistance, too little results in no movement at all. The optimal amount of pressure is precisely the amount that produces movement of energy.

BREATHING TECHNIQUE

Although some people encourage hyperventilation as a way to access an altered state of consciousness, I have found that deeper breathing does not have to be forced and can develop quite easily provided the principle of intention is understood and the context is safe. There is no question that continuous deep breathing *will* after a few minutes produce an altered state of consciousness. But one difficulty is that people who are ill often have markedly fragmented or obstructed breathing — an accurate reflection, by the way, of the energetic compartmentalization forming the backdrop of their symptoms — and so have real difficulty getting a full breath.

Breathing deeply whenever there is some discomfort (which would normally prompt us to hold our breath and tighten around the pain) facilitates energy movement just as well. Amongst other things, I find it gets the mind out of the way by giving it something to do. With the mind otherwise occupied, the body can speak its truth and energy can move.

Deep breathing can produce some strange sensations, such as dizziness, numbness and tingling, carpopedal (hand or foot) spasm, or tightness around the mouth. These are all quite common and rarely a reason for concern. If we persist with our breathing, we burst through to the void where we can experience the body in a completely new way, as a connected energy system or field, without borders or boundaries. Once there, breathing tends to become relatively effortless, and the strange sensations recede in importance as we become immersed in the void experience itself.

ENERGETIC PHENOMENA — PHYSICAL, EMOTIONAL AND MENTAL

A variety of physical, mental and emotional expressions can arise as a result of energy movement associated with experiences in the void. Emotional release can take almost any conceivable form and can involve the whole body. A specific sound — crying, laughing, shouting, groaning — will usually signal the release, giving a clue to its nature. Other common physical and mental experiences are myoclonic shaking and regression (see below).

Sound and emotion should be spontaneous to be effective. Making a lot of noise if we do not feel it, just to prove that we can, or perhaps to please our witness, is essentially a mental exercise and usually achieves little (although the 'fake it till you make it' approach does sometimes work). Spontaneously allowing sound, trusting the impulse to move, and being open to emotional upwelling, on the other hand, will facilitate the natural flow of energy and allow the body to speak its truth.

MYOCLONIC SHAKING — SPONTANEOUS ENERGETIC REBALANCING

Myoclonic shaking is an energetic release that takes the form of a vibration of the limbs, trunk or neck. This shaking, which can be fine or gross, marks the release of repressed energy into uncontrolled physical movement, which in turn serves to relax the muscles that had restricted it.

This very common physical principle is best illustrated by a weighted spring, or coil, hanging from a ceiling. When motionless, the spring and weight together contain potential energy (tension).

When oscillating, this potential energy becomes kinetic (movement or vibration). So, trembling or vibration signals a release of repressed energy and should be welcomed and encouraged. People sometimes have a spontaneous shivering or shaking experience and mistake it as a sign that something is wrong, or resist it because they think it makes them look odd, or because they dislike feeling out of control. Unfortunately, to resist is merely to miss a spontaneous rebalancing of our energy field.

ʘ *BRENDA*: RESTLESS LEGS

Brenda was thirty-five years old when she came to see us. She had chronic pain and was alarmed by her legs jerking uncontrollably just as she was falling asleep. Assuming that there was something seriously wrong, she notified her physician, complaining also of the sleep deprivation and fatigue her condition was causing her. Before long, she was taking a variety of anti-seizure medications. Combining these with the painkillers, anti-depressants and sleeping medication she was already taking for her chronic pain left her feeling like a zombie.

Unfortunately, it never occurred to Brenda or her physician that the shaking they were working so hard to repress might be a very effective way of releasing the tension that was contributing to her chronic pain. Brenda was astonished to find that if she allowed the shaking to take its course instead of fighting it, it stopped of its own accord after a certain time. And that when it stopped, she felt deeply relaxed and was easily able to fall asleep without drugs. The frightening condition she had subjected to any number of annihilating substances was nothing less than her body's own spontaneous healing response kicking in at the moment when her mind was least guarded, just as she was falling asleep.

REGRESSION — HOW PAST EVENTS INVADE THE PRESENT

The intensity of mental imagery encountered in experiences of the void can range from vague to vivid, and from fleeting all the way to a full-blown regression, in which we may re-experience traumatic events — accidents, abuse, the witnessing of terrible things. Such experiences tend to involve energetic phenomena occurring on physical, emotional and mental levels concurrently.

Re-experiencing can involve several sense organs — smells, sounds, visions and physical sensations can accompany the experiences. The result in some cases is an experiential gestalt that simulates the original experience in remarkable detail. Sometimes such events have not only been put out of an explorer's mind but were so effectively buried that they have never before been accessible.

Although one's first experience of regression can be quite dramatic and is often followed by a marked reduction in symptoms, such positive effects are usually only temporary. To really own the experience and gradually lessen the symptoms, it must be repeated until the energetic charge is reduced and no longer a big problem.

ॐ *DIANE*: POST-TRAUMATIC STRESS DISORDER

Diane had been in three car accidents and had been so affected by them that car travel began to cause her claustrophobia so intense that she wanted to get out of whatever vehicle she was in, even if it was moving. Diagnosed with post-traumatic stress disorder (PTSD), she had had several years of cognitive therapy without much improvement. During her first attempt at DIA, using nothing more than deep breathing and clear intent, she re-experienced the three accidents, and emerged feeling calm for the first time in years.

Later, using the same technique, she plunged into a childhood sexual abuse trauma. Out of this exploration, she understood in her body that her symptoms — especially her claustrophobic fear of being trapped and wanting to get out — were projections of the earlier trauma onto the accidents. Through repeated experiences in the void, Diane was able to reduce the energetic charge she carried until she was able to drive again without incident. Once she understood the source of her long-term anxiety and claustrophobia experientially, her terror was replaced by a deep sense of gratitude to life — for revealing and returning her essential wholeness.

ENERGY SLIVERS

An energy sliver can be described as an imprint of energy that comes about through the conversion of kinetic movement, or vibrational energy, into potential energy (tension) upon impact. In the first chapter, we saw how the body's myofascial tissue network is capable of transmitting, storing and modulating vibrational information. Mechanical, vibrational and electromagnetic energies flow away from the site of an impact and are lodged in the myofascial network. As a result, the kinetic energy of the impact is transformed into potential energy — which of course manifests as muscular tension.

Here is the origin of much muscle pain and associated syndromes. The chronic pain that people develop following relatively trivial accidents often has less to do with physical injury than it does with these energy slivers. A lot of time and money might be saved if we understood this, especially as these slivers can be extracted once we know they are there.

Slivers of energy travel into our bodies — just like slivers of wood or steel might — in a relatively straight line so the position of the body at the time of the impact is very significant. That the body will spontaneously adopt the correct position for the extraction of a sliver during DIA seems beyond belief until one has seen the phenomenon so often one almost comes to expect it. As the body nears the appropriate position, it often begins to shake, emotions flow, and there may be a regressive experience of the original trauma.

ॐ *PATRICIA*: A COMPLEX FALL

Patricia had had a bicycle accident some twenty years before we met her, and had remained in severe pain despite numerous and varied treatments and was taking up to twenty Tylenol tablets with codeine every day just to cope. The mechanics of her fall involved flying over the handlebars while still holding onto them. She had hit the ground chin first and cracked her jaw against the pavement, breaking her mandible, which had required surgical repair.

During DIA she spontaneously adopted a variety of impossible positions, each of which produced shaking at a certain point. Needles inserted during these positions were aligned along the energetic vector of the original trauma. Within three weeks of this approach, with sessions twice a week, she was off drugs and pain-free.

In order to keep herself pain-free, Patricia learned to practise dynamic meditation (see the section at the end of this chapter; see also chapter 13, Dynamic Meditation) and now uses facilitated DIA only occasionally.

SPONTANEOUS REALIGNMENT

A similar phenomenon might be called *spontaneous realignment*. During DIA and/or meditation, extraordinarily subtle micro-adjustments can occur that will gradually straighten out long-standing cricks, aches and pains. I like to refer to this phenomenon in jest as the arrival of the cosmic chiropractor. Yogis would call it *kriya* and associate it with rising *kundalini*

energy. But whatever we call them, we can discover these spontaneous adjustments for ourselves by following minute impulses
prompting us to move our bodies. Like any skill, it is practice that
brings results and, as we learn to trust the body, we can master
unbelievable skills in self-healing.

℞ *URSULA* — NECK INJURY

Ursula was thirty years old when she broke her neck flipping over
backward while water-skiing. She had had surgery for a ruptured
C5-6 disc but, although the surgery was considered successful, she
was left with severe pain in her neck and right arm. When she
came to us five years later she was taking 30–40 Percocets a day.
(Interestingly, she was an addictions counsellor but did not consider herself addicted because, since she had had surgery, her pain
was somehow 'real'.)

During sessions, her body seemed to want to arch farther and
farther backward, trying to reclaim the original posture of the
accident but the degree of hyperextension was never quite sufficient for her to effect a release. Since her frame was very small —
she only weighed about ninety pounds — I eventually tried lifting
her up into approximately the right position. As we inched closer,
her head went further and further into hyperextension while she
took deep breaths and sustained her moving-toward intent.

All of a sudden there was a loud pop and her body went limp
and relaxed. When she pulled herself together and stood up, she
told me all her pain had disappeared.

THE QUESTION OF APPLICABILITY

People often ask us whether interactive techniques such as DIA are
useful as a treatment for some specific condition — such as
fibromyalgia, multiple sclerosis or cancer. On the surface, it seems

a reasonable and simple question. After all, who would want to commit to a procedure or technique without some expectation that it will prove beneficial?

But the answer is not so simple. We generally do not understand that our questions limit the answers that can be given them. If our question assumes duality, as this one does, the answer cannot assume non-duality or wholeness. In other words, an answer must typically speak the same language and exist in the same universe as the question. If we remember that our energy field is an infinitely complex dynamic matrix of energetic information with varying degrees of coherence and that what we call disease is just a build-up or deficit of energy at a certain time and place, we will notice that this question of applicability contains implicit assumptions. It postulates a condition, the possibility of a treatment, the helpless patient, the knowledgeable physician and the idea that DIA is, like most surgical procedures, undergone to remedy a particular well-documented physical problem. In other words, it re-inscribes the whole universe of duality we have understood to be at the root of illness and pain. So, the only possible answer to the question's assumptions has to be, No! — not because DIA is not useful but because there is no such thing as a condition and DIA is not a treatment.

What we might otherwise say in response is that there are few contraindications to DIA — that is, that there are in fact few situations especially involving chronic pain or other symptoms in which it would be *in*advisable. The single caveat here is that it is best experienced by those who have a fully functioning and mature ego (experiential bodywork generally speaking is not useful for psychotics or those with arrested development). However, because DIA is interactive, the content of the interaction varies according to the situation and is never the same, and because its

applicability is not dependent on diagnosis, an experiential exploration of any situation can benefit almost anyone.

DYNAMIC MEDITATION: DIA SOLO

Ideally the principles of DIA, once experienced with a practitioner,
are taken into a daily meditation routine. The lasting benefit of DIA
is that it can establish a *referent* — a recognizable inner experience
of an expanded state of consciousness — which then can be more
easily recognized in meditation. Such states can be stabilized only
through experience. If for no other reason, daily meditation is
tremendously important as a tool of integration.

And although deep regressive experiences are unlikely to occur
during meditation, it is certainly possible to experience all the basic
elements of energetic release — if we are open to it. (As meditations
tend to assume stillness and silence, dynamic activity is unlikely to
occur unless we intend it.) That is not to say anyone needs to
change a routine they already do, and find beneficial. Indeed, if you
have a routine you already enjoy, all that may be necessary is to set
aside a few minutes in the course of it in which to allow physical
movement.

It is important to note that whether or not movement occurs at
any particular time is not the point. The point is to set up the
intention and give ourselves time for self-exploration. If we can
learn to do this, our bodies will teach us anything and everything
we need to know.

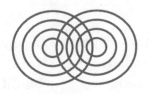

CHAPTER 12

THE EXISTENTIAL CONUNDRUM

Vanished the veils of light and shade
Lifted every vapour of sorrow
Sailed away all dawns of fleeting joy
Gone the dim sensory mirage.
Love, hate, health, disease, life, death:
Perished these false shadows on the screen of duality.
The storm of maya stilled.
— Paramahansa Yogananda

Sooner or later we all have to come to terms with our existential anxiety. Paradoxically, this confrontation often occurs just when we begin to recover from chronic pain or long illness. Just as we become aware that our pain or discomfort is lessening, just then, out of the blue, we may encounter a vast despair, a boundless anger, a colossal fear. How could this be? And why, just when things seem to be going well for a change, should we be called upon to fight a new fight? . . . Or is it a new fight?

At least part of the answer may lie in the ego's conviction of its separateness from other things — heavily underscored in Western societies by a political, social and juridical stress on individualism — and its need to defend itself against any threat to that separateness. One expression of this conviction is our mind's restless preoccupation with whatever it perceives to concern the self. One level of our mind acts like a bird in the middle of a lawn, constantly vigilant for threats from all sides. Illness and pain seem to justify this activity.

Unfortunately, this tends to mean that when life begins to go well, our very sense of self may begin to falter, especially if our illness or pain has been a significant part of our self-definition. With no battle left to fight in the body, all our fears turn inward and we meet them for what they are: saboteurs of the experience of wholeness and unity with *what is*.

Sabotage strategies make themselves known soon after we begin any serious attempt to heal. It is not that they were not always there but until we make a serious commitment to change, we generally remain blissfully unaware of them. Should we begin to explore the integration of our symptoms in earnest, however, the ego's strategies come flying out of the closet, thwarting the healing process through scepticism, anxiety and negative or even catastrophic thinking. Because the anxiety appears when the illness disappears, the equivalence of the two have to be understood and integrated, or else the illness will simply reassert itself as we wage an unwinnable struggle with our existential anxiety.

FEAR: THE EGO'S DEFENCE SYSTEM

The existential conundrum arises because of the contradiction that exists between our sense of separation (our sense that we are individual entities separate from other beings) and the fact that that sense of separation is ultimately an illusion. Separation leads directly to alienation, and the common conviction that life is a struggle to eke out an existence in a hostile world.

Such thinking is fear-full. The ego is structured around this fear, and fear is always called into play when ego's notion of self is challenged in any way. The ego's defence system whispers that the universe is dangerous, that disease is inevitable, that we should trust nothing — least of all our bodies. But the curious and paradoxical thing is, our physical symptoms are often little more than a physical manifestation of that same fear — a materialization, if you like, of our original existential anxiety.

It seems the mind just cannot rest: unoccupied, it grows desperate. So, if a difficulty is not immediately apparent, it will fill that lack with a generalized sense of impending doom. Or rather, it builds up unfocused energy — feeding from the deep underground well of existential anxiety we all live with — which we then frame as bad, suspicious, dangerous.

Just when physical symptoms lessen and things seem to be improving, for instance, fear begins to nag at us: 'Are the symptoms really being resolved? I wonder where that pain is. Let's see. . . . It's not really gone . . . it's just hiding. . . . This improvement is temporary, it won't last long . . . you'll see!' Whatever the actual situation, it keeps harping on and on, gleefully sabotaging our trust and confidence. It assures us that things are always bad and nothing can be trusted; and when things seem to be good in spite of it, we find ourselves going to extremes to prove our fears well founded.

It seems we cannot allow good things to happen to us without this sense of looming catastrophe showing itself. We start to get tense; the tension gradually creates pain; and pretty soon we are right back where we started. All that has changed is that our scepticism has been justified. . . . And a strange sense of relief accompanies the recurrence of our symptoms. 'The catastrophe has happened so we no longer have to fear it, and healing is impossible, so we don't have to risk it,' says the smug voice of our fears.

℞ *ELAINE*: INJUSTICE AS PAIN

Elaine was a forty-three-year-old woman who could achieve a pain-free state through DIA but who seemed unable to maintain it in spite of a daily routine of stretching, relaxation and meditation. Immediately following DIA, and for a while afterward, she was both pain-free and thought-free. She found this state delightful but could not hold on to it. We had long discussions about this and soon realized she was facing a ruthless, fear-based mental strategy based in her own style of alienation.

Elaine admitted to thinking that the world — and her life in particular — was full of injustices in need of redress. These thoughts would surface repeatedly and if they surfaced when she was in a pain-free state, she would get tense and before long her pain would return. Once that happened, the pain itself would consume her attention, giving her a focus for her anxiety and, significantly, providing validation of her feelings of injustice. In a very real sense her pain *was* the world's injustices focused in her body.

Despite knowing exactly how she was sabotaging this peacefulness she so enjoyed and bringing pain back into her body, Elaine had great difficulty letting go of her need to see the world as riddled with unfairness — in fact, her identity seemed to depend on it. (This is not to say there are not injustices in the world, just that Elaine did not have to carry tension and pain in her body to prove it.)

ILLNESS AS A SOLUTION
FOR EXISTENTIAL ANXIETY

Medical and psychological practitioners have long noted that diagnosis of some rather serious conditions — such as multiple sclerosis, cancer, irremediable chronic pain and lupus — are often associated with a kind of euphoria. Less well known, perhaps, is the fact that anxiety will often recede when *any* diagnosis is made, even if that diagnosis is relatively meaningless. For example, many diagnoses are simply a translation of symptoms into medical jargon — chronic pain syndrome, chronic fatigue syndrome, fibromyalgia and the like. Such diagnoses are little more than labels for the symptoms, yet for some reason they have the capacity to relieve anxiety and even produce its opposite, elation.

Even stranger, this diagnosis-elation can build, getting bigger with each diagnosis. I will never forget one man who had accumulated an extraordinary list of diagnoses — cervical disc injury, asthma, irritable bowel syndrome, peripheral neuropathy, peptic ulcer, diabetes, depression, macular degeneration, hypertension, high cholesterol and chronic pain syndrome, to name just a few. His weekly drug intake looked like a marketing brochure from a large pharmaceutical firm. Yet he seemed totally unperturbed. Indeed, the more labels he acquired, the happier he appeared to be. It was almost as if his illnesses were possessions or badges of honour, proof positive that he was a great guy who could put up with a lot, and who could tough out the worst of conditions.

And, in fact, he was not that sick, day to day. As I got to know him better, it became clear that his need for attention was the primary energetic wound lying behind the physical manifestations. So potent was this need, the fact that some of the drugs he was taking would almost certainly hasten his demise seemed lost on him.

It would be hard to guess the meaning of the kind of euphoria this fellow so vividly demonstrated were it not for our knowledge that the ego is always painfully, if subliminally, uncertain of its identity. A medical diagnosis can solve some of this uncertainty by giving us body parts — unwell, or malfunctioning body parts, but body parts nonetheless.

We might rephrase the underlying meaning of diagnosis to the ego as, *I am sick, therefore I am.* To have a disease, after all, one must first exist. If a heart is diseased, there must in fact *be* a heart. It gives one an authenticity and a distinction, and solicits the sort of care many may only have experienced as infants.

Furthermore, a diagnosis gives us the impression that we know something about ourselves, or at least that someone else does. In an unpredictable world, this might be seen by the ego as a significant advantage. But it is a huge disadvantage in healing because, in order to get better, we are going to have to give up precisely this sort of security ('my unease which I have manifested in parts of my body has been named and is known') and this identity ('I am sick, therefore I am'). And giving these up, of course, dumps us right back into our primal angst.

ADDICTION AS ANOTHER SOLUTION

If we cannot manifest an illness to soak up this angst — which haunts us all in some degree — we will sometimes substitute an addiction (which will often produce bodily illness, in both the short and the long terms). In the meantime, they function either to consume the energy of the anxiety (e.g., workaholism) or dissociate us from it (e.g., drugs and alcohol). Either way, we have an *a*-holism — a lack of wholeness.

Once an illness arises, it may take over the function of absorbing anxiety, and so have the curious effect of alleviating an existing addiction. Thus, a-holisms are really second-order effects — visible outward expressions of internal angst or existential despair. Since they arise from and reflect this primary split, any resolution of addiction must involve a resolution of the split. Unfortunately, such an understanding has not yet permeated medicine.

THE EXISTENTIAL ELEPHANT

In his book, *Travels*, Michael Crichton tells the story of his confrontation with anxiety while on a walking safari in Africa. Hunkered down in the dark of his tent after sundown in a game park, he imagined every cracking, swishing or scrunching sound outside was a wild animal. After tossing and turning for an hour or two, getting increasingly nervous and unable to sleep, nature demanded he go outside to relieve himself. Creeping from his tent and feeling rather vulnerable, he shone his flashlight in a circle around the camping area to be sure there were no wild animals about and found himself nearly face to face with a huge bull elephant, munching calmly on some vegetation, the light from Michael's flashlight reflecting in his eyes.

Crichton's next comment is telling: he reports that once he knew there really was a huge wild animal outside his tent, his anxiety evaporated. Of course, he also knew, wild elephants being what they are, that there was not much he could do but surrender to the situation. So he relieved himself, jumped back into his sleeping bag and went straight off to sleep. The story beautifully illustrates the fact that rational explanations can function as an antidote to anxiety.

Unfortunately, situational anxiety is not the same as existential anxiety. For existential anxiety, one could posit that the only antidotes are death or enlightenment. A confrontation such as the one just described relieves situational anxieties. But if we try to relieve our existential anxiety by, for instance, buying into a fairly meaningless diagnosis, all that happens is that we become imprisoned in a delusional self-definition. And, more tragically, we constrain ourselves to fulfill the prognosis — which often dictates ever-deteriorating health and even death.

THE EXISTENTIAL LOOP

Briefly, existential anxiety reappears as we move toward healing and — aided and abetted by self-sabotaging rationalizations — can incline us to revert to familiar symptoms in order to resist or assuage it. Unfortunately, without a good understanding of this puzzling mechanism, we are doomed to circle around the existential loop endlessly.

This condition — which at its despairing worst is truly like a dark night of the soul — is at the core of the healing process. The bind we face is that *a tension-free body can hold onto nothing*. We have to be prepared to give up everything our ego tells us defines us. To turn away from our identities — even if they are composed of negatives (sick, depressed, in pain) — is terrifying, especially when we are, in fact, in continual pain or severely depressed. And so the ego's various strategies act to keep us from moving in the direction of this release, which looks as if it may cost us our identities.

THE HOLE IN THE SIDEWALK

There is another little story that illustrates how slowly we learn our lessons. If we read this as a parable of our relationship with illness, we see our 'I' reproducing the same symptoms repeatedly until we find a way to understand that we are able to do otherwise.

The story goes like this:

Autobiography in Five Short Chapters, by Portia Nelson

Chapter 1 — I walk down the street. There's a deep hole in the sidewalk. I fall in. I am lost. . . . I am helpless; it isn't my fault. It takes forever to find a way out.

Chapter 2 — I walk down the same street. There is a deep hole in the sidewalk. I pretend I don't see it. I fall in again.

I can't believe I am in the same place; but it isn't my fault.
It still takes a long time to get out.

Chapter 3 — I walk down the same street. There is a deep hole
in the sidewalk. I see it is there. I still fall in . . . it's a habit.
My eyes are open. I know where I am. It is my fault. I get out
immediately.

Chapter 4 — I walk down the same street. There is a deep
hole in the sidewalk. I walk around it.

Chapter 5 — I walk down another street.

EXISTENTIAL FREEDOM

A life free of the dictates of the ego-self is a life free of much of the
trouble we all take as part of our human lot. And despite what the
ego might intimate to frighten us, this freedom does not mean the
annihilation of the self. Ego death is not a physical death, nor is it
even an end to the ego. In fact, it is only an end to the illusions and
delusions of the ego and its lust for power, which in fact disables
rather than enables us day to day. Given this, it is amazing how
difficult it can be to contemplate a different relationship to our
egos. Many people would rather die than alter this fundamental
relation — in fact, they would rather die than acknowledge it *can*
be altered.

We do not realize what we are doing to ourselves when we
choose to remain trapped in a small, egoic self. But an unbearable
illness or pain can shake us out of such complacency like nothing
else because any serious attempt to heal forces us to look at who
we are. And if we look closely, we will see that the ego is a false self
and that false self is always structured around an illusion.

Think back to your teenage years. Or observe teenagers you
know. They have problems: a sense of injustice, a need for attention,

for money, for sexual expression, for security. Whatever their problems, they feel them intensely. So intensely and so deeply, they start to identify themselves with their problems. (Think of the strange way our language has of allowing us to say both, 'I'm Michael' and 'I'm lonely' or 'I'm anxious about my security' or 'I'm shy' or 'I'm dumb.' In fact, I-am-X means only I am feeling this way just now but the slip into self-definition seems to be built right into our grammar.)

Now consider your adult self. Same problems, right? Years of therapy, dozens of workshops, intensive meditation, travel, gurus, interpersonal struggle, perhaps drugs, perhaps drink — none of it has changed the fundamental issues that arose during the stage of ego development, to which our egos then subscribed as self-defining. Without our defining problem, or problems, we seem to assume that our individuation must be less vivid. (And we soon learn that even the positive self-definitions we counter the negative ones with are fraught with anxieties nearly more powerful than the negative. 'Am I really talented?' ' . . . popular?' ' . . . clever?')

We are anxious enough to have a self, however, that we willingly bear the pain. What would happen if the self did not arise, and yet we existed? What — and where — would we be? To an ego, the question is terrifying. It opts without question for continued ill-health, unease and pain, anything to confirm its existence, its individuality.

WALKING DOWN A DIFFERENT STREET

So, is enlightenment the only answer? Not necessarily. In fact, there is a feasible and humanly realizable solution. After all, the anxiety that is at the root of our unease — from deepest existential angst to passing apprehension — is just energy. It is not an aberration but our very life current. To imagine that we should try to rid ourselves of it, then, is self-destructive, not self-protective.

What if we allowed ourselves to understand that anxiety is good

— even when it does not feel that way? If anxiety is energy and energy is life, then it does not require a solution. It really does not require anything, except a re-framing of its meaning into something positive, or at the very least, something that is supposed to be there. (For example, many people have recovered from disabling fears — such as a fear of flying — by translating or re-perceiving their mental and bodily energy sensations as excitement, not fear.)

Such re-framing is the equivalent of walking down a different street, in the language of the story above. If we understand that our anxiety — our mental and emotional energy — is good and natural, then we can stop being anxious about our anxiety. In other words, if our anxiety ceases to attract our fixed and negative attention, it will cease to make us either ill or unhappy, or both.

To get to know anxiety as energy and to let it express itself in our bodies! To succeed in doing this is to experience anxiety as something quite pleasant — even ecstatic — and to feel the sense of wanting to run and hide become a sense of *presence*.

BEYOND THE EXISTENTIAL SPLIT

Transcending the existential split is so fundamental a shift that we could say it occurs at the level of the spirit. When something that fundamental changes, there may be no initial discernible change at the material level. In other words, our physical symptoms may or may not change. Actually it is surprising how often they do change — sometimes dramatically so — but whether they do or not is not as important as the feeling of centredness that arises when we no longer feel split down the middle. The change occurs in an instant at the level of spirit and may be imperceptible to others. After that first shift, the effects reverberate into the body-mind at varying speeds.

The mental level, which contains the scepticism, can take many months to resolve, as we struggle with our old negative patterns. And lasting change at the physical, symptomatic level just takes however long it takes. But one thing almost everyone notices is that the new perspective gradually accumulates new experiences that counter the old mental arguments, cynicism and rationalizations. As time goes by, new referents become established in the psyche, the grip of our alienated psychic defence system begins to wane and we begin to feel a clear and vivid connection to life that until that time had been unthinkable.

CHAPTER 13

DYNAMIC MEDITATION

Kundalini is a terrific burning fire of the underworld.
This fiery power is in very truth like liquid fire that
rushes through the body when it has been aroused
by the will.

— C.W. Leadbeater

*W*e need not have bodywork to have the experiences of DIA. If we generate the intention to move toward symptoms while in an expansive and relaxed state in the course of a daily meditation practice, all of the DIA phenomena previously described can be experienced.

That dynamic experiences tend *not* to occur spontaneously in meditative states is probably due to a lack of intention and a restrictive expectation of the practice. Formal meditation has often been represented — and therefore experienced — as quiet sitting or walking. The meditator focuses on the breath, a mantra or an image and either tries very hard not to move her body or, at best, assumes that her body will not move spontaneously. This conscious and unconscious expectation is one reason that movement does not occur.

Many years of meditation can pass in this way, sometimes actually accentuating the mind/body block. Then suddenly, sometimes quite unexpectedly, things can change. When relaxation reaches a certain depth, it is as if the mind/body block begins to give way and mind-body awareness is manifested without warning.

This change can begin if we change our posture, or allow ourselves to make sounds. Or we may wonder one day, in a deeply relaxed state, what it would be like to stop running away from a long-standing discomfort. . . . And, perhaps for the first time ever, may find ourselves knocking on the edge of our pain, moving toward it without resistance, finally achieving the connection without necessarily understanding why we are drawn to do it.

This may happen just because the tightening or tensing we may not even be aware of in our normal state of consciousness dissipates with our new curiosity and lack of fear concerning our pain, our moving toward our pain. When we approach tight or sore areas in a relaxed and open state of awareness, shifts can occur that would otherwise be impossible, though the connection usually takes us by surprise.

ব *CORA*: UNCONTROLLABLE SHAKING

I will always remember Cora. She told us her arms had started shaking uncontrollably while she was in a deep state. She could only imagine that her many years of meditation had somehow opened her to possession by evil spirits and the thought terrified her so much that she stopped meditating for good. Not long after that, unfortunately, a car accident left her in chronic pain and — clouded by increasing doses of analgesics and frightened by her pain — she could not bring herself to do the creative work by which she had for many years made her living. The once vibrant artist had lost her connection to spirit.

Cora remained in despair for several years before the intensity of her pain brought her to our centre. Diving into the void during DIA, she experienced the same myoclonic shaking down her arms that she had previously associated with demons. When I suggested that it was simply the release of long-held tension in the muscles of her arms and shoulders, something seemed to click for her and she relaxed into the experience she had so long resisted. The result of this simple shift was extraordinary: her pain decreased dramatically in minutes and when she got home she found she could paint — and wanted to paint — for the first time since her injury.

Of course, such results rarely come so easily. Most of us need more time and more practice but Cora's experience demonstrates the five most important principles: intention, relaxation, moving toward the pain or symptom, trusting the body and letting go. Her symptoms probably shifted quickly because she was familiar with altered states of consciousness and only needed to reframe her experience to trigger the healing that was waiting to happen.

LETTING GO

As previously mentioned, letting go is frequently assumed to be a quiet affair and is often portrayed as a striving for detachment so that our problems no longer touch us. For those with a well-established mind/body split, this detachment can be misinterpreted — that is, mis-*embodied* — as dissociation. Unfortunately, this means that some meditators are in fact practising dissociation, practising severing the mind's awareness of the body from the body. In fact, detachment and dissociation are quite different. And until we understand the difference, trying to imitate a letting go by denying rather than honouring our emotions only deepens the two solitudes of the mind and the body.

Despite our expectations, then, when we first hold the intention to reconnect what we have so long held separate, the results can be anything but quiet. Letting go of anger means feeling it in the body. Expressing it might mean beating a pillow, pounding a punching bag or screaming with rage but it does *not* mean sitting quietly trying to ignore hot emotion inside. To do so, in fact, is a perfect statement of the ego-mind's mistrust of the body.

If we want change, we must change; and in order to change, we must do what we have not done before. Unfortunately, for most of us, this doing what we have not done before includes expressing our feeling unashamedly, consciously. Most of us habitually express our emotions — the negative ones especially but not exclusively — with a certain amount of shame, and a fair dose of denial; in other words, without much respect for them as feelings or for ourselves as bearers of those feelings. Instead, we choose to protect ourselves and our egos by dissociation in order not to be present as witnesses of our emoting.

Say the body holds rage and the mind rides roughshod over it, grimly insisting, 'I refuse to acknowledge this anger because it is mistaken (*or* is embarrassing, *or* is connected to shameful memories I refuse to acknowledge, *or* too precisely unmasks present conditions in my life, *or* because I cannot predict the consequences, *or* because I may be misunderstood).' Real letting go has nothing to do with what is correct or with what is logical or even with what is comprehensible. It has nothing to do with the sort of truth that would stand up in a court of law. It means respect for the body and the expression of whatever feelings arise from it without censure, honouring the body's intuitions — what we call our gut feelings. Without the recognition of this truth, the ego triumphs over the body's wisdom at its peril.

When we cease to be curious about our feeling, or alive to its origins or its meaning, we either hate — or begin to revel in — our sense of being out of control, and our minds shut down. In this way, anger, for example, becomes theatrical, detached, blurry. Or, perhaps we notice ourselves red in the face and banging the table, or red-eyed and snotty-nosed, decide we look silly, and never again allow even this sort of compromised expression of emotion.

To find a way of expressing emotion in a context that is not destructive, humiliating or productive of some unacceptable consequence is tragically difficult for many people. And yet it is the greatest barrier to their healing. As I have hinted in earlier chapters, I have found that putting time aside every day for what I call dynamic meditation — a crucible in which feelings can be experienced in the body without restriction — where the mind can remain engaged, curious, aware without interfering, can be life-altering.

THE PRINCIPLES OF DYNAMIC MEDITATION

Making noise just because we have now reframed noisy as *good* is fruitless, however. (No sooner does the ego understand the principles of dynamic meditation than it begins trying to make the body produce feeling, sound and movement — only to get frustrated if it does not.) The ego is still striving to run the show, using will to force an effect but it will never work because nothing the ego can do will heal the split.

What does work is not willpower but willingness. That, and the cultivation of an awareness that does not act, or what is often called *presence*. Willingness and presence open us to allowing movement, sound and the non-judgemental expression of feeling. It opens us to anything that wants or needs to happen without trying to make any particular preconceived thing happen. And that is really what letting go is all about — allowing whatever. If a meditation is quiet, that is fine, and if it is noisy, that is fine too. When our daily meditation sets up the same conditions as DIA — willingness, moving toward symptoms and self-witnessing — then we will more and more find ourselves in the void without need of DIA's external witness.

Dynamic meditation requires a delicate balance of welcome

and intention but is essentially very simple. The steps below map the route into the void-like space you are seeking. These steps do not assume that you have a regular meditation practice. If you do, dynamic meditation is best opened to at the end of your regular routine. Play with it to see what suits you best. You may be amazed at the effect it has on the quality of your regular practice.

▼ Achieve a state of restful alertness
▼ Ask for help and open the heart
▼ Move awareness toward the symptom
▼ Breathe slowly and deeply (full yogic breathing)
▼ Welcome the unexpected
▼ Practise regularly!

Now let us look at these points one by one.

▼ACHIEVING A STATE OF RESTFUL ALERTNESS
Quieting the mind is not easy. It is in the mind's very nature to move. Before opening ourselves to any expressive movement or sounds, however, it is helpful to be familiar with some form of relaxed awareness. Since it was described earlier (see chapter 4, Transcendence and Transformation), I will only briefly touch on it here.

One thing to remember is that there is a difference between what meditators call *monkey mind* and the essential movement of the mind. Monkey mind is that chattering, distracting, exhausting, addictive mind that most of us live with day to day. Strangely, quieting that irrepressible monkey can be frightening at first, as it is what we instinctively know is keeping us from the darker reaches of our selves, our memories, our concerns, our unanswerable feelings. Distracting as it can be, monkey mind is in fact the curtain that shields us from both our known and unknown depths — those places most of us, often without realizing it, would rather not go.

To use the mind itself to stop thinking is virtually impossible. It is putting the fox among the chickens, in a sense. But to learn to use the mind to observe the mind, to watch oneself thinking, is certainly within the reach of most. (As mentioned earlier, learning a formal meditation technique from a trained teacher is the best route, but for those who have no established practice and no chance to learn from a teacher, I offer a short instruction in the last chapter of this book. Remember that it is just a skeleton and take the opportunity to learn from experienced meditators whenever it arises.)

▼ ASKING FOR HELP AND OPENING THE HEART

Opening the Heart is part of some meditation techniques but if it is not part of yours, then take a minute or two to focus on the Heart chakra and its attributes of warmth and compassion.

However odd it might feel at first, asking for help can be a great adjunct to opening the Heart. It does not have to be a big deal. Merely being open to help in whatever form it may come is sufficient at first (or, if you are inclined, a more formal appeal to guides, the divine or cosmic forces). Whatever or whomever you choose to ask for help is irrelevant; you might even choose to ask your higher self. What is important is that we accept that we do not have all the answers and that we are open to answers coming in unexpected ways.

Even though it is sometimes only when we realize that we have no other option that we begin to consider letting ourselves be more present with what is going on in our hearts, that moment is not too late. We may ask symptoms to go away, try to ignore them, shut them out with painkillers and chemicals, fetishize them with expensive tests (X-rays, CT scans) and so on. But there comes a time when we begin to realize that no matter what we do, this pain is *our* pain.

When that time comes, we may consider listening. We may consider what the disrespect that closing our Hearts, plugging our ears and screwing shut our eyes to it has been. We may begin to wonder whether opening our inner ears and our inner eyes and our Hearts to it might be like. It is, after all, *us* and we might begin to wonder, what would happen if we began listening to our own cries of pain?

It is when we can truly acknowledge to ourselves that the predicament we find ourselves in has no rational solution, is nobody's particular fault and is never going to go away, that the deep pain we feel can begin its work of tearing open the tightness around our Hearts. Combining humility and the ability to ask for what we need (*Knock and the door shall be opened*, or *Ask and ye shall receive* as the biblical texts put it) is the simple opening that healing looks for.

▼ MOVING AWARENESS TOWARD THE SYMPTOM
Moving toward uses our inner wakefulness to take our attention — mentally and physically — right up against our discomfort while we remain deeply relaxed in meditation. If the lower back were sore and stiff, for example, we would slowly manoeuvre it side to side, forward and back, deliberately moving into the pain's edge but without force. When the pain intensifies, we are close to the place where a subtle adjustment may occur.

To force an adjustment or push into the pain too far would only pull us out of relaxed awareness and back into tension and we would lose our opportunity. To sit on the edge of our discomfort, moving minutely into our pain, is the way to really listen to that pain and to let it guide us to the change it wants to achieve. Used in this way, our pain becomes an incomparable guide to its own resolution.

This respect for what is, this presence, is a completely new way of being for most of us — one which others have called the *wisdom of no escape*.

▼ BREATHING DEEPLY AND SLOWLY

As we move toward pain, and as that pain intensifies, we tend to brace against it by tensing and holding our breath, and so block the energy that is moving us toward a release. One way to minimize this reflex is to breathe deeply and slowly. Deep breathing that uses both diaphragm and thorax is often called simply full yogic breathing. Deep, slow breaths help us relax through intense discomfort. With practice, even big increases in intensity can be handled, and previously unmanageable acute pain — such as muscle cramps — when explored, can lead to equally intense releases.

Do not be discouraged if you are unable to master deep breathing quickly. Usually our breath-holding is so automatic it just happens, despite our best intentions, the first few times. With time, however, most people can break the habit. The first thing is to learn to notice that our breath is held and, each time we notice that it is held, to re-establish the intention to move toward, move toward, move toward.

▼ WELCOMING THE UNEXPECTED

The qualities of gentleness and being open to whatever happens will often produce dramatic results where all else has failed. If we push on the edge of pain too forcefully, it just never budges. However, if we lean gently against it without pressure, sometimes something gives way.

Dramatic shifts tend to occur without warning when circumstances allow forces to act in concert and unhindered. And this quality of the unexpected and especially the *unexpected as gift* is useful to hold in mind — especially in the throes of painful symptoms when it can be very difficult to remember anything at all.

A few years ago, when I first started experimenting with dynamic meditation, in the space of a half-hour morning meditation I would sometimes experience in excess of thirty or forty tiny adjustments in my lower back and sacroiliac areas. Day after day, for many months, the corrections continued — not so much repeating as building, as though each adjustment allowed a further one, and as though the body were gradually balancing and realigning itself around a centre.

During this process, I became acutely aware of how much my years of racquet sports had misaligned my back. No doubt all that twisting and turning on the squash court had created layer upon layer of energy slivers until my back was one very complex and very tight energy knot.

Over time, patience, perseverance and increasing skill allowed me to gradually loosen and free my lower back — just as if I were untangling string. I am now able to make subtle adjustments almost at will and jokingly refer to my cosmic chiropractor making a house call. But it was not all smooth sailing. There were plenty of times when nothing seemed to be happening. I learned, for instance, that if I focused too much on an area that was bothering me, nothing would budge but when I allowed myself to explore freely — trying various positions, doing the opposite of what I had thought necessary, or just letting the body move spontaneously — I eventually got results.

I also had to struggle with those times when things seemed to be getting worse rather than better. At such times, doubt would fuel my natural scepticism and I would find myself sabotaging my own efforts. Perseverance got me through but, in retrospect, I began to notice that these times of doubt and scepticism were just the moments when my body was trying to untangle the densest — and most significant — blocks.

THE CADUCEUS AND *KUNDALINI*

Eastern traditions know what it can mean to open the flow of energy or *kundalini* up the back (see chapter 8, The Chakras). The released energy of the awakened serpent moving up the spine is felt as heat, tingling or physical movement. During the process, the individual may adopt bizarre postures, make spontaneous noises or facial grimaces. These sometimes bizarre phenomena, called *kriya*, reflect the many subtle adjustments that must occur to realign a body that has absorbed years of energetic insults.

Western traditions acknowledge *kundalini* without realizing it. Few physicians are aware that the familiar Aesculapian staff, the symbol of Western medicine, takes the form of two serpents coiled around a caduceus. The echo is hard to miss. If the Aesculapian symbol does refer to rising *kundalini* energy, as I have no doubt it does — especially as serpents in a Christian context would otherwise normally symbolize evil — then conventional medicine once understood more than it admits at present and took as its symbol healing snakes twining around a messenger-god's staff.

Let us hope that our lost knowledge may soon be recovered! The future good health of us all may depend on a rediscovery of these serpents' power. Certainly in my own experience, the feeling of energy (both hot and cold) rising up my back, the many subtle adjustments and odd postures suggest *kriya*. And the way the experiences led me on, day after day, for over two years, teaching me slowly to unravel the energy knots in my back, seemed testament to the fact that healing is within us always and will come to meet us the moment we are open to it — humble enough and brave enough to face our pain.

I also noticed as the months went by that not only was my back better but so was my general health. I rarely got colds or other infectious illnesses. The released energy seemed to have enlivened and strengthened my whole body; I slept better and felt full of well-being.

MYOCLONIC SHAKING

It is no more uncommon to experience myoclonic shaking during dynamic meditation than in DIA. Spontaneous myoclonic shaking should be welcomed and encouraged as a means of releasing deep tensions and emotions and, once we are familiar with it, even sought in pain or cramps as they arise or in emotional upwellings. Once *kundalini* is activated, the whole body may shake or shiver. It may begin with a shivering in the back or a shaking in the jaw and, to the extent we permit it, can become a consistent experience.

Of course, our tendency at first is to shut the shaking down. Cora, terrified, saw the energy outburst as the work of demons that had possessed her, and so slammed the door on what were in fact the first signs of her healing. It is important, then, to be aware that shaking and other unusual experiences might arise so that we can be open to them and be curious and even grateful rather than frightened. Shaking can open up the whole body energetically, shedding stress accumulated from yesterday and the day before and from many years before that. And with practice, it can be initiated quickly and with very little effort.

FEELINGS AND MENTAL IMAGERY

Similarly, the other manifestations of energy movement mentioned in connection with DIA — such as mental imagery, feelings and energy slivers — may also be present during dynamic meditation (see chapter 11, Dynamic Interactive Acu-Bodywork).

Mental imagery often accompanies a release of tense and tight muscles relating to the moment the tension got lodged there. Often the body moves in such a way as to remind us just what we were doing when the tension was generated.

If I release my low back, for example, I can feel, see, taste and smell the squash court where I twisted it countless times over the years. But particular imagery is not important. The release of energy cysts may or may not be accompanied by imagery and it does not really matter — all that is important is the release. It is mastery of tension-release that frees us, not the content of our experiences. The specifics of what comes up may be interesting and it can certainly be deeply nourishing and informing to explore them, but there is little value in dwelling on images if it moves our focus away from mastering the release technique.

Ironically, letting content just be, rather than analyzing it, is more important the more traumatic the original experience was. For example, if the imagery relates to abuse, some response of retribution might come to mind that might detract from the real business of releasing the trapped energy. In fact, if we get caught up in the imagery, we can completely miss the point of the release. One way out of this trap is realizing that life's traumatic experiences are the vehicles that motivate us to learn about healing, and that such learning is an incalculable gift, for it leads us to accept and even welcome painful experience and to have compassion for ourselves and for others.

THE SUBTLE BODY

After a while, the bizarre activity — weird movements, feelings and postures and the subtle adjustments they both provoke and permit — often settle into a profound, calm yet lively state of dynamic nothingness and we find ourselves immersed in the fourth or ground state of consciousness, or *turiya*. (Some people have called it bliss but this word often seems to be taken to mean some kind of dissociative, vacuous or drugged contentment that has no relationship to life, the very opposite of real bliss. In fact, dynamic nothingness has very little to do with feeling good — although it does feel remarkable. It is a state that transcends good and bad.)

The violent movements have ceased not because we are controlling them — far from it. They have stopped because the energies we habitually both repress and feed (with neurotic attention) have been spent. Calm arises from the absence of blocked energy; a sense of aliveness is generated from energy's smooth flow. We enter an extraordinary state in which the psychic splits have been temporarily transcended.

The unusual experience of deep calm and dynamic presence catches the ego completely off guard and leaves it at a loss. The mind goes blank. The chattering monkey mind we are usually unaware of as the backdrop to our daily lives just stops. And wonder of wonders, the emptiness behind that backdrop is not barren, as we had feared, but alive!

And even when the experience is new, there is often a deep recognition. It is as if we remember the emptiness of our *original face* — or what we were like before we plunged into the world of duality. We are once again beyond the personal and therefore beyond emotion and very often beyond pain. Just totally present, totally in the body, in an ecstatic open flow.

FINDING THE CENTRE

This dynamic nothingness might be described as the centre of our being, a place of freedom and belonging. Since nothing is there, nothing can harm it/us; it is a safe and fearless place. (And without the need to defend, the ego is out of a job — which perhaps is why it goes to such great lengths to prevent our discovering our centre in the first place.)

Of course once we have found it, we are never quite the same again and the struggle is on to establish such beingness as a daily, functional reality.

In my view, we should find this centre first thing every morning. By finding the centre before engaging in our daily lives, we can begin the day in a state of grace, feeling connected to everything else in the universe and responding through the day to everything we encounter from that place.

▼ PRACTISING REGULARLY

Regular practice is essential for the development of dynamic meditation just as it is for any other skill. If we wait for a health crisis before learning, let alone practising, our path will be that much harder. Finding our centre should be something we practise as a support to daily life, spiritual growth and renewal, not a panicked response to catastrophic experiences.

Nor should we expect any particular result on any particular day. The commitment to regular practice is what gets results. Otherwise we are just doing crisis management. Regular practice gets us over the hurdles that would otherwise pull us back into the state of alienation. It enables us to face the inevitable moments of doubt, lack of trust and apparent setback.

It also happens to de-stress the physiology. By regularly removing the energetic sludge before it blocks the pipes, so to speak, we can do a lot to keep the body energetically clean. This in turn can lead to a state of super health — reflecting our cultivated field coherence — a state in which illness rarely arises and good health right into old age becomes a realistic possibility.

DOWNSTREAM EFFECTS

Suffering is the inevitable path that must be trod on the way to consciousness, the inevitable price for the transformation we seek . . . if we take up our suffering consciously, voluntarily, then . . . it produces true transformation.

— Robert A. Johnson

$\mathcal{W}$e are so used to thinking of our bodies structurally and of our symptoms as defined by their local anatomy (*leg* cramp, *stomach* ache) that field effects — which can be anything but local — can prove a real challenge to our minds. As a result, when our symptoms move from one part of our bodies to another, the relocated discomfort is usually viewed as a new symptom and its true energetic identity goes unnoticed.

For example, migraine refers to a painful headache and other symptoms arising from dilated blood vessels supplying the head area. So what can one think when, as a result of an energetic intervention, migraine pain shifts to the lumbar spine? Without foreknowledge, the mind either misses the connection entirely, or dismisses it as insignificant.

Let me use an example from my own experience. One day after a few months of dynamic meditation, I developed a pain in the back of my left knee, the same knee I had injured decades earlier in a motorcycle accident. At first I thought nothing of it but over the next week the knee became quite swollen and painful. I could not fully straighten it and found it difficult to put much weight on it.

There was no ignoring it by the end of the week but by that time I was just as aware that my back pain had lessened in proportion as my knee pain had grown. In the past, I might have dismissed such a coincidence but this time I took note. It occurred to me that I was experiencing what might be called a *downstream effect* — a shift of energy from one place to another. (Although such an idea might be startling to some, it is actually quite feasible because the body's myofascial matrix is known to conduct vibrational energies. Chinese medicine views the phenomenon as the movement of *qi*.)

With that thought, I welcomed the new pain and awaited further developments. However, as the weeks dragged on and the pain dragged on, I started to wonder if I was being naïve. I began to get grumpy, irritable and depressed. But more than anything else, I began to get frightened. I wondered whether I might have something seriously wrong.

Sudden or unexpected energy shifts in the body can be quite disturbing. After all, there is nothing quite like serious pain arising in a new place to make us doubt our progress and run for cover, so to speak, by taking some symptom-altering medication and abandoning our commitment to a transformational, whole-field solution.

WHAT IS A DOWNSTREAM EFFECT?

When a log-jam in a river breaks up, the logs move freely with the currents awhile but often get jammed in a new location somewhere down-river. This is essentially what is meant by a downstream effect: a quantity of blocked energy has been released in one part of the body but becomes trapped or blocked again in another part of the body. And while small quantities of energy shifting and re-forming might do little more than cause some mild discomfort, the movement of a big block can completely change the structural dynamics of the body's myofascial matrix.

So when a deeply entrenched symptom moves for the first time, the shift commonly manifests as an aggravation and quite often one that is less bearable than the original. For example, a pain in the low back might be relatively manageable but if it moves to the neck and gives rise to a headache, it can be immobilizing. No matter how disturbing the block is in its new site, however, a downstream effect constitutes a change — and in energy work change is always better than no change, as it is the first hint of response, the beginning of a dialogue.

In spite of this, when the only way into a place of deep healing is through an increase in suffering, most of us fiercely resist. Even a good understanding of the healing process and its perils can wear thin after a few weeks in unfamiliar territory and intense pain. Prolonged pain may trigger doubts that tempt us to choose the relative comfort of our old situation over the sense of helplessness that can arise when everything we do seems to lead us into worse trouble.

Damned if we do and damned if we don't, we often prefer to stick with the devil we know than permit a new and unfamiliar discomfort, particularly if the new pain is severe. After all, how can we be certain in the face of new and persistent pain that the treatment path we have chosen is the right one?

HOW TO RECOGNIZE A DOWNSTREAM EFFECT

One way to recognize a downstream effect is to know as much as possible about them beforehand. Listed below are some of the clues by which we can distinguish downstream effects from new and distinct pains and discomforts. I have listed them briefly at first, then expanded on them in the following pages.

- ▼ *Inverse concurrence*: the new symptom becomes noticeable at the same time the old symptom is lessening.
- ▼ *Similarity*: the quality and overall effect of the new symptom is similar to the old.
- ▼ *Turbulence*: there may be associated myofascial twitching in the surrounding musculature.
- ▼ *Impermanence*: downstream effects, when not resisted, tend to be of limited duration.
- ▼ *Reversion*: attempts to circumvent the new pain, by altering body stance, for instance, tend to put the old pain back where it was.

▼ THE CLUE OF INVERSE CONCURRENCE

When a block of potential energy shifts position, symptoms in one area may dissipate and turn up in a different form elsewhere. The clue is in the inverse relationship. If the primary symptom is reduced or altered when the new symptom arises, then it is almost certainly a downstream effect.

Although we do not usually pay them much attention, such phenomena are immensely significant. We are given wonderful opportunities to learn from these shifts by observing closely and curiously whatever is going on and — resisting any temptation to interfere! — give our calm and vigilant attention to the mechanics of our energy transpositions in order to deepen our understanding of the quality of energy present in us.

▼ THE CLUE OF SIMILARITY

A second clue is in the symptom's characteristics. To convince yourself that you are dealing with downstream effects and not a distinct pain or symptom, pay attention to its attributes — the quality, arc intensity and radiating pattern of any pain that is present and its associated symptoms — such as fatigue or heaviness, noticing any concurrence with the original symptom. For example, if the primary symptom was associated with a heavy clogging feeling and the new one is as well, or if the new pain only occurs at certain angles as a joint arcs through its range of motion and the old pain occurred at the same position, then the new symptoms are likely transpositions of the old.

▼ THE CLUE OF TURBULENCE

Downstream effects are often accompanied by a kind of myofascial turbulence — which may manifest as muscle twitching, cramps or spasms of varying intensity. This is because the energy is not completely stuck in the new position and is trying to move on and become part of the body's general energy circulation. Ideally, downstream effects are like pit stops in a long race — temporary stopping places where observations and adjustments take place. But then we should leave the pit-stop promptly, making sure we do not exit the same way we came in but galvanizing our intent to allow healing to continue and trying our best not to get frightened and back away from further changes. We want to keep moving toward whatever we are facing in the moment.

▼ THE CLUE OF IMPERMANENCE

As mentioned above, downstream effects generally do not last as long as the original symptom, unless we resist them. Most transpositions will last no more than an hour or two, some a day or two (it is possible for a major transposition to hang around much longer, especially if there is significant resistance). However long their tenure, and no matter how unpleasant, transposed symptoms are passing and should be welcomed. If we react habitually, take painkillers, put on ice, bandage the area up or take other measures to resist pain or discomfort, a downstream effect may become entrenched and there is a risk of blocking further movement or, worse, reversion. We really want the energy to keep moving! Resistance of any kind will only get in its way.

▼ THE CLUE OF REVERSION

Reversion occurs when we try to avoid a downstream symptom through alteration of posture, movement or both, with the result that symptoms return to their original location. When a physical reversion happens, it is usually because our intention has reverted to moving away due to the unpleasantness of the downstream effect. Difficult as it may be, it is important to maintain an unbending intent, otherwise we fall back into old patterns.

If the movement of energy that is now caught in a downstream effect is a result of our intentional integration of a symptom, it is a tangible demonstration of the success of our intent. But having worked hard and psyched ourselves up to embrace a particular symptom, we are caught off guard when pain is transposed to a new location or changes its character, and the unfamiliar new pain is often met with habitual resistance. We return to the old strategy of trying to make the pain go away and this avoidance is a reversal of our hard-won intent. It is that reversal that allows symptoms to move back where they came from.

℞ *HAROLD*: BACK PAIN & HEADACHES

One very common effect is a transposition from the low back to the head — particularly in people exploring DIA for low back pain. Harold, a construction worker who had been off work for almost four years after injuring his back by heavy lifting, was thirty-five when he came to our centre. Although understandably depressed by his circumstances, he took little responsibility for his health and tended to blame his troubles on those who had tried to help him. After I explained some of the principles of DIA to him, he said he was leery of doing physical therapy because he had once had a severe headache after a session with another acupuncturist.

I recognized a downstream effect and realized that the acupuncturist had started a process she had not been given an opportunity to complete, so I warned Harold that if we worked together, he should not run away from transposed pains but should stay present and observe as well as possible whatever arose for him. By allowing for the possibility of another headache ahead of time, I hoped to prepare him by helping him realize that the headaches were coming from him, not from any therapist.

Fortunately, it all worked out quite well. Harold did develop a headache, which we relieved with two needles in the back of the neck where the neck muscles join the skull. Twenty minutes later, with his back pain relieved and no headache, Harold became someone I could talk to. Too bad he had not stayed with his acupuncturist a bit longer. He might have saved himself a lot of pain. But having a lot of Wood energy in his make-up, patience and perseverance were difficult.

THE LAW OF CURE

One of the fundamental theories of homeopathy, the Law of Cure,[1] takes note of the fact that, energetically, pain and illness are phenomena that register traumatic experiences as layers over time in a complex pattern. In the myofascial matrix we looked at earlier, the impact of each trauma to the cytoskeleton is superimposed on those the system has already stored, meaning that a realignment of the matrix involves removing the energetic slivers in reverse order.

The Law of Cure recognizes much the same thing, saying more or less that we go out the way we came in. In practice, this means that during DIA, dynamic meditation or other energy techniques, any of our life experiences can come up again, often appearing in reverse chronological order. For example, if we fell down the stairs at age two, broke an arm at age six, had a whiplash injury at age sixteen, then during the course of DIA we might experience neck pain followed by arm pain, followed by a memory of falling down some stairs. One particular client I remember would frequently get pain in his right shoulder when I worked on his very sore feet. He later told me he had injured his shoulder years prior to his feet acting up.

Another remarkable thing about the Law of Cure is that it can be quite predictive of the kinds of downstream effects one might expect: old injuries or scars, the sources of which predate the problem being addressed, may become sites for downstream effects in just the same way they reappear temporarily during DIA. It is important to remember that energy shifts occur with great frequency whether we recognize them or not. Serious students of healing will want to

1   The Law of Cure was formulated by Constantine Hering (1800–1880), one of the founders of American homeopathy. It states that symptoms are resolved from within to without, from innermost to outermost, from top to bottom and in reverse order in which they occurred (i.e., backwards chronologically).

learn to spot these shifts as they occur, for to resist them is to begin to undo all the good work we have done or, as happens all too often, visit our various symptoms over and over without being able to move forward.

℞ *JONI:* BACK PAIN & APPENDECTOMY SCAR

Joni came to see us with chronic back pain following a car accident. After one session of DIA, she complained of exquisite sensitivity in her appendectomy scar. The site was a bit tender at the best of times and she did not like to touch it but after this particular session of bodywork, it was really painful.

Thinking we might be dealing with a downstream effect, we stimulated the site of the scar with a microcurrent stimulator. Almost immediately, she screamed in pain and began retching. As the paroxysms of retching moved through her body, her back arched and contracted, moving back and forth, in great heaving waves — moving as it had not done in a long time. After several minutes of such movement, she settled down and announced that the pain in both her back and her appendectomy scar were gone.

It had never occurred to Joni that her appendectomy scar might have been related to her back pain. Nor did it occur to her that the pain in her back was blocked from healing because she was unconsciously protecting her appendectomy scar in such a way as to automatically trigger a setback every time there was any improvement in her back. Simply put, her attempts to avoid the appendectomy pain led her to holding her body in an awkward forward bend, which in turn put a strain on her back. Whenever her back felt a bit better, she would stand up a bit straighter, which put unacceptable pressure on the abdominal scar, which caused her to bend forward again. Thus she was caught by a downstream aggravation placed precisely between her back pain and freedom.

Once she had re-experienced all that was contained in her appendectomy scar (the vomiting and retching turned out to be a body memory of her post-operative nausea), her fear of discomfort in the scar receded and, with this downstream block opened up, her back was free to improve too.

Downstream effects are proof that healing is possible. Once we have had an experience of energy shifting as a result of applying a moving toward intent, we can repeat the experience at will and so confirm our ability to use intent to bring healing. This repetition gradually stabilizes our experiential understanding of the fact that mind (intent) can move energy and strengthens our faith in our ability to care for and relate to ourselves, the lack of which is usually a big part of our illness or pain.

So, if pain is our teacher, there is no need to feel anxious or resist it. Without resistance and anxiety, there will be no tension. Without tension, disease and pain are unlikely to persist. Ultimately, in fact, without tension, disease and pain are unlikely to arise.

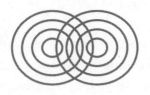

CHAPTER 15

EVERYDAY LIFE MEDITATIONS

*No matter how many committee meetings we have
attended, funny little motions of the shoulders and
weird cries are waiting inside of us. When we are in a
boring conversation, we could, instead of saying
something boring, give a cry. We can never predict
what might come out.*

— Robert Bly

*O*ne way to increase mind-body integration is to
commit to working with our pain whenever and wherever it presents
itself. That way we can use every moment of the day as an opportunity to be present with whatever is going on in our bodies.
Whether we are driving, washing dishes, walking, arguing, eating,
shopping, running for a bus or even sleeping, we can practise being
present in the body and moving toward discomforts as they come
up. Such mindfulness will gradually erase the distinction we may
have made in our minds between meditation on the one hand and
everyday life on the other, and also means that our mind-body
energies are never stagnant or stuck for long before we begin giving
them attention. For this reason, it is one of the quickest ways to
break habits.

Briefly, in everyday life meditations we simply bring the technique of moving toward into some daily activity that is posing a

difficulty, remaining open to some form of energy movement just as we have learned to do in sitting meditation. And in just the same way, to whatever extent possible in the situation, we should let anything come that wants to come, be it a physical, mental or emotional expression of energy movement. We neither block anything nor try to make anything happen but rather remain curious about, and have compassion for, whatever may want to appear.

WALKING MEDITATION

Walking is a pleasant part of many of our lives and so is a good place to begin to practise structured and unstructured healing meditations. In a walking meditation, we are not so concerned with the mechanics of walking but rather the *feel* of walking. Walking meditation aims to investigate whatever barriers we may have established to a normal gait and then to observe and to work with any pain that arises. This means experimenting with abandoning our compensation tactics (limping, favouring one leg, altering posture to avoid pain) while cultivating an inner-outer awareness and a new understanding of our fears.

Pain in the hips, knees or ankles presents an ideal opportunity for practice. Begin walking as you would normally, getting the feel of your rhythms, then let your consciousness slip away from day-to-day concerns. As you feel your body's rhythm, place your attention lightly on the whole cycle of your gait. Notice limping, lack of congruence, pain, tension, holding, leaning or other subtle alterations you have made over time as compensation.

Now slow down to identify difficult parts of your gait. And just as if you were learning a tricky piece of music, go slowly enough to make it impossible for your body to fake it by hurrying through whatever parts it finds hardest. Pay the process curious and compassionate attention throughout and, using intention, bring your gait as close to ease as you can. Remember, you are asking your body to communicate with you, not trying to force it to do something in a certain way.

As you work with your gait, you may find yourself faced with acute pain. Acute pain is a particular difficulty in any kind of meditation because it tends to make us flee the scene mentally and physically. Your response, however, should be the same: slow down and pay attention. Approach your pain as if in slow motion to find your edge and, moving back and forth between pain and no-pain, expose that edge and watch for myoclonic shaking. Stay with any shaking for a while, then resume walking. Watch closely for changes in your gait.

If there is a burst of pain during a particular arc of the gait cycle, close attention will probably reveal an effort to avoid that pain. A limp is a classic example of such avoidance. Unfortunately, a limp does more than just avoid pain. It necessitates a series of further physical adjustments to accommodate it, which in turn differently configure the body's tensegrous structure. If the pain is temporary, the body is able to return to its pre-injury state once that pain passes; but if the pain is chronic, the cytoskeletal changes become more and more difficult to reverse.

In the walking meditation, we do the opposite of limping: walking normally, noticing the pain as it arises and entering it with awareness, feeling the energetic block and seeing what is required to open it up instead of avoiding it. I got quite a bit of practice in this technique one time when my left knee flared up (this was the leg I had injured in a motorcycle accident many years previously). To begin with, I noticed an exquisitely painful arc through a particular ten degrees of flexion while walking. By paying my gait close attention, I saw that I avoided this pain by keeping my knee straight whenever my foot hit the ground. This strategy allowed me to disguise my limp so that other people would not see it. But I was fooling myself.

As I mentioned in the last chapter, this knee pain had all the features of a downstream effect: as the knee flared up, my back pain subsided; and there was a very similar ten-degree arc of pain in both. Further, I had myofascial twitches all over the place — there were points of exquisite tenderness around the knee joint that would set my whole leg trembling with trivial pressure. It was not hard to see how my avoidance strategy would sooner or later lead to a recurrence of the back pain.

So I resolved to mobilize intent and move toward the pain as much as possible. As I walked into the pain, I discovered my unconscious was extremely adept at pain avoidance. In fact, it seemed impossible not to try to escape it by altering my gait slightly. I persevered, however, walking more and more slowly, until I found the precise place in my stride where I went into avoidance and instead made myself lean slowly and deliberately into it. My reward was a searing pain that shot through my knee and almost pulled me onto the pavement. I tried again, going more slowly still, embracing the pain in fractional amounts by breathing deeply. I noticed that I was shaky and a bit dizzy.

Recognizing this as a sign of entry to the void, I pressed on and before long noticed some myoclonic shaking in my leg. The shaking increased more and more and soon my leg was trembling, shaking and kicking quite violently. After a few minutes, it subsided and I found I could walk almost normally without pain.

PRINCIPLES OF WALKING MEDITATION

Find a state of restful alertness and inner-outer focus while walking.

▼ Move toward pain physically and mentally.

▼ Notice how pain avoidance is automatic.

▼ Make your gait as normal and symmetrical as possible.

▼ Watch for myoclonic shaking, trembling or other signs of energy movement.

▼ Welcome the unexpected.

▼ Practise regularly — go for a walk every day.

CRAMPS

Cramps are a build-up of energy at a certain location, so they represent huge opportunities for energy retrieval. They often come on spontaneously, sometimes in the middle of the night, during yoga or stretching, or as the result of an unusual physical position, so we have to be ready to work with them at a moment's notice. Despite their unpleasantness — or perhaps because of it — they make great opportunities for a healing meditation.

ENERGETIC SLUGGISHNESS

Cramps became more interesting to me when we started to see carpopedal spasm (a crampy contraction of the hands or feet) in people during DIA, especially when they hyperventilated. The physiological explanation — blowing off too much carbon dioxide — had unfortunately blinded me to the energetic situation.

In time, I came to another more intuitive explanation. It had to do with the experience of helplessness engendered by the cramp. And I found those affected could frequently relate that sense of helplessness to other facets of their lives. It was as if the cramp was a metaphor for larger issues.

Metaphorically and literally, then, cramps are a retardation of energy as it tries to move outward. Such energetic sluggishness can have significant existential consequences, as is illustrated in the following case.

℞ RICHARD: ARM CRAMPS

Richard was a drummer in a rock band who came to us because he was getting painful cramps in both arms whenever he performed. It had been so painful for him to play that he had to quit the band; and, since drumming was his passion, this decision had been fairly devastating. By the time he came to see us, he had investigated every source of healing he could think of, from neurology to acupuncture, over several years without success and was in a good deal of despair.

During DIA, Richard developed the typical contractions of carpopedal spasm in his hands and wrists. In his case, however, I watched with increasing amazement as the cramping extended up his arms into his shoulders. As Richard's body began to vividly express energetic containment, his hands and arms contorted as if he were trying to grab onto something, his eyes full of fear and anxiety. We massaged Richard's arms repeatedly to help him bring the energy down to his hands as he struggled valiantly with the contractions until he got his hands warmed and opened. Frightening though the experience was, however, Richard's determination brought him a considerable reward: later that day, he gave us a drumming solo, pain-free for the first time in years.

During subsequent discussions, Richard admitted he tended to cope with his fears by withdrawing into himself to avoid social contact. He added that one outcome of his void experience was the realization that this 'withdrawal' was being enacted in the painful contractions as a literal energetic reality and not just an emotional one.

It is rare to see such a clear demonstration of the principle that *energy follows intent*. Moreover, the experience for Richard was life-changing because he came to see clearly how his difficulty drumming was a direct reflection of the way he had managed his existential angst.

CRAMP MEDITATION — MOVING TOWARD PAIN

We are usually advised to apply counterforce to cure a cramp. Such advice is based on acting against pain; and counterforce will often terminate a cramp in the moment. What is not well understood is that the counterforce further blocks the flow of energy to the periphery, and so maintains or worsens the condition that generated the cramp. In a cramp meditation, on the other hand, we use a moving toward intent, which means we want to enter the cramp consciously and go through it to see what happens.

At one time in my life, I used to get a lot of cramps in my feet. Because they were painful, I habitually tried to terminate them but at a certain point I recognized the potential they presented to practise a moving-toward intent. So after that when a cramp arose, I took off my shoe, lay down and breathed deeply into the pain. Excruciating as it was, it did not last forever and as the spasm settled down, I noticed the foot had warmed considerably.

For me, that experience confirmed that energy blocked in the lower leg was coming into the foot, and so my cramp meditation practice was born. I experimented daily until I no longer feared foot cramps — with the result that I rarely got them any more, unless I deliberately brought them on by flexing my toes — and my feet were usually warm to the touch. Later on, I was able to experiment with cramps in bigger muscles, like calf, thighs and buttocks with very similar results.

It is true that some cramps (such as a calf or thigh cramp) can be very difficult to negotiate. The trick is to sit right on the edge of the cramp until you work up enough courage to drop into it. Staying on the edge of a cramp — or any pain — can allow one the benefit of gradually opening an energy block without going so deeply into the pain that it becomes overwhelming.

PRINCIPLES OF CRAMP MEDITATION

▼ Recognize the opportunity presented in the cramp.
▼ Move toward the cramp. If it proves overwhelming, apply just enough counterforce with the antagonistic muscles to keep the pain bearable without terminating the cramp.
▼ Breathe deeply and slowly.
▼ Watch for myoclonic shaking, trembling or kicking movements.
▼ Make a loud noise if you feel like it.

NIGHT MEDITATIONS — MOVING TOWARD INSOMNIA

Many people have difficulty sleeping, and those with chronic illness are particularly prone to sleeplessness and interrupted sleep. Sleep can be disturbed by pain, whirling thoughts, muscle spasms, palpitations, restless leg syndrome, sleep apnea or just plain old anxiety.

Sleeping pills, anti-depressants, pain-killers and the like are usually taken to oppose, or act against insomnia whereas, as we have seen, deep healing always requires that we embrace our symptoms and receive their message. As most people know, sleeping pills may get one to sleep in the moment but an unhealthy dependence can quickly develop and the pills themselves can, in the end, actively contribute to insomnia, not to mention interfering with consciousness and day-to-day functioning. Sooner or later, most people realize that the negative consequences of taking drugs for insomnia outweigh the positive benefit.

In a night meditation, we move toward our sleeplessness rather than away from it. This can give us an entirely new way to approach the problem of sleep disturbance. After all, anxiety, whirling thoughts, cramps and restless legs are all the result of energy build-up. By moving toward them, we may be able to remedy our sleeplessness and to retrieve our blocked energies.

ENERGETIC OVERFLOW

A few years ago, I found myself waking up on occasion with back pain. At other times, anxiety and recurrent thoughts would keep me awake long into the night. It occurred to me that the difficulty might reflect a kind of energetic overflow: energy first stagnating because of recumbence, then overflowing into the head to stimulate mental activity. Moreover, here was an another ideal opportunity to test the concept of moving toward. If I was not sleeping, I reasoned, I might as well use the lost hours profitably.

So one night, when sleep would not come, I sat up in bed and allowed myself to wonder just what my body wanted. It did not take long to answer me. As soon as I relaxed into my symptoms, my torso jumped, my head and neck shook and my legs started kicking. After only a few minutes of this, my head cleared and I was able to go off to sleep. What is more, I woke the next morning with that delicious feeling of having had a really good night's rest.

It seems that anxiety can best be solved through meditation undertaken *at the time that the anxiety is surfacing*. The trick is to recognize that anxiety is just raw, unfocused or undirected energy and then relax into it and allow the energy to move the body. In a remarkably short time — often only a few minutes — the anxiety diminishes as the energy behind it discharges through physical movement.

The next time I woke with back pain, I began to move toward the pain in dynamic meditation. Within moments, my pelvis began to shake and tremor, and a sensation of heat moved up my back. After a few minutes of this, I could literally feel the stiffness easing; and as the physical movement subsided, my mind also became calm and clear. Sleep subsequently came easily, and I once again woke up in the morning feeling rested and fresh. These two experiences were remarkable both in their simplicity and their speed, and graphically demonstrated to me the profound possibilities inherent in seizing the moment to do some dynamic meditation.

Many people describe an annoying restlessness that comes on when they are trying to go to sleep. They are just drifting off when their legs start shaking, crawling or spasming. Such experiences are more common after an injury or trauma and can mean years of sleep deprivation — you may recall Brenda, from chapter 11, Dynamic Interactive Acu-Bodywork. Yet it rarely occurs to sufferers that such experiences can be deeply healing if not resisted, or that the pain of restless legs can be moved with prompt attention given it at the time the restlessness arises.

OTHER NOCTURNAL SYMPTOMS

We move through the void on the way to sleep every night. And since energy is free to move in the void, it is no surprise that it boils up as we pass this delicate threshold between waking and sleeping, particularly after an injury when the body is healing.

Other common night symptoms include teeth-grinding, tongue-biting, snoring, sleep apnea and palpitations. Teeth-grinding wears down the enamel on the crowns of the teeth, making them sensitive and susceptible to decay; tongue-biting is painful; snoring and sleep apnea lead to chronic daytime fatigue, and can cause significant marital tension; and palpitations, which are an anxiety response under normal waking conditions, can trigger a fear response. None of it is a perfect recipe for sleep!

Each of these conditions is a marker of energy congestion in the chest, throat or face, and each can be cleared quite quickly. Sit up the moment you realize there is a problem, enter a meditative state and with gentle, unforced attention be open to movement occurring in the head, neck, shoulders or arms.

This may result in significant head shaking, which can spread into the shoulders and down the arms. The shaking will usually subside after a few minutes and restorative sleep should ensue. It sure beats a uvulectomy as a way of dealing with snoring!

PRINCIPLES OF NIGHT MEDITATION

▼ Recognize the opportunity presented by insomnia.
▼ Sit up and assume your usual meditation posture.
▼ Move toward the specific symptom — whether it be pain, mental chatter, anxiety, palpitations, restless legs, snoring, apnea or whatever.
▼ Breathe deeply and slowly, unless the body wants to snort — in which case, snort away.
▼ Watch for myoclonic shaking, trembling, head-shaking or kicking.
▼ Keep the movements going until a sense of calm arises, then go to sleep.

Night meditations can be very enlivening. They can improve not only our sleep but our general well-being, especially if we at the same time remove the negative effects of sleeping pills and pain-killers from our systems — and all with just a few minutes stolen from the nightly battle with insomnia.

LUCID DREAMING — MOVING TOWARD FEAR

Most of us are familiar with nightmares and know what it is to wake out of a dire situation with our hearts pounding. Yet how many of us realize the opportunity contained in such a dream? A nightmare is a particularly intense dream and the more intense the dream, the more energy is in it. The habitual response of terror followed by waking relieves the immediate anxiety but can leave us disoriented and frightened. And waking from the dream means we lose the abundant energy of fear and the opportunity to learn to work with it.

But if we intend to move toward the content of a nightmare rather than run from it or wake out of it, we must first learn to be conscious enough while still asleep to make that decision. *Lucid dreaming* refers to dreaming while aware that we are dreaming, and more particularly to being aware enough while still in those dreams to influence them. In other words, lucid dreaming gives us the unusual and very valuable opportunity to experience two states of consciousness simultaneously. Such awareness is rare in waking life but it can be cultivated and its healing power accessed in a dream state.

I recall one intense dream in which a murderer was chasing me all over the countryside. Later in the dream, I found myself in the dining hall of a large castle. The guests were aware that a marauder was in the castle grounds and expressed relief that I was there to protect them. At that moment, a large oak door at the end of the room began to open with an eerie creaking sound, making it obvious that the intruder had come up the stairs from the courtyard below.

Feeling constrained to act the protector, I arose, terrified, to cross the room. But, as I moved toward the door, I became aware that I was dreaming — asleep yet awake at the same time. Then, perhaps because of my constant waking attention to the idea of moving toward pain and discomfort and through fear, I knew what I had to do, and it had nothing to do with escaping the situation, by holding the door against the threat from outside, or by jumping out of the dream. I knew I had to embrace the threat (which, after all, was only a projection of some part of myself) so instead of holding the door closed, I threw it open to greet the demon.

And then the most extraordinary thing happened. Within a moment of making the decision to stay present, I felt a surge of ecstatic energy running through me. Huge waves of a kind of electricity washed over me and I stayed in this rapture for a long time. Eventually, I awoke, serene and enlivened — not to mention amazed — instead of tense, disoriented and alarmed, and found that for about twenty minutes after I awoke I could revisit the feeling by bringing the dream's situation to mind.

That was my first experience of the transmutation of energy in the dream state and even today, although it happened many years ago, I can still recall the quality of that particular energetic experience.

PRINCIPLES OF LUCID DREAMING

- ▼ Intend lucidity before going to sleep.
- ▼ In the event a dream does become lucid, recognize the opportunity presented.
- ▼ Look at things to stabilize the dream images — such as your hands, buildings, vehicles, etc.
- ▼ When something begins to fade, look at something else.
- ▼ Move toward anything scary, remaining open.
- ▼ Stay present for as long as possible.
- ▼ When you do start to wake up, re-run the dream to recollect all the details.

All of the above healing meditations share the intention of moving toward in order to integrate pain, fear, emotions or other forms of blocked energy. The examples given are mostly from my own personal experience, as they reveal how I learned to apply this integrative intention in my daily life, waking or sleeping, when I met energies I might normally run from or block. We all have these opportunities. Let your creativity suggest ways of approaching situations as they arise. So long as your moving-toward intention is clear and earnest, results are bound to follow.

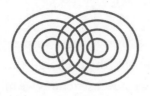

CHAPTER 16

SEXUAL HEALING MEDITATIONS

We may be on the brink of a transformational sexuality in which our sexuality becomes, in the context of a depth relationship between two people, a godding exchange so that the larger creative powers emerge to restore the body and the mind and to transform the spirit.
— Jean Houston

$\mathcal{D}$espite the so-called sexual revolution many of us lived through and can still recall, the healing and transformational potentials of human sexuality remain sadly under-explored and under-used. In spectacularizing and commodifying, legalizing and medicalizing sex in the West — in other words, putting as much distance as possible between our eyes, our minds and our uninhabited bodies as possible — we have forfeited much of our understanding of its potential, its power and its depths.

For the average person, this loss is personal and often unconscious. But for anyone working with people, the current legal and social attention to sexual boundaries between professionals and their clients causes particular difficulty. And, in energy healing, it is a difficulty that cannot be resolved by somehow excluding sexual energy from consideration in the work.

In fact, any refusal on our part to acknowledge and honour sexual energies in those we work with would merely mimic the very problem we see in nearly everyone with chronic illness or pain. Nor are we able to skirt these energies in dynamic interactive acu-bodywork (DIA) whatever strictures we might attempt to apply, just as those who practise dynamic meditation will find their own energies hard to avoid. Whether we are prepared to admit it or not, sexual energy is as central to the energy body as the heart is to the physical one.

In fact, as fear and anxiety — the energetic root of so much of our chronic illness and pain — are nearly impossible to sustain in a body in which sexual energy is flowing unrestrictedly, few discussions could be of greater interest in the treatment of chronic conditions than those around sexuality and our habitual restriction of sexual energy to body parts and contexts that are merely sexual. Like the heart and the circulation, our sexual energy is implicated in nearly every moment of our lives but is typically denied in all but a few. Very unfortunately — in fact, it is not going too far to say, cruelly — because of the significant social strictures around sexual issues, especially in contexts that involve working with the body, anyone wanting to heal the effects of sexual repression and dissociation (the so-called love/sex split) in themselves these days generally has to do so without professional help.

I mentioned sexual wounding briefly in chapter 8, The Chakras. In this present chapter, I will go over the origins and various expressions of the wound then suggest experiential ways of addressing it. (It is probably worth pointing out again that, as with any of the other energy blocks or splits, the conundrum of the love/sex split cannot be solved with the intellect. At best, the intellect can be brought to understand the impossibility of a rational solution, which clears the way for an experiential exploration of the dynamics of the split.)

THE LOVE/SEX SPLIT

To briefly recap, psychologists tell us that an almost tangible split develops between our loving and our sexual selves for two specific reasons: as a result of incest taboos — which demand that we limit sexual impulses around the people to whom we are most closely related emotionally, our family members; and through the general denigration of sexuality as dirty, immoral or uncivilized. The shaming in the biblical story of the Garden of Eden is a script our society has inscribed deep in its matrix.

Although an incest taboo is common to most of the world's cultures, its function seems to have been as much to maintain genetic, social, spiritual and even economic vitality as it was to provide an important opportunity to practise sexual self-regulation and a recognition of the power inherent in sexuality. Certainly, these taboos were never originally intended to denigrate sexuality itself but to put it in its place. In many traditional cultures, youths were mentored through their coming of age. So, for example, young boys near puberty might be taken aside by uncles, the young girls by aunts, to be taught the place of sexuality in their culture.

We have let go of these formal sexual mentoring systems and have for the most part failed to substitute much of anything, either publicly or privately, for them. With no one to help them, teenagers are left to their own devices when it comes to integrating their emerging sexuality. It is not surprising, then, that repression, misunderstanding, fear and even dissociation are a part of so many young people's reckoning with sex in our culture.

For instance, the incest taboo prohibits sexual intercourse between close family members but a young psyche living within a family is likely to interpret this stricture to mean that he must not have sexual relations with anyone very close, anyone with whom he feels at home, or anyone with whom he has strong ties. It has been speculated that, as a result of this taboo, a subconscious sense of impending doom arises later in life whenever a relationship reaches the kind of depth of feeling and/or the familiarity one has with family. The repression of sexual feelings in these situations gradually becomes automatic until — and this is the essence of the so-called love/sex split — *we cannot have sex with anyone we love.*

We can have sex, or we can have relationship, but not both at once. As a result, many of us arrived in adulthood feeling that it is only safe to allow sexual energy to flow freely with near strangers — that is, people with whom we have little spiritual or emotional bond — and we unconsciously struggle against intimacy out of an ingrained and subrational fear of this taboo.

Unfortunately, this fear becomes evident in long-term relationships just as the connection between lovers approaches spiritual kinship, at the moment it becomes very familiar, or familial. So we find our sexual connection with a lover will often break down just when we begin to lose our sense of them as *other*.

THE SEVERED *CHONG MAI*

One way of understanding the dynamics of unimpeded energy circulation in a sexual relationship can be found in the interrelation of yin and yang energies in the body and the intimate connection between the sexual (second) and Heart (fourth) chakras, which is mediated by an energetic vessel known in Chinese medicine as the *Chong Mai*. In the ideal situation, then, sexual communion involves a giving and receiving of energies at all chakras but most particularly at the Heart and sexual chakras. If the *Chong Mai* is severed (as it is in many people), then sooner or later one of those two chakras (Heart or sexual) closes and an energy backup develops that eventually douses the flames of passion.

When we are first in love, we do not know our partner well, so the incest taboo is still dormant and remains hidden while our projections onto our partner stimulate our chakras to open temporarily, giving us a taste of what is possible in relationship. In the next phase of relationship, romance generally fades and, in its place, a deeper spiritual connection or a comfortable familiarity arises. At this point, the more vulnerable of the two chakras will often close — in one or both partners.

If one or other partner closes the Heart chakra, then the other partner will eventually close his or her (and it is usually her) sexual chakra. Although the dynamics are in no way as straightforward or as predictable as this sketch may make them appear, this deterioration can be very confusing to partners whose experience of intercourse may have been extremely satisfying. As enjoyable sex fades mysteriously from their relationship, many couples split up and move on, feeling angry or hurt. The few who choose to stay together, however, gain an extraordinary opportunity to reach higher states of consciousness, if they are prepared to consciously transcend and integrate their love/sex split.

PHYSICAL SYMPTOMS OF A *CHONG MAI* SPLIT

In those who have developed a significant split as a result of trauma, consciousness has usually been dissociated from the pelvis by an intense desire to avoid the pain, shame or terror associated with it. Energy (consciousness) is diverted from the pelvis and accumulates in the upper body, leading to what is described as an excess of energy above and a deficiency below. The excess upper body tension can lead to migraines or tension headaches and a myriad of other symptoms including blood rushing to the head (blushing, flushing), acne, upper back pain, various pre-menstrual symptoms (such as irritability, mood swings or anxiety), breast lumps, pain in the hinge of the jaw (temporomandibular joint syndrome, or TMJ) and so on.

In others, the opposite dynamic occurs. Consciousness is dissociated from the Heart area in order to avoid the potential humiliation and terror of emotional vulnerability. The dynamic results in an excess of energy below and deficiency above. Common physical complaints can include low back pain, prostate problems, sexual acting out (with all its consequences) and heart disease.

In the more complete splits, individuals combine various coping techniques — masturbation, hypersexuality, repression and dissociation — to deal with the continuing pressure of unintegrated sexual energy. Masturbation temporarily releases congested sexual energy but of course does nothing to integrate it and further depletes vital bodily energy which can, in extreme cases, weaken the constitution. Frequent intercourse or intercourse with a variety of partners also drains vital energy and carries the additional risk of sexually transmitted disease.

Repression/dissociation can lead to compartmentalization syndromes with either an upper or lower focus. In its extreme form, multiple personalities can arise from sexual dissociations — among them, a Dr. Jekyll/Mr. Hyde split in which a pleasant dominant personality covers for a darker and more dangerous one.

TRANSCENDENCE/INTEGRATION

Those stuck in a love/sex dissociation can use the practices of transcendence, moving toward and integration we have looked at in earlier chapters to release sexual energy to flow throughout their bodies. In my opinion, such an approach — rather than the repression, which is overtly and covertly suggested — should be taught to young people at puberty as sexual energies emerge during those critical early teenage years.

Release and integration of sexual energy allows it to rise up the spine, often activating *kundalini* energy, to produce a calm, enlivened and even blissful state while repression of the same energy leads inexorably to illness through a painful and destabilizing dissociation of mind and body.

LETTING GO

The adage, *Good sex is better than no sex but no sex is better than bad sex*, is seldom heeded by couples whose sexual exchange has become blocked. Some people are so hooked on the value of sex that they would hardly consider letting it go even when relations are provoking arguments, anger or other negative responses. Others, who may find sex a self-conscious, unenjoyable chore, or a frankly uncaring self-indulgence on the part of their partner, prefer to just turn away from the experience altogether and may dissociate if pressured to engage in intercourse. (Such dissociation may help them cope in the moment but unfortunately only intensifies their underlying energy block.) Under such circumstances, a period of conscious, thoughtful abstinence has a lot going for it.

Although for many people the idea of no sex is terrifying (usually because the ego hears in it alienation, rejection and repression), conscious abstinence has many advantages, not the least of which is the possibility of better health. In fact, the conservation and redistribution of sexual energy is by far and away the most effective way of recharging the body and keeping it healthy — so effective that those who master it often remain vital and energetic far into old age. (Complete abstinence is not necessary for energy conservation, which can, in men, be achieved by learning not to ejaculate and, in women, by learning to own and to circulate their sexual energy.)

Periods of conscious abstinence also provide us with a chance to back off, to learn to feel sexual energy dancing in our bodies, to value it as energy and stop throwing it away and, finally, to integrate it psychologically and bodily into the wholeness of our being.

Compare the alternative. We live in a society apparently mesmerized by a homogenized, superficial sexuality and suffering epidemic levels of sexually transmitted disease, chronic fatigue and degenerative conditions from burn-out; yet, while sales of tonics and immune stimulants sky-rocket, we frantically toss away the most fundamental energy we have — our sexual energy.

MOVING TOWARD BLOCKED SEXUAL ENERGY

One way to transcend and integrate sexual energy is to do just what we have suggested with pain, anxiety or insomnia: set up an intention to move toward the energetic block in an altered state of consciousness and find out what the energy wants to do. This will be different for each person, depending on the specifics of their *Chong Mai* block. The key is to move toward the specific difficulty — whatever it might be.

For those with pelvic congestion who experience pressure to discharge, moving toward will likely mean working with the idea of non-ejaculation, while simultaneously opening themselves to emotional vulnerability, so that a redistribution of sexual energy can occur. This is not as tormenting as it might sound! When we succeed in allowing sexual energy to flow in the body, sexual tension actually lessens and leaves us deeply enlivened.

Meantime, for those more prone to pelvic dissociation, moving toward might well mean working with some upper body symptom — such as headaches — while simultaneously opening to disowned pelvic energies. In such a situation, orgasm might be helpful if it succeeds in pulling excess upper body energy downward. The important thing is to try doing the opposite of the habitual.

KUNDALINI

To touch on this topic once again, *kundalini* energy is our basic energy or creative force, which is said to lie dormant at the base of the spine until mobilized. Since it is fuelled from the second chakra and the *mingmen*, it will almost certainly activate once we begin to work with our sexual energy while consciously withholding orgasm.

Confusion on this point can easily take an aspirant back down the road of repression and exacerbate any symptoms or imbalances. Little wonder it is generally considered dangerous to try to open the *kundalini* prematurely, or without skilled guidance. However, by the time we are manifesting chronic and severe physical symptoms, it may seem a bit late for caution. At that point, *kundalini* awakening is often long overdue and, in any case, may even be occurring spontaneously (particularly in trauma cases), presenting as itself as spontaneous myoclonic shaking and other *kriya*-type manifestations.

Unfortunately, instead of seeing these phenomena as positive, the medical system tends to pathologize spontaneous energy discharges (myoclonic shaking) as seizures and suppress them with drugs. This misunderstanding and the suppression that follows only freezes individuals midstream in the chaos of their transformational journeys.

There are many yogic techniques to cultivate *kundalini* energy, from breathing exercises (*pranayama*) to meditation postures. Those interested can pursue such techniques through yoga or meditation teachers. I simply want to put the thousands of years of study of *kundalini* next to the experience of myoclonic shaking here. After all, there is nothing new under the sun — especially where our energy bodies are concerned.

MOVING ENERGY UP

For those with excess pelvic energy, the Heart chakra is quite likely to be closed or deficient, and orgasm is often being used to relieve the excess pelvic tension. Abstinence will provide the opportunity to open a new pathway. Once we decide to abstain, we need to set aside time daily to meditate with a view to moving blocked sexual energy up and into the body to open the Heart. If we are meditating regularly anyway, nothing much needs to change. Meditation begins in the usual way. After a few minutes of quiet introspection, place your attention on the lower chakras, paying particular attention to areas of tension, tightness and congestion. Again, this is no different from any other dynamic meditation. We simply intend to move toward discomfort in the pelvis, as we would move toward discomfort anywhere else in the body. Meditation tapes or music can be useful to assist in holding intention.

Absolute trust of the body is essential. Look for movement, myoclonic shaking or other energetic signals. Of course, these can start anywhere but, if there is significant pelvic tension, it may want to start in the pelvis. Pelvic movements that may occur should be respected and the body permitted to move as it wants. Be prepared to feel all the feelings that may be held there — shame, guilt, anger and fear. There is no sexual healing without facing the totality of the repressed energy and opening to those energies, as feeling requires vulnerability, which is precisely what opens the Heart chakra.

The pelvic movements may become quite vigorous or even violent but generally they will evolve into a sensation of energy moving up the back, warming and enlivening the upper body. This is the *kundalini* flow, the energy that opens the Heart and reconnects the sundered *Chong Mai*. Keep going as long as you like, as long as there is energy to move.

After a while, when you feel the energy has moved sufficiently, let yourself quiet down slowly and enjoy the peaceful feelings that may now be present. With practice, you will find you can achieve a calm, refreshed state in which sexual energy is present as a background buzz that envelops the whole body. This quiet yet dynamic state is the quintessential feature of transcendence and integration.

MOVING ENERGY DOWN

For people with excess energy above and deficiency below, a slightly different technique may be required. Dissociation from the pelvis rarely occurs without good reason, and sexual abuse may have laid the groundwork for the energetic dissociation in childhood. Such people yearn for emotional closeness, as they relate primarily through the Heart chakra but typically feel violated when their attempts at emotional intimacy elicit a sexual response from a partner. One big difficulty they often face is that their legitimate desire for closeness makes them energetically transmit a come-on, which attracts the very experience that alienates them. Sex brings terror and forces them to dissociate further.

Such women (this split is usually seen in women) often have boundary issues and must learn to say no before they can willingly say yes. Abstinence provides them the opportunity to insist that their boundaries are respected. When those boundaries are honoured, then bit by bit more physical closeness can be tolerated.

A helpful meditation for this gestalt must address the four issues of: dissociation; bringing energy congested in the upper body down; bringing *kundalini* energy up, and negotiating the chaotic mixing of upper energy and *kundalini* that is likely to occur in the region of the solar plexus or power chakra.

This can be a very difficult task. Dissociation is always harder to approach than containment because in some ways it is a deeper

imbalance. What begins as containment often progresses to dissociation so that, as we reverse the dissociation, we confront the
containment that was always there underneath.

First, we have to intend to come back into the body. Then begin
meditating, looking for movement or myoclonic shaking wherever
it might arise. Rhythmic drumming, or music that is passionate or
that enlivens earthy energies can be helpful. Look for loosening of
congested energy in the upper body manifesting as shaking in the
head, neck or arms.

Once the upper body is moving, intention can be directed to
the pelvis, which may not want to move if it is dissociated. Energy
loosening above and *kundalini* rising may generate feelings of anger, helplessness and shame as they meet in the personal power
centre (the solar plexus or third chakra) and recreate the helpless
feelings that generated the original dissociation. It may manifest
as an uncontrollable vibration in the pelvis that is felt as both terrifying and awesome.

Memories of previous violations may come flooding into consciousness accompanied by waves of anger that demand expression.
If we stay present, we can meet our power — power which was unavailable to us at the initial wounding. Our legs may kick, repressed
anger may flame hot. Shouts of *No! No!* or *Get away from me!* are
common and must be honoured and felt as deeply as possible.
Memories of previous violations feel just as terrifying as they did
the first time. But when they are met again in an environment
where healing is intended, the fury released can be triumphant.

ଯ *KEN*: EPILEPSY

Although there is clearly a predominance of male pelvic tension
and female pelvic dissociation, it would be a mistake to divide

these two energetic imbalances along gender lines, so, as the following case demonstrates, the imbalance more commonly seen in women can and does occur in some men.

Ken was forty-five years old, had been diagnosed with epilepsy at age seventeen and had been on anti-epileptic medication ever since. He told us he always had problems with relationships, being unable to sustain a romantic interest beyond the first few weeks. Sooner or later, usually sooner, he would be on the move.

In fact, it turned out his whole life had been about moving. His parents had made their living building houses, living in them for a while, then selling them, so they were always moving. He had been abused sexually by a teacher as a boy and he thought this might be related to his difficulties with relationships. As an adult, Ken had continued to move about, never settling for long, but he was beginning to tire of drifting. He suffered for some time from a chronic low-grade depression and when we met he was beginning to wonder if he would ever find his zest again.

It seemed clear to us that if Ken were to recover, he was going to have to capture some of the energy that was firing his epileptic seizures. After some discussion, he reduced his medication in preparation for our ten-day residential program. There, during interactive bodywork, he let the energy he knew as 'epileptic' flow through his body.

We noticed immediately that Ken held his pelvis as stiff as possible as the seizure progressed. With some encouragement, he was able to gradually loosen it and permit the flow of energy downward. Eventually it all came together, the block loosened and — after half an hour of fairly violent activity — he came to a place of absolute calm.

He told me that, for the first time he could remember, he felt whole. 'I thought I knew what self-acceptance was,' Ken confided, ' . . . but I had no idea it could be a body experience.'

Ken's situation emphasizes graphically how an illness that superficially seems unrelated to the love/sex split can require sexual healing to resolve energetically. With a blocked pelvis, Ken's sexual energy was diverted to his upper body. The excess energy above produced epileptic seizures; the deficiency below produced an inability to sustain romantic interest.

Without access to his sexual energy and with a body full of seizure-dampening, anti-epileptic drugs, it is no wonder Ken was depressed. To risk a seizure by reducing those medications — something no physician could ever condone — to get out of his particular drug trap demanded enormous courage, resolute self-responsibility, earnestness and clear intent.

PRINCIPLES OF A *CHONG MAI* MEDITATION

▼ Recognize the opportunity presented by abstinence, chosen or not.
▼ Achieve a state of restful alertness.
▼ Intend to remain present and move toward any sexual tension.
▼ Breathe deeply and slowly.
▼ Watch for myoclonic shaking and let the pelvis move in any way it wants to, resisting fantasy (it is movement that mobilizes energy, not discharge).
▼ Use inspiring music to move energy up, earthy music to pull energy down.
▼ Make noise if you feel like it.
▼ Practise regularly.

A GRADUAL HEALING

Those who bring sexual healing into their lives and relationships should be aware that the inner work is gradual, not swift. The most marked feature of the integration of sexual energy is the first taste of freedom from sexual addiction or aversion. Once this freedom is tasted, reversion is unthinkable. Sexual relations are no longer established from need nor shied from in fear. Each partner is free to give the other what the other desires rather than taking what they want or think they need.

For someone with a Heart chakra block, this might mean being present emotionally without anticipating sex. For those with a second chakra block, it might mean being present sexually without feeling violated.

THE INNER TEACHER

Healing the love/sex split will be a different emotional and spiritual experience for each person who undertakes it, but nearly everyone will find his or her physical health significantly improved by the integration of sexual energy. Daily meditation becomes the sacred space in which an enlivened energy body full of freely flowing sexual energy slowly grows. Gradually, pain disappears without painkillers; fatigue disappears without caffeine; flexibility increases as stiffness melts; and other inexplicable symptoms simply go away. And with daily practice, consciousness becomes increasingly aware of the energetic dynamics of illness: a block in energy flow, a materialization of that blocked energy, and finally, a pathology.

As our sexual energy becomes integrated, the upper chakras begin to open and we may become aware of capabilities related to higher consciousness. In Eastern thought, these special powers are called *siddhis* and are thought to emerge as the *kundalini* energy moves up toward the vertex. The Heart (fourth chakra) opens in compassion, the power of expression rises from the throat (fifth chakra), the third eye (sixth chakra) opens to clear sight, and the vertex (crown chakra) opens to the transcendent and the resolution of duality itself.

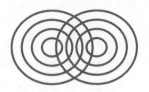

CHAPTER 17

ACUPUNCTURE TECHNIQUES

. . . There has never been a doctor anywhere, at any time, in any country, at any period in history who ever healed anything. Each person's healer is within.

— Marlo Morgan

$\mathcal{A}$cupuncture practitioners often ask us what protocols — that is, what point or sequence of points — facilitate entry to the void. It is always a tough question to answer because there really are no specific point protocols.

Although it would normally be considered poor medicine to initiate treatment without a diagnosis and treatment plan in place, in the case of chronic conditions, where real healing is a process that arises spontaneously out of the unknown, the opposite is often true. Further, as we have hinted in earlier chapters, to consider an individual separate from the condition being addressed, and the practitioner as separate from both for the sake of forming judgements (e.g., a diagnosis and/or a treatment plan) both deepens everyone's mind/body split and fractures the gestalt of the healing process. If, on the other hand, we are willing to admit to not knowing — as risky as that may seem at first — we usually find that what we need to know arises when it is needed, as an intuitive response to a particular situation.

So the real answer to the question, 'Which acupuncture protocols facilitate entry to the void?' is that the question contains a classic misunderstanding of the process. Heretical as it might sound, knowledge of advanced theories and particular acupuncture points and protocols are unnecessary to healing. In fact, conscious ignorance as a starting point, based on humility, curiosity and genuine *unknowing* are much more effective in addressing complex and chronic situations. So, whatever a trained practitioner already knows is usually more than adequate.

FORMULA-BASED ACUPUNCTURE

Chinese medicine — which includes acupuncture, moxibustion, herbal medicine, cupping, qi gong exercises, tuina (massage) and so on — is a very complex set of systems. Over the course of centuries, acupuncture alone has become so complex it now takes many years of study and much hands-on experience to master and the number of formulas and treatment protocols alone are so immense that no one could ever remember them all. Unfortunately, this vast body of knowledge has inclined instructors to deliberately emphasize technical skills and memorization during training, just as conventional medical schools in the West have done.

Again, the difficulty with conventional diagnosis and treatment protocols is that the vital holistic principles of *intent* and *context* are often overlooked. The existence of point protocols, coupled with the natural desire to relieve symptoms, can lead to an over-valuing of needling technique, accurate diagnosis, proven protocols and classic syndromes over core principles, and leads to a near eclipse of both the individual's uniqueness and the profound nature of an authentic healing relationship.

This is no small issue because when much energy is diverted to ego-centred intellectual activity and problem-solving, the practitioner gets pulled out of her Heart into her head, and is thereby dramatically limited in her ability to participate in deep healing. As I pondered this unfortunate situation, it became apparent to me that the mental effort of trying to make a correct diagnosis and pre-scribe a specific treatment regime actually destroys the very thing we are trying to bring to the forefront of our healing practice — the integrity of the interactive explorer-witness continuum.

Too much focus on knowledge means time wasted trying to think through imponderables. Why not instead admit them as impon-derables — literally, that which cannot be thought — and ask them to reveal their own complex natures and their own solu-tions? If the knot knows best how it is knotted, perhaps we would do better to allow not-knowing as a valid, perhaps essential, part of the healing relation and humble ourselves to ask the body-mind itself to offer information and eventually a solution out of a sincere relationship and a healing intention. However challenging it can be to get over considering not-knowing a lack, a negligence, even dangerous, the rewards of doing so are well worth the effort!

When we operate from a place of unknowing — rather than from a pretence of knowing — there is suddenly no division between the two people engaged in DIA. When both admit they do not know, the masks are off and, paradoxically, the truth may be seen more clearly. Such a simple admission of our common ignorance is the way out of duality. But it takes trust that this is exactly the right way to start, and more trust still to resist the temptation to know *before* we start.

I am not suggesting we dispense with knowledge altogether. We do need a structure within which to explore the infinite depths. But I want to speak for those of us who make a point of avoiding mental gymnastics and instead act from our whole selves and from core principles in whatever discipline we adopt. And while there is certainly more value in some needle placements than others, frankly, my experience leads me to believe even this value is slight compared to the value of intention and intuitive response to the immediate, interactive situation at hand. Intuition is based on the possibility of somehow going beyond, or transcending, the knowledge of a particular discipline. If the most memorable healing experiences arise from a place beyond theory, why not consciously develop the intuition, the courage and the curiosity to go beyond, rather than endlessly learning new skills and techniques?

It is not too much to say that when intention and context are understood and all parties are present and willing to stay open to whatever comes, diagnosis, theory and precise needle placement are almost superfluous. A sailing analogy might clarify what I mean. When sailing, we normally *intend* to go in a particular direction before we raise the sails, and if that intention is in complete accord with the direction the wind is blowing then we sail faster. If we raise the sails optimally, we would go faster still but as long as intention and wind direction are congruent, we would still move forward however the sails were raised, or even if they were not raised at all.

Intention in interactive work is like going in the direction the wind is blowing, whatever that direction might be, and accepting to go that way and no other wherever it might take us. Needle placement is like raising the sails tolerably well. (Again, if we lack intention, good needle placement will not achieve much, because it will be like fighting the wind. If, on the other hand, we have congruent intention, then perfect needle placement is relatively unimportant.)

Once I understood this fundamental point, I realized that the therapeutic ritual was reducible to some simple principles that can be learned fairly quickly. Of course, there is always more to be learned, and techniques can always be improved. But the more we can reduce the urgency to expand knowledge for its own sake, or for the sake of the ego, or to bolster our insecurity, or even to mask our lack of true healing intent, or our unease at unmediated enquiry *with* rather than *on behalf of* the explorer, the more we can heal our own mind/body split and let go into the Heart zone.

REDUCING THE FIVE ELEMENTS
TO THREE BASIC CIRCUITS

First, just as in homeopathy or any other holistic discipline, we want to get right away from treating symptoms and work with the individual who has the disease rather than the disease itself. And we want to ground the experience in a clear intention to recover the flow of original energy. In my experience, a return to that principle can be done with minimal fuss using five element constitutional typing supplemented by the six-temperament perspective discussed in chapter 6, The Six Temperaments.

You may recall from earlier chapters that, using the French energetics model, three energy circuits arise out of the five elements, each representing a zone of influence — the front, side or back of the body (see table 1).

Zone	Elements	Energy circuit
BACK ZONE	Water / Fire	Tai Yang–Shao Yin
SIDE ZONE	Wood / Fire	Shao Yang–Jue Yin
FRONT ZONE	Earth / Metal	Yang Ming–Tai Yin

Table 1: The three zones and their circuits

BACKWARDS ASSESSMENT

The magic of the three-circuit design is its simplicity: it makes it possible to circuit test for constitutional type. Although this might not seem particularly remarkable, it is actually the complete opposite of the generally accepted approach. Normally, practitioners try to decipher constitutional type cerebrally, coming to a diagnostic conclusion before needle insertion is attempted.

Working backwards like this — from solution to assessment, as it were — might be confusing were it not for the forceful guidance of the energetic phenomena we encounter during DIA. The combination of intention, breathing, acupuncture, acupressure, sound, movement and abreaction will frequently generate big energetic responses — often emphatically on one particular circuit. And if one circuit over the others produces an exaggerated response, then we can infer that the circuit in question contains a good deal of original energy. From there, an intuitive focus on selected elements within the circuit will often reveal an individual's constitutional type without further calculation.

Of course, if I were very experienced and very astute, I could probably look at an individual's skin tone, the light in her eyes, the shape and colour of her tongue, ask her a number of simple questions, feel her pulses and come to a reasonable conclusion about her constitutional type. But people who are chronically ill often have so many energetic layers and masks covering their basic constitutional type that their original energy is deeply concealed.

I used to think I was a bit slow and basically a poor diagnostician but over the years I have found that very few of my colleagues feel they know any better. Indeed, many will candidly admit that they are often going on guesswork while assuming an air of confidence — which means that quite a few of us in practice are as energetically masked as our clients. It is difficult to see how original energies can be located and reintegrated when so much lies hidden on both sides.

With this in mind, I want to touch on an approach I have found very helpful to provide a structure through which my own intuition can flow. Being somewhat technical, it may be of little interest to some readers. Furthermore, in presenting this material, I do not in any way mean to suggest that my approach is the right one, or that others should use it. Each person's intuition is unique and must be trusted and followed as it arises in feelings and hunches in the moment.

SESSION STRATEGIES

▼ SESSION 1: THE FOUR GATES

A simple way to get started in the first session is by opening the Four Gates. These points move energy in a general way. I use them not to do anything specific but rather as a way of introducing the body to being needled and as an opportunity to teach people how to breathe in deeply as a needle is inserted.[1] (See further in Appendix 1, Void Exploration/DIA.)

The points of the Four Gates are Liver-3 (Great Pouring) Large Intestine–4 (Adjoining Valleys) and are located in the valleys in the muscles of the hands and feet, between the first and second digits. Next I explore the entire body surface with acupressure, starting on the feet, working up the legs, abdomen, chest, neck, shoulders and face, noting the location of any points of tenderness along the way and noting which zone — front, side or back — is most affected. This gives me a clue as to which circuit to test in the future. Success in this first session is very much dependent on sensitivity and feedback because it is here that boundaries become apparent and here that trust, rapport and mutual respect either develops, or is strained.

---

1   This may be a novel instruction for some. In certain situations, people are counselled to breathe out with needle insertion rather than in.

▼ SESSION 2: CIRCUIT TESTING

I generally begin the second session by checking for tenderness at the source points of the three basic energy circuits and correlate these with the zones of tenderness I found in the first session (front/side/back). These source points are located in the hands and feet, and if tender will often indicate that the particular energy circuit involved contains significant stagnation. If the tender spots correspond with an affected zone discovered in the previous session, so much the better. (See appendix 2, Selected Acupuncture Points, for details of the specific points.)

Correlation of a symptomatic zone with tender source points suggests which circuit to test first. A noticeable energetic response when the source points are needled confirms the significance of the circuit. If, on the other hand, there is no response, I simply move on and test another circuit, either during the same session or at another time. All three circuits can be tested in this way and if one of the circuits engenders a significantly greater response than the others, often that is the circuit which contains original energy. From there, it is simply a question of focusing more closely on each individual organ to find the likely constitutional type.

Once again, after inserting the needles, I check the whole body using acupressure, this time moving more freely and intuitively while encouraging the explorer to dive into the void through expression of sound, movement and feeling. Such expression gives me experiential feedback that further guides my hands and my needle placement. In this way, the relationship moves deeper and deeper into an unknown, where the separation between us gradually disappears and the interaction becomes increasingly fluid and intuitive.

▼ SESSION 3: CONSTITUTIONAL TYPING/
  DEVELOPING RELATIONSHIP

Between the second and third sessions, I meditate on the first two
sessions and try to correlate the experiential findings with what is
being revealed constitutionally through our developing relationship. Often, people will get curious about five element constitutional typing, learn about it themselves, then tell me what they
think their constitutional type might be; and their opinion is often
far more accurate than anything I could come up with.

As information flows from a variety of sources, I focus on the
likely constitutional type, using fewer and fewer needles. This
alternation between experience and theory gradually narrows the
possibilities until sooner or later, often fairly quickly, we hit the
button, and this button gives us a pretty good idea of the constitutional type.

However, even when we do not hit the button, if we are in the
right zone, our sails are up and the boat is moving with the wind.
Initial needle placement is only the beginning, a way of starting a
process of exploration, not an end in itself. The experience in the
void guides further interaction and any further acupressure or
needle placement arises out of the needs of the moment. Sometimes very intuitive people begin to involve themselves in the process by telling me where they need needles or moxa — graphically
demonstrating how interactional work connects people to their
inner healers.

MOXIBUSTION

Those who are constitutionally worn out can find needles too
painful to bear. In such situations, we will often move to *moxibustion* which, although less well known in the West, is an integral
part of traditional acupuncture.

Moxa is dried and powdered mugwort (*Artemesia vulgaris*). When moxibustion is used, the mugwort is burned over an acupuncture point to put heat into it. Moxa comes in many forms; sometimes cigar-shaped bundles are burned right on the acupuncture needle. Other practitioners pinch the powder into small mounds and light them with punks. The moxa smoulders slowly and when it gets near the skin and begins to feel warm, the individual signals 'hot' and the moxa is removed. Moxa smells a little like fragrant autumn leaves when it burns and the sensation of warmth over the acupuncture point is remarkably comforting and soothing.

Moxibustion is not just a gentler way to address a particular point. It differs from needling — which stimulates or disperses existing energy — in that it can actually put new energy into the system. Although such an idea might seem surprising, it has long been acupuncturists' common experience that a little moxibustion, used at just the right place and time, can have truly far-reaching effects; and it is now well established scientifically that complex interdependent systems are highly sensitive to just such minute inputs.

Because it can put energy into the system, moxibustion is extremely beneficial to the many people these days who are energetically depleted or run down. It is also very helpful to people who are constitutionally frail or energetically cold. Cold types have cold hands and feet, like hot weather and like to bundle up to keep warm. Frail types tend to be tired, have low tone in their body tissues, catch colds easily, or are immune deficient generally. Often they have had painful experiences with acupuncture or bodywork in the past and may be adamant they do not want needles again. Any of the constitutional types may require moxa but yin constitutional types — specifically Metal and Water — seem to require it more often than others.

THE CURIOUS MERIDIANS

Another simple option for an initial needling protocol is to work with a set of circuits called the *extraordinary* or *curious* meridians. These circuits are regarded as the primary energetic reservoirs supplying the main meridians and can often access energy in a general way across entire zones regardless of constitutional type.

While this may seem to argue against bothering with constitutional typing at all, the advantages of understanding our own constitutional tendencies are profound. Such an understanding can help us to appreciate and celebrate our own original energy and can go a long way to helping us accept parts of ourselves we have considered flaws, parts we might have felt inclined to hide or deny. Moreover, using the curious meridians without any sense of constitutional type is a bit like putting up a sail without bothering to match the sail to the boat.

The main advantages of using these meridians are the small number of needles involved and their general applicability to complex situations. A combination of curious and primary meridians will often produce a simple, elegant approach to DIA because the number of needles can be minimized. One specific curious meridian, the *Chong Mai* (see chapter 8, The Chakras), being the central energetic pillar, taps directly into the *mingmen* (Gate of Life) and has more potential than most to activate the *kundalini*. Because the *Chong Mai* energetically fuels all the other circuits, including the other curious meridians, opening it can open up the entire energy system of the body with a single needle. Such an approach can be incredibly powerful if used at the right moment — so, for those who want to get really simple, Spleen–4 is perhaps the only point anyone actually needs to know. Opening the *Chong Mai* can be much like just throwing up the biggest sail available and letting the boat go in whatever direction the wind wants to take it. Of course, you need to be careful you are not in a hurricane before you hoist the sail.

YIN TUINA

For people with long-term pain, blood stagnation or other chronic condition of long-standing such as Parkinson's disease, multiple sclerosis or Reflex Sympathetic Dystrophy, a more gentle approach is usually required. *Tuina* is Chinese therapeutic massage. Most people are familiar with the yang form, since it resembles an ordinary Swedish massage with hands-on contact of variable intensity. Yin tuina, however, is completely different and less well known.

Yin tuina uses very light or no contact with little or no visible movement, rather like Reiki or Therapeutic Touch. For people who cannot tolerate needles at all, sometimes simply putting hands on the painful areas, or even holding the hands an inch or two away from the skin can gradually soften and enliven areas of long-standing pain or dissociation. Yin tuina demands patience, the ability to sense subtle cues from the energy field and great persistence. In cases of long-term dissociation, this extremely gentle, attentive, non-invasive approach can sometimes be the only acceptable way to interact, to develop trust and rapport, and attract consciousness back to dissociated areas.

NOT TREATMENT BUT CATALYST

It cannot be emphasized enough that in DIA, acupuncture needling is not a treatment but a *catalyzing event*. Further, a needle can facilitate movement into the unknown only if we truly wish to go there. Intention is key. Without intention and without a measure of trust, needling itself may not do very much. It is clear intent that gets us into the void. So when signs of transition arise — such as increased breathing, sweating, dizziness, abreaction and unusual movement

— we should resist the temptation to interpret these experiences negatively and realize instead that we are on the threshold of the unknown.

At this threshold we have a choice. We can get frightened, pull out the needles and postpone the encounter until another day, or galvanize our intent and move forward into the unknown. In my experience the void is where healing is, where hidden mystery (healing) begins to answer manifest mystery (pain) — where those blocks that prevent our bodies, minds and spirits from regaining their innate health begin to speak.

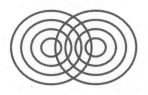

CHAPTER 18

CANCER AND THE DEATH MYSTERY

If a disease is on a terminating or downhill course, a transformational process is manifesting. The obvious transformation toward which that person is heading is physical death, but there may also be a transformation on this side, in the living. . . . One way or another, through cure or death, it resolves the symptoms and the disease.
— W. Brugh Joy

*H*olistic philosophy can have an extraordinary impact in the journeys of those facing life-threatening illnesses such as cancer. Self-limiting conditions and acute problems can be addressed with less than perfect integrity, but most common cancers — breast, colon, lung, prostate — bring our mortality itself into sharp relief and require our whole and concentrated attention.

A MEDITATION ON DEATH

Somewhere in the National Gallery in London, England is a remarkable painting of a Benedictine monk in fervent contemplation of the skull he holds in his hands. Wandering in the gallery, I was spellbound by this painting which spoke so eloquently of the mysteries of death, transformation and transcendence, and the intensity of our relationship with them.

Many religious traditions emphasize the benefits of a meditation on death. Some recommend that we educate our lust by visualizing the decay and putrefaction of the desired one's body after death; others suggest meditating through the night in a graveyard until our fear of death is dissipated. Terminal cancer patients can feel forced to similar meditations — except that the beloved body is their own and the graveyard reeking of fearsome death is an internal one. Yet those who can bear the looming face of their own death in their soul's darkest hour may find in it a wisdom and a clarity not available to most.

Life-threatening cancers ask us to walk beside our own death. Not only that, they ask that we learn to face another sort of unknown, for in both their progress and in their mysterious remissions, they lie outside rational enquiry. One might therefore hope the conundrums they pose — like Zen's teaching koans — might spur an exploration of the supra-rational in the medical establishment but, instead, cancer's puzzles seem only to engender more and more bizarre and furious attempts to fight this supposed alien in our midst. Burgeoning oncology departments, billions spent on genetic research, an out-of-control vitamin and supplement industry, frustrated rhetoric at cancer conferences and an overwhelming reliance on mutilating surgery: it is a frenzied picture. Still, the enormous apparatus we invoke seems too often utterly helpless against an enemy we cannot seem to understand no matter how brightly we illuminate it.

A TRANSFORMATIONAL IMPERATIVE

But what if cancer is not really an enemy at all but rather a messenger calling us to the kind of transformation of consciousness available only through our intense, inborn fear of death? Is such a suggestion an absurd denial of the obvious, or an affirmation of wholeness? Let us consider. The mind imposes a psychic division: *self* (normal cells) and *not-self* (cancer cells). But, seen as an energy field, both normal cells and cancer cells are self. And, in fact, as far as we know, despite the ongoing search for infectious or environmental factors, in most cancers there is no specific external agent, no single virus or bacteria we can pinpoint that might be causing cells to go awry. So although an external carcinogen may well trigger cancer in some, it has no effect on others.

At the end of the day, then, it seems an illness that arises out of no other thing than ourselves. Yet when cancer is discovered in us, we feel invaded. And it can seem harsh medicine to appear to deny the existence of a disease that has a propensity to kill. For this reason, and all it implies, I have always hesitated to work with cancer patients. Despite this, some have found their way to our clinic and a few have had extraordinary experiences there, two of which I would like to relate. Before I do, though, I want to talk a bit more about field theory as it might pertain to cancer.

CONTAINMENT/DISSOCIATION IN CANCER

In contrast to regional pain syndromes, we have seen in multiple personality disorder that compartmentalization need not be somatically limited. The complex, superimposed wave patterns of vibrational fields may affect every part of the body — and beyond — simultaneously. Psychosomatic compartments might therefore be restricted somatically, or they might not. But what about more complex, non-local phenomena? Theoretically, such phenomena could arise when a cell, or group of cells, responds to an alternate vibrational generator with a different organizing frequency; or alternately, if a group of cells somehow becomes de-tuned, and fails to respond to any organizing frequency whatsoever.

In other words, what if a group of cells through stress, pollution, infection, deterioration and the many other insults life offers lost their ability to attune to the body's central vibrational generator, the Heart? These cells might become disorganized, out of control — they might start looking and acting like cancer cells. In fact, cancer may be a unique expression of the ego's compartmentalization strategies, in which contained and dissociated energies break through the containment barriers to spread throughout the body.[1] Since these energies have likely been out of attunement with our field frequency for many years, cancer spreads as if it is listening to the beat of a different drummer, or perhaps not listening to any drummer at all. No wonder cancer appears an alien force. The cancer cells might represent energies long disowned, rejected and projected by the ego. To accept cancer as self, rather than rejecting it and demonizing it as not-self, then, means the destruction of some of the ego's dearest illusions.

The idea that cancer might reflect a field disturbance is not new. Many years ago Harold Saxon Burr intuited that cancer occurred as a disturbance in the energy field long before it manifested as a pathology, and further understood that if the disturbed energies could be harmonized, the disease process might on occasion be arrested.

A wealth of anecdotal evidence from all cultures across all times suggests that alterations in the field can bring about immediate and radical changes in the physical body. The super-human strength of a mother lifting a car to release her trapped child, patients leaving their wheelchairs, using muscles wasted by disease to run out of burning buildings, and spontaneous remissions in terminal cancers all exceed rational explanation.

---

1   I have alluded to some of these strategies in chapter 3, Qi and Blood Stagnation, with specific reference to myofascial tension patterns in the body.

A simple energetic explanation — based on coherence theory — however, can provide some understanding. Coherence theory suggests that perhaps such emergencies release enough energy to bridge our psychic splits, producing a coherence sufficient to these extraordinary abilities. And spontaneous remissions may in fact be vivid expressions of a more lasting bridging as the result of a profound inner transformational process.

THE STATE OF THE FIELD IN CANCER

To further understand the overall state of the energy field in cancer, let us look more closely at the characteristics of the cancer cell. First, it is de-differentiated — that is, it has reverted to a more primitive state; in addition, it replicates quickly compared to most other cells; it appears unregulated in its activity; it spreads beyond organ boundaries; and it acts as if disconnected from the body's organizing principle — the Heart's vibrational rhythms from which the body's energy field gets its coherence.

So, if vibrational coherence were re-established, is it unreasonable to suppose that the disconnected cells might re-differentiate and re-attune to the larger whole? And similarly, is it unreasonable to suppose that the myriad random cancer cells that tend to relocate throughout the body — the metastases — might be reintegrated? If so, then re-establishing coherence might be a more creative approach to the puzzle cancer poses than our present one, in which we focus on attacking tangible malignancies with drugs, surgery and radiotherapy.

One difficulty with these approaches is that the microscopic metastases are frustratingly beyond the reach of chemo- or radiotherapy. Conventional cancer therapy is basically a warfare model. Indeed, the diagnosis of cancer generates such fear (and sometimes self-loathing) that many people react in panic. Unfortunately, once that kind of unreasoning fear sets in, every decision, every move, every strategy generates a dissonance that can only increase the fragmentation of our energy field.

One way out of this dilemma is to stop trying to *treat* cancer at all, and instead set an intention to move toward symptoms while in an altered state of consciousness, in order to learn what they have to tell us. In doing so, we can shift attention from the terror of the diagnosis to the possibility of transformation. I hope the following two stories, which prove nothing in particular in themselves, will show what can come out of such an approach.

℞ *BARB*: PAROTID CANCER

Barb was a tall, fragile-looking woman of fifty-five who had developed a rare malignant parotid gland tumour — perhaps, she thought, because her neck had been irradiated when she was a small child —which had metastasized to her lungs. Barb came to us not to explore her cancer but rather because of an incapacitating pain in her back and right foot that her physicians had not been able to attribute to the tumour.

Despite the apparent distinction between her foot and back pain and her parotid tumour, I felt there was little point in avoiding the issue of her probable death from her cancer as it was so clearly a factor in her situation. So during our first meeting, I looked her in the eye and emphasized the importance of exploring her deepest fears without reservation.

'You know Barb, cancer involves the death mystery and if you really want to deal with this pain, you are going to have to look directly into that mystery until it holds no more fear for you.'

'I'm not sure I know what you mean,' she replied, a little nervously.

'Those of us who have not been diagnosed with life-threatening conditions can deny our fear of death — we may not even be fully conscious of it yet,' I ventured. 'But this cancer has pushed it right in your face. . . . Although as human beings — able to generalize from what we see of other human beings' lives — we all know we will die, we normally face this fact in our own time, in our own way. If cancer asks us to confront it before we are ready, however, then disfiguring surgeries, chemotherapy and radiotherapy in the name of 'life' can become a strange sort of self-destructive cloak to what we cannot bear to imagine. But if we are willing to feel our fear and become curious about our death, we have a chance of discovering something much less frightening than we might have expected.

'That being the case, you could choose to go right into the psychic experience of dying and see what happens. . . . It's easier said than done, of course. . . .' I added, almost as an afterthought, watching her expression. 'Not the least because it is a lonely experience. You see, none of us have yet been where you are. . . .'

'Fair enough,' she replied. 'But I'm not sure I understand what you're getting at. I still don't know what you mean by the death mystery.'

'I'm not sure I do either,' I admitted. 'It's amazing how we all try to avoid understanding it. People will allow themselves to be mutilated when they have cancer, without considering that the surgery is itself a kind of death. And one that, tragically, holds little promise of transformation. But when fear takes hold, it's easy to lose balance. . . .'

We chatted a little more and eventually Barb seemed to see that something different was being offered her and expressed a willingness to give it a try. Her life, she told me, was not worth living as it was. After her first acupuncture session, however, the pain in her back and leg intensified so much that, two hours later, she could hardly sit still. Being reluctant to reach for her pain-killers, she took

me aside and asked if there was anything I could do. Not knowing
what else to suggest, I asked her whether she wanted to lie down
and take the opportunity to go deeper into the experience.

And that is when something quite extraordinary happened.
Barb cried for a few minutes, expressing her pain, then her breathing deepened and slowed until it seemed she was hardly breathing
at all. This went on for what seemed an eternity — perhaps three
or four minutes. As she emerged from this limbo, she explained
what had been going on.

'You know,' she said '. . . life is pain and death is nothing. And
I'm caught in the middle with nowhere to go.'

I was struck by the tone of this statement. It was clear that it was
spoken from her heart and that what she expressed was a core belief. I
sensed an opening. Caught in an irresolvable dilemma, Barb's existential pain had been so amplified by her physical pain that she could
not let go into either. A resolution was crucial and the opportunity
was here and now, while she was so open to her own truth.

As gently as possible, I threw out an idea. 'You know, Barb,
death is part of our lives every day. Parts of us are dying every
moment that we live; everything around us is both living and dying at once. If you look at it this way, the idea of death may seem
like nothing, but the truth is we just don't know. Death is an unknown, that's all, and an unknown is not necessarily the same as
nothing. And if death is not necessarily nothing, then in the same
way, life might not necessarily be pain either.'

It did not seem like much but the impact was extraordinary. A
chord was struck, a light came on in Barb's eyes and she visibly relaxed, drifting once more into the stillness of the void out of which
had come her Heart statement. As I watched her remarkably slow
breathing, I wondered how consciously she had returned to that
place which so closely resembled death. When she came back

again, five minutes later, the pain that had bothered her for six months was gone.

LACK OF COHERENCE

Of course this story is not really about cancer at all. It simply illustrates one woman's grappling with her fear of the unknowable — death — which had begun to manifest as a fear of that other unknowable — life. Whenever we feel caught in the middle as she did, with no escape, it is because a core belief is threatened. The ego is structured around these core beliefs, which it feels it cannot relinquish.

In life-threatening situations, when the ego realizes that death is near — that it is doomed whatever path it chooses — the door is paradoxically open to transformative visions of life, self and death. Barb knew there was no way out and, at the moment of transformation, all of us in the room could feel her energy field palpably shift toward coherence. And it seemed that in that moment, her pain dissolved.

Before she left us, Barb took me aside and almost whispered, 'You know, when I came here, there was a wall between me and somewhere I desperately wanted to be. Now that wall is gone.'

℞ DONNA: BREAST CANCER

Donna was forty-one years old and had metastatic breast cancer when she came to our residential clinic. She had been treated with a mastectomy, adjuvant chemotherapy and radiotherapy but a few months before coming to see us her cancer had recurred. Like Barb, she had come to the clinic for her pain rather than her cancer. Although in her case, her physicians had inferred the pain was in fact due to her disease, it was keeping her awake at night and her insomnia was draining her energy, leaving her exhausted, and it was this that she wanted to address at our clinic.

Once again, it seemed clear that the issue of the death mystery could not be ignored. So, I looked Donna in the eye and came directly to the point. 'You do realize that the five-year survival for this illness is pretty close to zero, which means that there is no intervention here or anywhere else that can promise you much?'

'Yes, I do,' she replied. 'I'm not looking for miracles. . . . I just feel there's something else, something missing. . . . After reading your book, I really want to try . . . going into the void.'

We talked about fear and about death and I urged her to focus her exploration on her feelings around dying rather than attempt to get relief from her symptoms or to prolong her life.

'Does that mean I shouldn't hope for my pain to be a little better after a session of DIA?'

'I'm afraid it means you shouldn't hope for anything in particular,' I replied. 'Unfortunately, you can expect nothing, no one can expect anything from their void experience — we have to go in without expectations because expectation colours the experience and its outcome. It shifts it away from integration and wholeness and inhibits the coherence we're looking for.'

A little disappointed, Donna entered the void and as she did so the fear and tension she was holding began to release. She shook like a hummingbird. The shaking started in her feet, moved up her legs and eventually erupted from her mouth in song. And the extraordinary thing was that after the session she *was* pain-free — as she had hoped — and slept as she had not slept in months.

It turned out that the singing that had erupted from her was not incidental. Over the course of the week's residence, she sang more and more, the sounds coming from deeper and deeper in her body so that by the end of the program she sounded like a shaman in a deep trance. Her songs and chanting resonated through her body and we could almost see sound reverberating up her spine.

But more was yet to come. About a month after she returned home, Donna's abdomen swelled up with fluid and cancer cells, which is usually a pretty bad sign. The fluid was aspirated as a palliative measure with the expectation it would recur but, strangely, the fluid did not re-accumulate and her cancer subsequently went into remission.

Six months later and still in good health, Donna returned to the clinic for a few more DIA sessions. In one of them, she disappeared into the far reaches of the void. On her return, she described a journey that had ended in a large mountainous valley, strewn with grasses, rocks and a few pine trees. An old woman with long, greying hair sat on one of the rocks. She wore boots made from an animal's pelt and had a colourfully decorated shawl draped over her shoulders.

As Donna approached, she noticed the old lady had a kindly face, full of wisdom and love. It seemed natural to sit near her feet, so she did, indicating that she was willing to listen. The old woman told her a number of things: first that all would be well; next, that she had things to do and that she was to get on with them; and that she could return to the valley to visit whenever she wished.

Donna was in the void for no more than ten minutes but when she returned to ordinary consciousness, she said her journey seemed timeless and she had clearly been changed by it. She was calmer and more determined than ever to live.

In the end, Donna's remission was to last more than three years. She restructured her life, fulfilled a number of the things she wanted to do and died peacefully.

A COHERENT FIELD

These remarkable cases suggest to me that cancer, perhaps more than any other illness, has something profound to teach us and furthermore, that that teaching has something to do with facing and transcending our existential fears — our fear of life and our fear of death. It is not that it is not possible to face these issues at other times and in other ways but a terminal diagnosis does present a certain urgency to complete tasks that most of us would rather ignore for as long as possible.

It seems to me that whatever is behind cancer is demanding transformation and will even kill the physical being, if necessary, to complete its process. If we are willing to allow the transformation to take place, to surrender and let the forces re-shape us, then the emerging field coherence may spontaneously reintegrate areas of fragmentation and disease may revert to health.

Indeed, I wonder whether such an astonishing thing did not happen in both these women. After all, in a newly established, strong and coherent field, what can aberrant cells do? They can take advantage of the healing vibration to regain their ordinary nature and function, and become part of a healthy energy system, or, if they are damaged beyond repair, they can leave the system. Under such circumstances, disease finds the tables have turned: now aberrant cells must resonate with the health of the system or die.

TREATMENT OPTION OR ADJUNCT?

Whatever conventional treatments people may choose, cases like these graphically demonstrate the importance of exploring the energetic issues surrounding cancer — in particular the existential angst that manifests as a fear of death and the energetic fragmentation that arises from it. But exploring these issues should not be misconstrued as another treatment option, nor should the exploration be undertaken with the idea that somehow it will prolong our existence.

Wholeness includes both living and dying and when we find a way to come to an acceptance of that then the frantic questions about diagnoses, treatment options and prognoses recede a little. And in the breathing space that ensues, we might be able to go where few go willingly in this life — into the mystery of letting go and of surrender.

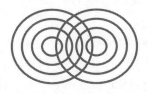

CHAPTER 19

THE WATER–FIRE SECTORS

When pain is accepted for what it is . . . a lesson and a warning,
and deeply looked into and heeded, the separation between pain and
pleasure breaks down, both become experience — painful when
resisted, joyful when accepted.

— Sri Nisargadatta Maharaj

A remarkable feature of constitutional typing is that the same pathology can have very diverse energetic origins; and, vice versa, people of similar constitutional type can manifest completely different symptoms. This only underscores the fundamental tenet of both homeopathy and Chinese medicine that it is the one seeking treatment who is important, rather than whatever symptoms or diagnosis they may be carrying. A conventional diagnosis is often like the tip of an iceberg — an unreliable indication of what lies under the surface.

By way of illustration, let us look at several apparently diverse problems in the Water and Fire sectors — and see how the five element model can guide us to a deeper understanding of the manifestation of various illnesses.

ॐ WATER — *PEARSON*:
REFLEX SYMPATHETIC DYSTROPHY

Pearson was a seventy-four-year-old man with pain in his right leg and foot, which had been diagnosed as Reflex Sympathetic Dystrophy (RSD).[1] Several physicians had told him that he had a deteriorating condition that was irreversible and untreatable. He had tried to learn all he could about his condition but, unfortunately, nothing he found ever promised much hope. Not surprisingly, when I first met him he was frustrated, frightened, angry and depressed.

RSD is a peculiar type of pain syndrome that differs radically from the pain of the more commonly encountered myofascial tension syndromes. It often begins in an extremity after a relatively trivial injury but then never goes away. People with RSD say the pain is excruciating, way beyond what would be expected from the magnitude of the injury, and is often triggered by the lightest touch. Other bizarre symptoms can occur, including temperature changes, abnormal sweating, unusual changes in skin colour, skin thickening, edema (boggy tissue swelling), and skin and muscle atrophy. In advanced cases, the atrophy can progress to immobility, contractures and osteoporosis. In sum, it is a strange and little understood condition.

Pearson actually first noticed pain in his right foot when he was eleven but it was much later in his life — after failed surgery for a foot neuroma — that he was diagnosed with RSD. He had also had surgery on both hands to relieve painful Dupuytren contractures, with mixed results. When I first saw him, both his hands and feet showed evidence of tight and contracted connective tissue. He confirmed this tightness was nothing new.

As we got to know him, Pearson revealed that he had been

---

1   RSD is now known as Complex Regional Pain Syndrome, type 1 (CRPS 1).

adopted as an infant and did not know his biological parents. He began to wonder whether it was this early disruption that could have made him so eager to distinguish himself, to go it alone and to control his life. As an entrepreneur, he had a strong work ethic and made his fortune through single-minded effort and long hours of work. And he had been very successful. But his body and his spirit seemed to have paid a price: his connective tissue had gradually dried out, his skin became dry and withered, his tendons tight, his emotions stunted, as though a quality of dryness pervaded all levels of his physical, mental and emotional body.

Why life stresses should have affected him in this way rather than another was the question. Why was Pearson developing these chronic fibrotic conditions; and what was it about him that led him to keep choosing surgery when it had repeatedly failed to help him?

FIVE ELEMENT DYNAMICS: TAI YANG–WATER

Pearson was likely a Tai Yang–Water constitutional type. The work ethic, the push, push, push like an engine that could not stop, all pointed to Water. He was tightest down the back, legs and under the feet — also consistent with the Water constitutional type. The confusing thing was how the symptoms of skin and tendon dryness fitted into the picture. Five element theory associates dryness with Metal, while tendon or fascia problems are generally associated with Wood.

But let us look at what energies he had difficulty with. The decisions he had made to avoid change and uncertainty (Water) and the difficulty letting go (Metal) pointed to Metal and Water avoidance. The Wood, Fire and Earth sectors were all represented. His creative energy was moving (Wood), he lived his passion (Fire) and had accepted his rewards (Earth).

Letting go, accepting chaos and welcoming transformation

seemed to be the sticking points. When there is no letting go, energy that should move from the Earth phase to the Metal moves instead toward Water. If there is a block there, it moves on toward the Wood sector again, where in Pearson's case, it had added fuel to the pre-existing work ethic.

Pearson had become the engine that could not stop. He suffered the *chaos of resisted surrender* with aridness materializing in his connective tissue. Meantime, because the Water energies needed to soften the tissues were not readily available, his energy impacted in the Wood phase, expressing itself through a combination of overwork, anger and depression.

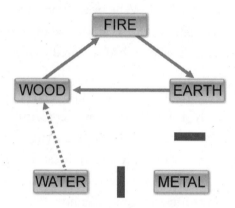

Figure 1: Pearson's energy diversions

WATER'S PERSISTENCE

The path before Pearson was a steep one: to let go and surrender to transformational forces, to open to his pain, to own his feelings and to trust his body again. It was quite a challenge for a seventy-year-old with an attitude but, to his credit, he persevered with an earnestness and commitment one rarely finds outside the Water element. In the end, it was his original energy that saved him.

But it did not happen overnight. When Pearson first came to us, he was reluctant to let anyone touch his foot. Bit by bit, he gradually permitted contact, beginning with gentle holding and gradually progressing to massage and acupuncture. When we started DIA, I noticed that there was pain everywhere, not just in his foot, and that the dryness was similarly present throughout his body. The other foot was sore, the hands were sore where he had had surgery, and the tendons in both feet were tight and sore, and everything was dry.

Progress was slow and protracted but, over two years, Pearson made steady gains. He just kept at it, like a long-distance runner. As time went by, he learned to meditate, mastered the art of restful alertness and the skills of letting go. There was a gradual change in his outlook. His anger melted away, he spent more time in the garden and less time fuming over work issues. His wife noticed he was easier going and more open emotionally. And although there was never a big or sudden change, when we looked back over the time since we first met, the overall shift was incredible.

Pearson still has pain in his feet but he is no longer frightened by it. His disease — once thought to be relentlessly progressive — is no longer progressing. All in all, he is getting better. But most impressive is the enormous change in his attitude. Pearson now laughs and looks forward to tomorrow.

ᚱ FIRE — *DANIELLE*: ULCERATIVE COLITIS

Danielle was a forty-five-year-old woman with ulcerative colitis, who came to us after the stressful experience of a lengthy hospital admission prompted her to consider a different approach to her difficulties.

Danielle's early life was a story of abuse and repression in the name of religious piety. She described her childhood home as a prison where she and her siblings were expected to work from dawn until dusk, rarely allowed off the property, discouraged from outside friendships, beaten regularly for trivial transgressions and humiliated for displaying any interest in the other sex. At the same time, she was sexually abused by two of her older brothers.

At fifteen, during a rare outing, she fell madly in love — a breath of fresh air for a girl suffocating in a straitjacket. But unfortunately, when she invited her new friend home to meet her parents, they promptly banned her from ever seeing the young man again. She was heartbroken and decided never to love again. With her heart betrayed, and sexuality a sin, Danielle had no option but to contain her energy in her middle, a sure recipe for some problem arising in the digestive system.

FIVE ELEMENT DYNAMICS: TAI YANG–FIRE

While the intestinal focus of Danielle's symptoms might have pointed to an Earth or Metal constitutional type, there were so many triggers up and down the back that a Tai Yang (Fire or Water) constitutional type seemed more likely. Moreover, from a five element standpoint, Danielle and Pearson were not so dissimilar. She had the same push-push way of approaching life that is typical of Tai Yang but she was definitely more fiery in nature, the heat perhaps backing up into the intestine. Furthermore, Danielle's early experiences had led her to her own unique energetic diversions. Where Pearson had bypassed Metal and Water, Danielle's energy had primarily bypassed Fire and Water.

Danielle's Heart wound blocked movement into Fire, so her Wood energy had flowed across to Earth, causing tension in the stomach and solar plexus area. From there, letting go was haphazard, a mix of constipation, pencil-thin stools, loose stools and diarrhea.

Then the Water phase, with all its potential energy, would have been very difficult for her to tap into — for the dual reasons of fear and shame — leaving her energy cycling around the stomach and intestines.

OPENING TO PELVIC SHAME

Danielle's entrapment was particularly difficult as it was complicated by the curse of silence and a sexual taboo. As the energies of the pelvis were obviously going to be very important in the healing process, it was with relief and some awe that we noticed Danielle begin to allow more and more pelvic movement as she went deeper into the void. Eventually, she had to get up on her hands and knees to allow the powerful surges to pass through her body, laughing (an expression of Fire) from her belly as she did so. At last, she fell into a deeply relaxed state and had her first normal bowel movement in five years.

The strong waves passing through her pelvis and back provoked much thought and introspection. She understood the significance of the pelvic movements and related it all to the sexual guilt she

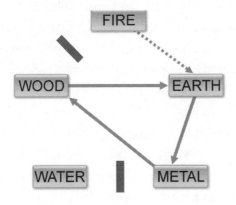

Figure 2: Danielle's energetic diversions

had acquired from her family situation, religious upbringing and broken heart. Gradually she came to realize that her body, far from betraying her, was the container for her lost feelings and was calling her back home. Further, the recognition of her parents' betrayal allowed her to better understand her current relationship difficulties.

Meanwhile, Danielle learned how to meditate and relax. Later, she introduced a dynamic meditation into her daily routine, in which she allowed herself to explore the forbidden pelvic movements and began the difficult process of healing the *Chong Mai* split. Her bowel movements reverted to normal and, for a while at least, she has been able to stop most of her medications. Whether she can maintain these improvements remains to be seen, since so much depends on her being more present in her body and disciplined with her daily routine.

☞ WATER — *JOYCE*: MULTIPLE SCLEROSIS, OSTEOPOROSIS & COLITIS

Joyce was a thirty-one-year-old woman who came to us with three different diagnoses: multiple sclerosis, colitis and osteoporosis. Her main complaints were leg weakness and numbness, mainly in her right leg, which caused her to limp and occasionally to trip or fall. She considered herself weak, fragile and sickly and presented such a convincing image of frailty I at first wondered if we could work with her at all.

Oddly, in contrast to her apparent frailty, the pulse at Joyce's wrist turned out to be strong and vibrant. I recall wondering whether the dissonance between her presentation and pulse might indicate she was more robust than she looked; and, if that were so, that perhaps her difficulties stemmed from a considerable mind/body dissociation.

FIVE ELEMENT DYNAMICS: SHAO YIN–WATER

I felt intuitively that Joyce was a Water constitutional type because of the aura of fear in her language and behaviour — although she was probably more a Shao Yin (Kidney) type than Tai Yang like Danielle or Pearson. Such people can become quite adept at dissociation as a way of not feeling their existential angst. Indeed, this was probably at the root of the weakness in her legs, which in time came to be diagnosed as a neurological disease. But without awareness of this dynamic, she really had no way of tapping into her own inner healer.

Joyce's strong pulse was indeed a harbinger of things to come: she was anything but frail. Further, she was aware of her tendency to dissociate and had made a decision to end it before she came to see us. The Shao Yin–Water constitutional type often responds to moxa, and true to form, moxa and needles on the ankle Water points induced a fine vibration in her, which she at first found terrifying but later related to as ecstatic.

Further, as she surrendered to the process, she started kicking her legs in a way that she had previously thought impossible. As the experience deepened yet further, she oscillated between ecstasy and

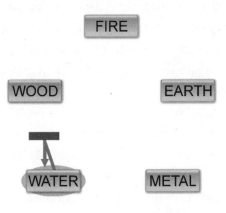

Figure 3: Joyce's energetic diversions

terror until she was able to feel that the two were actually energetically equivalent. At some point, it suddenly dawned on her that her habit of mental interpretation — rather than simply feeling her angst without judgement — was what prompted her to dissociate.

Joyce's intuition of the deeper root of her illness led to a transformation, one that allowed her to begin to trust her body again. Such transformations can be dramatic to behold at the time of their unfolding but they have to be maintained, and of course it is one thing to achieve a shift in attitude, quite another to reverse an illness that has long since manifested on a material level. A regular body-centred meditative practice — such as tai chi — can be a big help in this regard. The body-befriending process has to be practised and maintained over the long haul or else the tendency to fall back into old patterns can be too hard to resist.

♌ FIRE — *NIGEL*: HEART DYSRHYTHMIA

Nigel was a fifty-five-year-old man who came to deal with his chronic anxiety, smoking addiction and periodic attacks of tachycardia (rapid heart rate). On occasion, these attacks had been nearly fatal and had landed him in more than one coronary unit over time. Nigel was outwardly self-confident: his conversation was assertive verging on bombastic and his conduct was calculated to give the impression of a carefree, high-spirited personality. However, he also had a short fuse, was quick to anger and on occasions became bellicose and abusive with the smallest slight or apparent criticism.

Nigel had high shoulders, suggesting a tension band around his chest, and simply exuded heat from his head, chest and hands. During DIA, sometimes with only one or two points on the Water/ Fire axis, he would erupt into torrential shouts and insults, which would stop as quickly as they began, leaving him calm, controlled and back to his usual self. After these sessions, if his heart rate had been high beforehand, it would fall back to normal.

FIVE ELEMENT DYNAMICS: SHAO YIN–FIRE

From a five element perspective, Nigel was probably a Shao Yin (Heart)–Fire type, who tended to accumulate too much heat in the heart area, likely as a result of constantly resisting fully feeling the vulnerability of his Fire energies. Consequently he needed repeated cooling down but the Water sector, where cooling could take place, was equally off limits because the transformational Water energies would have forced an encounter with a similar vulnerability.

Day to day, it was clear, Nigel was much more comfortable cycling around the Wood-Earth-Metal energies (being creative, receiving the fruits of his creativity, letting go and moving on), always taking care not to stray too close to the deep sadness and sense of betrayal that is very much part of the Fire experience. This strategy worked quite well much of the time but if a block in receptivity ever occurred (Earth sector), such as a sense of being slighted, criticized or unacknowledged, then the heat would back up into the Fire sector, giving rise to tyrannical outbursts, a rhythm disturbance in his heart and an intense desire to smoke or take drugs. Ironically, many of the drugs he liked to use, such as nicotine or cocaine, although they calmed his anxiety in the moment, actually aggravated his condition over the long term.

Put simply, as a Shao Yin–Fire, Nigel's difficulty was that the idea of allowing a full experience of his original energy looked too much like Heart-break to be something he could consider approaching, let alone embracing. Unfortunately, the constant resistance to *feeling* the Heart-break was pushing people away, inducing self-destructive habits and even forcing a *literal* heart-break through potentially life-threatening rhythm disturbances. And while it was not difficult

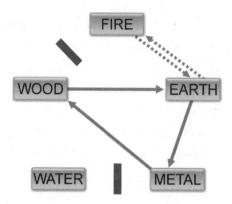

Figure 4: Nigel's energy diversions

to relieve his excess heat with acupuncture, such an approach was only a short-term solution. A longer-term solution would require Nigel to be more present with and *feel* his broken Heart, so the heat would not accumulate in the first place.

Nigel quickly understood his situation and had every intention to do what he could about it. But, of course, being present with original energy is a lifelong challenge, and our everyday worlds — worlds that we have built more or less consciously to hide from just this energy — tend to work against us at every moment. Here, again, is where the space of meditation can provide us a place and a time outside our daily lives. In this space apart, we can cultivate such presence by opening to the flow of emotion during daily meditation practice. Over time, the integration of these energies into daily life just becomes a natural extension of the practice.

♌ WATER — *LEO*: DEPRESSION & FORGETFULNESS

Leo was a fifty-four-year-old long-term meditator with chronic depression who feared that his increasing forgetfulness was a harbinger of early Alzheimer's. Not one to take medications for any reason, he was more drawn to exploring his depression through alternative approaches such as DIA. At the outset, he seemed like a Metal constitutional type: he had the classic indicators of feeling disconnected from life and searching for something intangible. However, the DIA experience seemed to suggest something different, as there was major tension and holding in the back Tai Yang area, the Water sector.

As we got to know him, the most significant thing about Leo seemed to be the complete lack of flow in his life. He had not managed to find a satisfying creative outlet, could not receive the gifts that had come his way and was unable to let go of petty resentments. He knew that a change was needed but his only notion of how to go about achieving it was through effort and, so far, that had not worked. He was frustrated in his job, his family life, his sex life, and had little in the way of an outlet apart from exercise, which he pursued obsessively.

FIVE ELEMENT DYNAMICS: TAI YANG–WATER

If Water were Leo's constitutional type, then his active, push-push exercise routine suggested he was more Tai Yang than Shao Yin. Either way, it seemed he had just not found a way to mobilize his inner potential and bring it creatively through the Wood sector. As it was, with nowhere else to go, his Water energy got diverted into Fire where it manifested as excessive exercise and a big sex drive.

Leo recognized he was wasting his potential but had no idea how to turn things around and merely felt compelled to exercise more and more. Perhaps because this was not really his passion, the fruits of such efforts were largely unhappy: long hours of exercise distanced him from his family and left him fatigued, so he could not really respond to the love offered him. As his energy was blocked from moving on to the Earth sector, it got diverted to

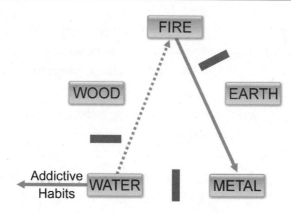

Figure 5: Leo's energetic diversions

Metal, where it manifested as chronic depression. Meantime, his addictive habits were gradually draining his essence.

I guessed that Leo's extreme exercise regime was probably accomplished by some mind/body dissociation, which might actually have been stabilized by his long years of meditation. This hunch was confirmed when he told me that he sensed his meditations, while engendering calm, were mostly cerebral and left him with a feeling that he was simply covering something over.

Although Leo only had two DIA sessions, they were sufficient to reveal the source of his angst and also suggested what he might do about it. Leo saw that he could choose to inhabit his body, stop using exercise, sex and even meditation addictively, stay present with his angst and find a way to express the energy more creatively (i.e., to actively engage the Wood sector). A full mind-body encounter using dynamic meditation could be very helpful in mobilizing his sexual energy, bringing it up into the body and opening his Heart chakra. At the very least, if Leo were to fully inhabit his body and feel the full force of his angst rather than running from it, his fear of impending Alzheimer's would almost certainly recede.

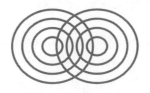

CHAPTER 20

THE WOOD–FIRE SECTORS

There comes a time in a man's life when to get where he has to go —
if there are no doors or windows — he walks through a wall.

— Bernard Malamud

*N*ow, with the help of a few more vignettes, let us look at the Wood and Fire continuum, which, you may recall from earlier chapters, spans the energies of expansion and creativity (Wood), to the spontaneous expression of being fully in the moment (Fire) and involves the Jue Yin and Shao Yang axes.

☿ WOOD — *NICK*: BACK PAIN

Nick was a forty-five-year-old man who came to us with chronic low back and leg pain from a serious car accident some five years previously. Perhaps because of poor experiences with therapy in the past, he was very ambivalent about DIA and voiced confusion about doing any hands-on interaction. As an expression of this ambivalence, for several days after he arrived he would come and stand at the door of the acupuncture room hesitating to come in, as if immobilized by a mysterious force. We did not try to push him at all, letting him take his own time to settle into the program and begin to trust us. It turned out to be the right approach because after he had one particularly sleepless night of tossing and turning, something shifted and he became keen to take a dive into the void.

Nick turned out to be highly sensitive to acupuncture, requiring minimal stimulation to initiate myoclonic activity in his legs. As a result, he had good releases with every session, which in turn motivated him to go deeper, and to explore the idea of physically moving toward his pain — that is, letting his body move spontaneously and adopt different positions on the basis of intuition.

With this kind of intention in place, Nick started expressing his long-held frustration through shouting and movement. During one session in which he began arching his back, I got my feet into his back and pulled back on his legs. Suddenly there was a loud pop as a subtle adjustment took place. In another session, he started shaking everywhere to such a degree that several people had the impression there was a cold wind in the room — particularly coming off his feet. After this experience, he was pain-free for the first time in years.

FIVE ELEMENT DYNAMICS: SHAO YANG–WOOD

From a five element perspective, although Nick's initial fearfulness might have suggested a Water constitutional type, his ambivalence, rage, hip pain and the presence of Wind all pointed more to Shao Yang–Wood.

Prior to his injury, Nick had been functioning adequately both at work and at home, receiving the fruits of his actions and generally cycling successfully around the Wood-Fire-Earth sectors. But, being a Wood, he likely never allowed himself to feel the full force of his creative energy. So, although he was functioning adequately, he probably had much more innate potential than he was willing to admit, and was storing much of this untapped energy in his body as tension.

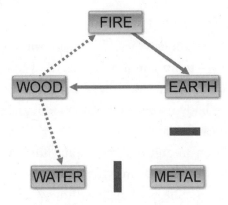

Figure 1: Nick's energy diversions

Such a situation is energetically precarious because, without deliberate cultivation, most people do not have conscious access to the Metal and Water sectors (representing the skills of letting go and transformation), leaving few options should tensions build up to the point of becoming symptomatic. So when the accident came along, things changed dramatically. When he became unable to work, access to the Fire and Earth sectors was blocked and Nick's energies had nowhere to go other than to stagnate as pain in his low back and legs. Further, backed-up energy in the Wood sector left him frustrated and indecisive; and, in the Water sector, fearful.

Nick's energetic potential became apparent the moment he entered the void and surrendered to the wind-like energy moving through him. Although his present focus is necessarily on how to access this experience at will so he can be pain-free, the challenge in the long run will be for him to find a way to channel the energy more creatively so that it does not back up in the first place. This will likely require a commitment to a regular dynamic meditation routine, while at the same time keeping his eyes open for any creative openings that might fire his passion and make him more excited about life.

ঽ WOOD — *JANET*: LUPUS

Janet was a twenty-four-year-old woman with Systemic Lupus Erythematosus — more commonly known as SLE, or lupus — a debilitating condition in which the body makes antibodies against itself, attacking body tissues such as the kidneys and joints. It is a condition that can be fatal.

Janet had been in and out of hospital for several years and, when we saw her, was being treated with various immune-suppressing drugs. She was anxious, fidgety and paranoid, suffered from nightmares and had frequent suicidal thoughts. Janet had had an emotionally restrictive upbringing in a deeply religious family and had experienced several years of physical and sexual abuse from a trusted member of the family. So underneath the fear she was justifiably angry.

FIVE ELEMENT DYNAMICS: JUE YIN–WOOD

Initial circuit testing pointed to a Wood constitutional type, which seemed to make sense given that that element is often the source of internal and external conflict. And, given the predominance of anxiety and timidity, she was probably Jue Yin rather than Shao Yang. In any case, being Wood she was likely unwilling and probably unable to feel the full force of her rage, which would have put her in conflict with the rules of conduct she had learned from her upbringing. Further, a conflict in the mind can very well express itself in the body. Or to be more precise, SLE might well have been a material manifestation of her inner state — a helpless and self-destructive war against her very life force, which was an internalized version of the struggle against her instincts that her upbringing had imposed on her. Whatever its history, the end of this psychic war could not come too soon.

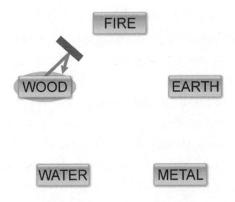

Figure 2: Janet's energy diversions

Janet turned out to be well primed. All she needed from us was a little support. When we let her know that we respected and acknowledged her feelings of rage and injustice, that they were acceptable and understandable, we found her more than willing to express them. In her very first session, with very little stimulation, she let loose a torrent of rage using language that would have made a rap musician blush. As sounds of murderous anger and vilification came pouring forth, it became increasingly clear to all present, including Janet, how painful it must have been to hold these feelings inside for so long.

Janet's initial progress was quite astonishing. Almost overnight she turned from an anxious, panicky, frightened person into the picture of calmness and strength. Her pain had brought her to an unburdening and her cries of rage and sorrow had opened a vital well of compassion for herself, to which she had had no access before this moment.

Whether Janet can maintain her gains will depend on how bravely she can use her new discipline of meditation to contact, get to know and learn to honour her original energy. Her commitment to herself was high when she left us and she understood the tremendous importance of respect, curiosity, courage and gentleness in the long road back to original self.

ઋ FIRE — *TRUDY*: RELATIONSHIP DIFFICULTIES

Trudy was a thirty-five-year-old woman who came to us with heavy periods, menstrual pain and migraine headaches. She was a high-energy type who always seemed happy and outgoing. Trudy liked to try new things. It was her style to try anything and everything. On the other hand, she was disinclined to stick with anything for long, particularly if results were not instantaneous. She told us she had been through two marriages, changed jobs fairly frequently and broke off with any boyfriends who displayed serious interest. She seemed unable to make any kind of long-term commitment to anything or anyone, arguing that the thing she cherished most was her freedom.

Trudy's up-front, cheerful disposition pointed to a Fire constitutional type but it turned out that she was not always as happy as she liked to appear. Happiness was the face she wanted to project to the world; sometimes, however, it was merely a mask — there to cover up the sadness of unfulfilled dreams.

Although her self-image was all about freedom, Trudy was discovering that she was in fact anything but free. Her inability to hold a steady job meant she was always in financial trouble; and her reluctance to make commitments meant she did not have the kinds of relationships she said she wanted. And she was aware that her biological clock was ticking — considering her physical symptoms, it seemed likely that she might soon lose her opportunity to have biological children. In other words, she was beginning to see how fragile her freedoms were. Her trouble was that, like so many of us, she seemed incapable of translating her understanding into action.

FIVE ELEMENT DYNAMICS: JUE YIN–FIRE

Acupressure examination revealed many trigger points in the upper chest, back and shoulders, indicating a significant upper body tension band — perhaps to protect her Heart from the terror a committed relationship might bring. Such a band can be typical of the Pericardium (Heart Protector) or Jue Yin–Fire constitutional type. Meantime, the menstrual pain pointed to significant stagnation of energy in the pelvis.

So it was a safe bet she could not feel the full force of the Fire element. But in addition, she clearly had trouble receiving what relationships had to offer — which meant she had trouble in the Earth sector. So her energy was probably forced into the Wood, Water and Metal sectors, into the areas of creative or directed energy, of letting go and transformation.

Trudy had little trouble letting go. On the contrary, she was always letting go and moving on, imagining that such movement represented freedom and change. The predictable cycle of changing domiciles, jobs, boyfriends and so on, she began to realize, represented only the appearance of transformation. Real transformation, of course, is an internal process that changes the way we deal with

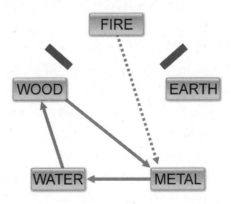

Figure 3: Trudy's energy diversions

our original energy, so that we can become more present with what is.

Interactive bodywork revealed the extent of her fear and un-happiness. A seemingly endless torrent of deep sadness and terror flooded from deep inside her and, in her amazement at meeting herself this way, she began to see that her desire to be free was just a mask for a deep fear of experiencing the full vulnerability of liv-ing from her Heart. As of this writing, Trudy has begun what she hopes is going to be a long-term relationship. She is understand-ably terrified.

℞ FIRE — *GOTTFRIED*: HEPATITIS-C

Gottfried was a forty-five-year-old man who had contracted hepatitis-C after receiving a contaminated blood transfusion. He had been told that his disease would slowly progress until he went into liver failure. As he recalled his experiences, he could scarcely refrain from exploding with anger and his rage was tinged with the bitterness of having been betrayed by a system that was sup-posed to look after him when he was ill.

FIVE ELEMENT DYNAMICS: SHAO YANG–FIRE

When anger is explosive and tinged with bitterness, it points to the Fire end of the Wood-Fire continuum, the so-called Shao Yang–Fire, as opposed to the Shao Yang–Wood, where the anger is often held as a general belligerence. If Gottfried was indeed a Fire constitutional type, he likely had not really found his life's passion (Fire) and had probably always had difficulty with anger, which in the normal course of events he would have sought to contain. Prior to contracting hepatitis, the strategy of containment worked well and he had built an outwardly successful life cycling his energy round elements other than Fire. He had created a successful business as builder/contractor (Wood), received the fruits of his work (Earth) and let go to reinvent himself more than once. But the fundamental transformation of his relationship to the Fire in him had to wait until a situation arose that forced him into the void (Water) and an associated confrontation with his repressed Fire energies. Hepatitis-C was exactly such a situation because it took away the compensatory energy diversions and left him face to face with his original energy.

After contracting hepatitis-C, Gottfried could no longer work, so there was no way to dissipate his energy through his usual workaholic behaviour. He literally backed up into the Fire and Wood sectors and found himself feeling furious and bitter about his predicament.

After circuit-testing confirmed the Shao Yang circuit was active and a couple of sessions had allowed him to familiarize himself with the process, Gottfried decided to dive deep into the void. In one session, he experienced an agonizing, scorching pain that worked its way up the right side of his body, which he later described as a white

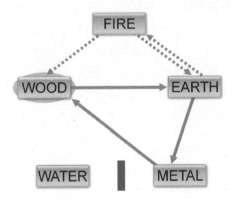

Figure 4: Gottfried's energy diversions

light going into and through his liver, literally cleansing it from the inside. He came out of the session feeling quite different and convinced that his hepatitis was gone.

The transformation was remarkable and noticeable to others. He seemed totally different, calmer, balanced and even joyful — I no longer felt any anger or bitterness around him. I ran into him a year later and he was still feeling well. Of course, whether the biochemical markers for hepatitis-C are actually gone is another matter, since they usually stay around for life, but Gottfried himself was not concerned. His sense of his own health remained vibrant and he was more interested in enjoying every moment that life had to offer him. Meantime, the hiatus of the past year had afforded him an unusual opportunity to explore his passion for painting, something he had never had time for in the past when all his energy was focused on managing his business affairs.

Lest it appear that Gottfried is now simply ignoring his condition, it is worth noting that the sense of betrayal that lies at the root of the Fire experience — though often triggered by an external event (such as contracting hepatitis-C) — might better be understood as a betrayal of the Self by the self through the denial of original energy (in this case the passion of the Fire element). Once that original energy is rediscovered and embraced, the attention focused on the trigger can simply evaporate. In other words, the attitudinal shift associated with transformation is usually not based on denial but lies in an authentic reaffirmation of original nature.

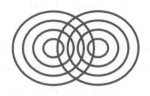

CHAPTER 21

THE EARTH–METAL SECTORS

To see something totally the mind
must be free from all fragmentation
and the very nature of fragmentation
is the centre from which one is looking
— J. Krishnamurti

*I*f you recall from chapter 6, The Six Temperaments, the Earth and Metal sectors have been paired together as
the Yang Ming – Tai Yin energy axes. The Yang Ming axis is concerned with the front of the body and the digestive system (Earth
with Stomach and Spleen, Metal with Large Intestine and Lungs).
The Tai Yin axis is concerned with personal boundaries and spans
the distance between separateness and closeness — Earth types
preferring more closeness, Metal preferring more space.

℞ EARTH — *BONNIE*: FOOD ALLERGIES & TRAUMA
Bonnie was an affable forty-two-year-old woman who, in addition
to chronic pain, complained of fatigue, a sensitive stomach and various food allergies. One day, some three years before we met her,
she had injured her low back and right wrist when a barstool she was
sitting on collapsed. She had made her living as a freelance graphic
designer but was now no longer able to work at the computer and

lost her financial security. Her life started to unravel. Her husband divorced her soon after her accident and over the next few years her kids began to grow up and leave the nest. Eventually, she lost her home and began to spend what money she had left flying around the world in search of an elusive cure.

FIVE ELEMENT DYNAMICS: YANG MING–EARTH

From a five element perspective, Bonnie's cheerful disposition combined with a sensitive stomach pointed to a Yang Ming–Earth constitutional type, and significant Earth source-point tenderness seemed to confirm it. As Earth types are vulnerable to losing their centres, it is interesting that her accident itself was a metaphor for such a loss (a collapsing stool could be understood as a literal loss of centre), as was losing her home and family.

During initial DIA sessions, in which we applied moxa to Earth points, Bonnie repeatedly went into peals of laughter (Fire) before choking and coughing up large quantities of phlegm from her lungs (Metal). Several sessions went this way before her right hand and wrist started to shake. Remarkably, immediately the shaking began the coughing stopped. Subsequently, if she consciously stopped her wrist from shaking, her coughing started up again. It was as if there was a coughing-shaking switch that appeared while she was in the void.

One of the questions we held as we went into sessions was, why was this wrist injury, which might have been shrugged off by others, so devastating, robbing her of her marriage, her livelihood and, finally, her home. At least part of the answer probably lay in Bonnie's constitutional type. Being an Earth with a block in the cycle of giving and receiving (manifesting in food allergies on a physical level), it was a good bet she had difficulty feeling the full force of her Earth energies. She was much more comfortable being creative, having a good time, letting go of things she found irksome and moving on. Prior to her injury, she was able to function quite successfully circulating her energy round the Wood, Fire and Metal sectors. But once her injury barred access to the Wood sector, her energy ended up oscillating between Fire (laughter) and Metal (coughing up phlegm from the lungs).

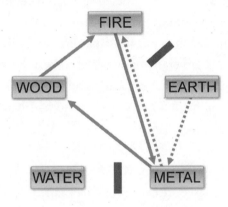

Figure 1: Bonnie's energy diversions

By opening to myoclonic shaking in her wrist and then her arm, Bonnie gave her energy another pathway to move along in place of the repetitive laughing/coughing. Furthermore, the more she let go into the wrist shaking, the more her wrist symptoms improved, which led to a remarkable lifting of her fatigue and depression, as she began to intuit a possible way out of her difficulties.

In the long run, however, although recovery of her wrist function would enable her physically to work again, until her fundamental Earth imbalance is addressed, Bonnie may remain unable to fully receive and process physical, emotional and spiritual nourishment. To reverse her fatigue and slowly deteriorating health, Bonnie will have to work to recapture her lost Earth energies by

nourishing herself with regular meditation, wholesome food, enjoyable exercise and, most importantly, a meaningful home base.

℞ EARTH — *SIMONE*: HEADACHES

Simone was a forty-five-year-old woman of Middle Eastern descent
who came to us with incapacitating headaches. Although they
were frequently classic one-sided migraines, they would occasionally appear in the front of her head and at other times in the back.
It was an unusual and puzzling pattern. A typical migraine is
one-sided and is generally considered to be related to the Wood
element. But in Simone's case, the standard treatment of releasing
the Wood element had not worked: she had baffled more than
one acupuncturist.

FIVE ELEMENT DYNAMICS: TAI YIN–EARTH

Where theory-based interventions had failed, however, exploration from a place of unknowing yielded fruit: an acupressure point
exploration revealed many trigger points in the front zone — up
the legs, over the abdomen, chest, neck and face, indicating significant stagnation in the Earth sector (Tai Yin and Yang Ming).

Given that the acupressure exam made an Earth type a distinct
possibility, Simone's home and family orientation made her more
likely the Tai Yin type. As Simone's story unfolded, it became
apparent that her move to Canada had been a reluctant one, and
even though it had been many years, she still had not come to
terms with her separation from friends and family. Such a wrench
was pretty well guaranteed to put an Earth constitutional type —
for whom home connections are particularly important — out of
balance. However, Simone also had difficulties in other sectors.
She was 'hot above and cold below' and had a Caesarean-section

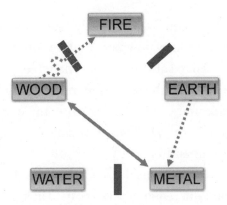

Figure 2: Simone's energy diversions

scar, suggesting stagnation in the pelvis (Water), and had a stressful job she worked at for security rather than passion (lack of Fire). She also tended to manifest a low-level anxiety (Water), which she in turn focused on her headaches.

With difficulties in three energy vectors — Earth, Fire and Water — Simone's natural energy tended to oscillate between Metal and Wood. But she also had a big band of tension around her neck — no doubt aggravated by her phone and computer duties at work — a tight diaphragm (typical of Earth constitutional types) and a tight band in the pelvis. So there were several reasons for excess energy diversion to the head.

Wood congestion probably produced the lateral headaches while the Metal sector was probably congested by a reverse flow up the front Earth zone (reversed because of the pelvis block). The occipital headaches, which were the least frequent, were probably due to the Tai Yang, through the Fire element, acting rather like an overflow channel.

Through experimentation based on mobilizing the Earth energy using moxa on Earth source points and massaging up the leg Tai

Yin (Spleen) meridians, we eventually found a way to release the excess head/neck energy downward. Attention to original energy in this way seemed to shift enough stagnation to facilitate a subsequent release down all the various meridians passing through the neck (front, side and back). Furthermore, the moxa and massage facilitated entry to the void, which permitted Simone to adopt a moving-toward intention.

It was a rewarding series of sessions and although, as of this writing, Simone still requires periodic help in keeping these pathways open, she now understands the genesis of her headaches and, as her Earth constitutional type comes into balance, she feels she will likely become increasingly skilled at releasing them on her own without resorting to drugs. (Ironically, this may also be the moment that her headaches cease to arise.) She plans to find more ways to meet her need for community (Earth) and find work that is more satisfying (Fire), at which point I can imagine she might even find herself lastingly headache-free.

℞ METAL — *CAROL*:

WHOLE-BODY STIFFNESS & ACHING

Carol was a sixty-four-year-old woman who came to us with generalized muscular aching and rigidity, a stiff neck, hips and back, which she felt was being aggravated by family stresses (she had had more than her fair share of hard-to-fledge kids and aging parents) that left her feeling chronically tense and anxious. No stranger to therapy, she had done years of counselling but had gradually become so stiff that she now had to do an hour of yoga every morning just to get herself limbered up for the day. She volunteered that she felt she lived in her head and wanted to get out of what she called her 'cerebral mode'.

FIVE ELEMENT DYNAMICS: YANG MING–METAL

Carol had trigger points all down her sides, on her shoulder tips and on her hips, which seemed to point to a Wood constitutional type. However, when she participated in DIA, using a moving-toward intent while we did some circuit testing, she opened wave upon wave of grief — indicating she was more than likely a Metal.

If Carol was indeed Metal, her active disposition and rigidity pointed to the Yang Ming type. But whether yang or yin, she would have had difficulty feeling the full force of her grief, so that her Earth energy would have diverted to the Water sector, leaving her rigid with resistance to the chaos of surrender. Stiffness and difficulty with real transformation were the result of her inability to allow the necessary letting go. In some respects her focus on cognitive therapy had even been a hindrance, as she was beginning to intuit, absorbing her time and energy in a distorted form of creative expression — an anxious problem-solving without any real passion or fruition. This lack of exuberance (Fire) may have diverted her Wood energy to her Earth sector, where it manifested outwardly as family problems.

After engaging her original Metal energy and releasing some very

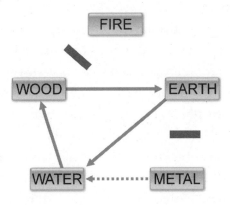

Figure 3: Carol's energy diversions

old grief, the deep authentic timbre of which was moving to hear in her voice, Carol completely surrendered to her experience. Her surrender translated into a dissolution of her stiffness and a restoration of full and free mobility that expressed itself in waves of what seemed almost celebratory movement throughout her whole body.

Carol told us later that hearing the sound of her own voice expressing the depth of her grief had been profoundly transforming. She said that despite all the therapy she had done, she had never heard herself simply give wordless, thought-less visceral *voice* to her grief. There had always been words, a narrative; never just the awesome sound of her own pure grief coming from deep within her, out of her organs and out of her very bones.

℞ METAL — *ED*: BACK PAIN

Ed was a thirty-five-year-old man who had injured his back in a car accident. Although his back injury had not seemed very serious at first, the pain gradually intensified until it became so severe that eventually he agreed to a rhizotomy, an operation in which the nerves to several levels of the thoracic spine are severed. His pain continued despite the operation, however, and he became severely depressed.

Ed confided to us that he had frequently contemplated suicide and had actually attempted it once or twice; adding that he not infrequently put his life at risk on the road, driving his truck as if he did not care whether he lived or died. At the same time, remarkably, he stubbornly insisted that he was perfectly emotionally healthy and had no baggage he wished to explore. Such people leave few avenues of approach. I eventually voiced some frustration at not being able to make a connection with him, explaining that to claim that one has no problems while actively contemplating suicide was a confounding display of denial — at which point, Ed appeared to soften, as if for the first time he were considering the impact of his behaviour on others.

FIVE ELEMENT DYNAMICS: YANG MING–METAL
Given his rigid mental posturing and outgoing nature, Ed was likely another Yang Ming–Metal constitutional type but, unfortunately, we had no way to circuit-test as he would not permit any acupuncture or even acupressure. Here was a situation where a bit of analysis was helpful. If Ed was in fact Metal, he probably could not feel the full force of his grief, which would mean that his Earth energy was being diverted into the Water sector, leaving him with increasing rigidification and prone to injury.

Ed had survived this way before his accident because his other elements were functioning adequately. He had a passion for music — singing and playing the piano (Fire) — and had received the rewards of his passion (Earth). But his injury had left him with a pain he could not receive (blocked Earth), had interfered with his ability to express his passion (Fire) and had left him with no vision of his future (Wood). With no way out and no way to move, his energy had been forced to return to the source (Water). This desire to

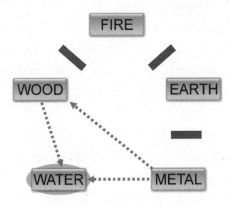

Figure 4: Ed's energy diversions

return to the source had expressed itself somewhat violently in Ed's thoughts of suicide — likely a confused desire for the 'death' that precedes transformation.

Ed's most curious manifestation was his shaking jaw, which he of course dismissed as insignificant but which to my mind looked like myoclonic shaking — a cause for hope, perhaps. And while he was reticent to try acupuncture, he was willing to try some ear balancing (auricular therapy). While we explored his ear with a microcurrent stimulator, we encouraged him to breathe, to sing if he felt like it and to look for shaking. With this mild catalyst and a lot of encouragement, Ed started to shake everywhere at the same frequency as his jaw. Afterward, he reluctantly admitted the experience was quite pleasant, even ecstatic.

When Ed left us, there were indications that he might be thinking about re-evaluating some of his firmly held beliefs; and, although he remains in pain, his body has had the experience of energy release and found it pleasant — both signs that the door to healing might be cracking open.

☡ METAL — *JOE*: VISIONS

Joe was a fifty-five-year-old First Nations man who came to us with low back and knee pain. He had also been struggling with depression for many years and, after exploring various conventional and alternative treatments without success, intuited that there might be deeper issues to explore and decided to come to work with us.

FIVE ELEMENT DYNAMICS: TAI YIN–METAL

Joe did not talk much but when he did he usually had something profound to say. He had about him an air of reverence that seemed to quell idle chat in his vicinity. His yin manner and bearing pointed to Metal or Water but when a body scan revealed a large sebaceous cyst on his right upper chest, just over the point Lung-1 (Zhongfu, Middle Palace) — the lungs being the yin organ of the Metal element — it seemed that his body was letting us know without delay that he was indeed Tai Yin–Metal.

During DIA he went off into the far reaches of the void right from the first session, returning to describe visions and insights that seemed to go beyond his personal memory. In one, he journeyed into a hellish world where he saw the devastation of his people through smallpox. In another, he soared with ravens and eagles (and reported that shortly after this vision, he was out walking with a friend when an eagle feather fell out of the sky right into his friend's hand).

Then in one extraordinary session, Joe saw many of his people being killed in a big battle, which he intuited was the famous battle at Wounded Knee. After this vision, he was amazed to find that his knee pain had disappeared for the first time in ten years — amazed, but not altogether amazed: as we worked, Joe was beginning to understand something of the power that lay buried in him and how that power created pain and depression when it went unused.

From a five element perspective, however, there was a bit of a

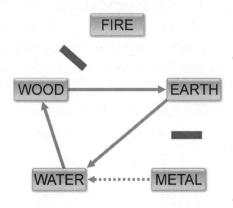

Figure 5: Joe's energy diversions

puzzle to sort out, because a sore back and knees are more often associated with the Water element. So why did Joe, ostensibly a Metal constitutional type, have chronically sore knees? We looked at the possible energy diversions that might have brought this about. If Joe was indeed a Metal constitutional type, he would have had a hard time tolerating the full force of his Metal energies. Habitual suppression of his original energies — and his gifts — would have left him little option but to push himself through life (Water) doing things that really did not engage or excite him, utilizing his creative energy for security rather than passion (Wood and Earth), a sure recipe for depression.

When we force ourselves to go through the motions this way in life, we inevitably drain our Essence (*jing*) and this, in time, can stagnate energy in the Water channels regardless of our constitutional type, giving rise to low back pain and/or knee pain. That previous acupuncture had not worked well for Joe may well have been because the acupuncture was directed at moving the Water channel stagnation, where the symptoms were located, rather than addressing the loss of original energy, which was located in another sector.

Not only were Joe's knees significantly improved when he left us, he felt profoundly different in himself. Although maintaining and developing his gifts and engaging the powers he discovered will call on everything Joe has to give in the coming years, in the long run, he feels strongly that he must cultivate his gifts, take them back home and find a way to use them to help his community, which he feels suffers from a lack of visionary leadership.

WHAT DOES IT ALL MEAN?

If there is anything to be learned from all of these stories, perhaps it is this: there comes a point in life when it is time to let go of the constraints the ego has set upon us and move toward transpersonal experience. In our society, few people publicly acknowledge that an illness may be one of the most potent agents of that transition.

In fact, if we listen to the message of our symptoms and treat our illness and our pains as a treasure of sorts, we might not only save our lives but enlarge and deepen them in ways we could not have anticipated. Making the assumption that things are actually *right* even when they appear wrong radically alters our life experience. If we then shift our intent to move toward the thing we are tempted to resist, fear, dislike or avoid, we will have an opportunity to surrender to the transformational forces that are automatically engaged.

If illness were more respected and honoured culturally, we might be more inclined to move *with* the forces that take us toward trans-formation. Far from being the evil or the failing our society has made of it, it is in fact the envoy of our wholeness, the representative of the very thing we need to take us back to real health.

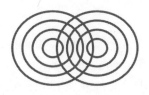

CHAPTER 22

THE UNBROKEN FIELD

Stay in that love, go deeper and deeper into it, investigate yourself and love the investigation and you will solve not only your own problems but also the problems of humanity.
— Sri Nisargadatta Maharaj

$\mathcal{W}$hen the mind stops and we give up making distinctions between this and that, or here and there, or yin and yang, and intuit the underlying unity or wholeness of life, then a healing occurs; and in that moment it could be said that the field, habitually fractured by umpteen mental distinctions, is unbroken. It is this direct experience of the unity underlying diversity that is the goal of introspective techniques such as meditation. So for those readers who have no formal meditation training or instruction, I want to offer a short generic breath-based meditation that may help you get started. As a beginner's guide, it is not intended to take the place of proper teaching and is really only a quick overview for those completely unfamiliar with meditation techniques. Further, because some of the concepts have been discussed elsewhere, there will be some unavoidable repetition, for which I apologize.

If you are new to meditation, try not be too concerned about which technique is the best. There are many techniques out there and the particular form you learn is probably not as important as the commitment to a daily practice. Once you have learned one form, you will be better able to judge which form and which teacher are best for you. (Remind yourself to stay open to new methods and new ideas. If you catch yourself thinking that the particular form you have learned is the only correct way, check yourself: this voice is not likely coming from experience nor from wisdom.)

Why, one might ask, is meditation so important if our symptoms have receded after a few sessions of DIA? One answer to this question is that it can be very challenging to maintain the releases and the diminution of pain that DIA can bring. We tend to slip back into our old ways and in so doing restructure our old symptoms. Old behaviours just do not die very easily. So in order to maintain improvements and keep energy flowing smoothly in the body, it is of great importance to mobilize those energies that tend to get stuck and to do it every day, through some kind of meditative discipline. The benefit of the encounter with an expanded state of consciousness in DIA is, as we saw earlier (chapter 11, Dynamic Interactive Acu-Bodywork), that it can establish a *referent* that then is more easily recognized in meditation.

CREATING A SACRED SPACE

Meditation certainly helps maintain good health but it also gives us much more. In fact, it can give us however much we are open to receiving and consequently it can quickly become an extremely important part of our lives. Even though we may begin our practice with no greater aspiration than to maintain an open channel to our physical or emotional body, it can quickly take on a sacred quality and the place we do it can become a sacred space. And, before long, everything else we do in the day is palpably affected by the time we spend with ourselves. It is at this point that we realize how truly vital our meditation is, not only to our own well-being but to that of our families and communities.

So, before you begin, consider what space you can give this healing and perhaps sacred practice. Setting aside a space in your home in which to meditate will do a great deal to establish and nourish your practice. It does not have to be much. A small room is ideal but just the corner of a bedroom or other similar space will suffice. A futon or foam mattress, a few pillows, some tissues and perhaps a few meaningful objects or images are all you need.

Begin practising daily. After a while, just entering your sacred space will begin to move you into an altered state and prepare you for fruitful energy work. As your skill develops, so will your ability to consciously transmute contained and rejected energy into creative energy. This means that energy that is no longer dumped, contained, acted out or made conscious as illness can instead be retained, transmuted and used to enliven the field.

GETTING STARTED

If the idea of sitting in the lotus position fills you with dread, please relax. The lotus position is best suited to those who have been using it from a young age.[1] Sitting comfortably either cross-legged on the floor, with your pelvis raised above the level of your knees and slightly tipped forward for maximum stability or in a chair with your thighs level with the floor and your feet flat on the ground (or on a raised surface, if necessary), is just fine for our purposes here. Whatever is comfortable for you will do as long as energy can travel up your spine and you can breathe comfortably. Having your back supported is fine, too, if you are planning a quiet meditation.

However, if you want to be open to the development of some

1 Beginning meditators and those concerned with the authenticity of their meditation posture may take some comfort in the fact that Maitreya Buddha, 'the Buddha to come,' or the Buddha of the future, is often pictured sitting in a chair with his [sic] feet on a lotus foot rest.

dynamism, then better results can be obtained by sitting upright with nothing behind your back. This can be done in the formal lotus position or cross-legged but, again, for many people sitting upright in a chair may be preferable. The important thing for dynamic meditation is that your back is free to move should some dynamism begin. If you prefer, you can start your meditation in a comfy back-supported chair as if for a quiet meditation and then change your posture when you anticipate doing dynamic work.

Whatever posture you choose, sit quietly with your hands resting on your thighs or over your knees, depending on your posture and your proportions, palms open upwards or palms down comfortably on your legs. If you choose to sit in a chair, your feet should be planted squarely but comfortably on the floor.

THE MEDITATION

You might want to have a friend read this particular section onto a tape in a slow, steady, restful voice, then play it back to yourself while you meditate.

Take a few deep slow breaths, letting go a bit more with each one. Take a moment to feel your feet on the floor, your stomach, your shoulders, your hands, as many places as you are moved to visit with your attention. Do not try to change anything, just put your attention on them. You may notice them relaxing just from the support of your compassionate, non-judgemental awareness of them. You may also be surprised at how much sensory aware-ness there is in parts of your body that you do not usually give much attention to. You may find your feet, for instance, feel as sensitive as your hands. Let go your anxieties, worries and concerns for the time being as you commit to being with yourself for the next fifteen or twenty minutes.

Now bring to mind a beloved figure — a guide or helper who has some deep meaning for you. He or she might be a religious leader, a deity, an angel, a healer or a teacher; some people have a special relationship with a particular animal spirit, or you may choose to ask an aspect of nature — a tree, a flower, the ocean — to be your teacher. Ask for assistance in your meditation from any or all of your guides or helpers. Also ask them to help you be in the world in peace on this particular day. Focus on your guides for a few moments before letting them drift back to where they came from.

If the idea of guides and helpers is not comfortable (and remember your relationship with your guide or helper in meditation is not one of worship but simply one of focus, appreciation and inspiration) then bring to mind a safe, quiet, inspiring place — such as the seashore, a favourite spot in the woods, or even a room in your house, or perhaps a cottage. Continue to breathe gently and slowly. Be careful not to over-breathe; just a gentle, steady, full breathing rhythm that you find easy and comfortable.

Now, gradually and with the least amount of effort, bring your attention to the point where your breath enters your nostrils. Feel the air as it passes in and passes out. Note the sensations that accompany each breath as it flows in and out of the body. Notice your chest rising and falling, and your abdomen rising and falling. Notice how the breath nourishes the body. Notice how the nostrils flare a little with the in-breath and collapse a little with the out-breath. Notice whether the nostrils and nasal passages are open or partially blocked and what that feels like. Notice how the breath seems able to flow to every nook and cranny in the body — taking you anywhere you put your attention — into your big toe, your navel, the hair on your head, or your fingertips. Do not put any effort into your watching; it does not help — just pay some attention in a gentle, relaxed sort of a way.

As you do this, you will notice sensations, thoughts and feelings appearing spontaneously in the quiet you are creating. Sensations and feelings arise in the body, thoughts arise in the mind and, after a while, they pass away. They all come and go like bubbles rising to a surface and breaking. Do not try to follow your thoughts, just notice them passing like clouds in the sky. When you notice your mind watching a thought a little too eagerly, or beginning to follow and elaborate it, as it doubtless will, gently, without irritation or judgement, notice what has happened, let the thought go on its way and return to the breath.

After a while, you will begin to see how thoughts take your attention; how they will take you off on a tangent if you allow them to. Remember that it is the nature of the mind to think, just as it is the nature of the lungs to breathe. The object is not to fight the nature of the mind but to change your relationship to it and to the thoughts that occur.

After a while, you will see what meditation strives to teach experientially: to be able to know your self as distinct from your thoughts. Meditation is simply a way of learning that when you notice that you have gone off on a tangent, pulled along by your identification and fascination with your thoughts, you can gently detach yourself and bring your attention back to the self that simply exists, back to the breath. As you once again begin noticing the in-breath and the out-breath, you begin to teach yourself that your emotions are not you, your thoughts are not you.

Note the slow, deep rhythm of your breathing. Note the whole breath cycle from its beginning to its end, clearly, sensation by sensation, without strain. When other sensations arise in the body, let your awareness recognize them *as* sensation. Do not think of them as 'body', or as 'leg', or as 'pain', simply note them as sensation, notice them coming and notice them going and return to the breath. Similarly, when an emotion arises in the body, let it flow through you without resistance. Do not try to hold it back or swallow it down; rather, breathe into it, move toward it and let it occur. Think of your feelings as energy; they need not have content; you need not focus on their content. Just surrender to your breath, experience your breath. Do not try to get anything from the breath. Do not concentrate on it; just barely graze it with your concentration and allow awareness to penetrate where sensations arise of themselves and by themselves.

As you settle into quietness, you will gradually feel a kind of full-body awareness, a global sensation of presence or feeling that spans the whole field, from the top of your head or above to the tips of your toes or just beyond. Within that wholeness, you may be able to discern areas of tension or tightness, areas where energy seems to be flowing and areas where it seems to be blocked; areas of pain and tension and areas of no pain. There may also be areas that feel unlike the rest of the body: some may feel numb, others may have other qualities, sensations or feelings.

You may notice twitches. Twitches often happen around the eyes or elsewhere in the face but they can occur anywhere. You may notice sensations of movement, a flow of something like electricity — either up the back or down the legs or any other place. Over time, you may feel sensations in your various chakras. In the root chakra you might feel some tingling or movement; in the second, some sensations of sexual energy. Notice your lower back, which might be a little tight from sitting in an unfamiliar position without support. There may be a pulling sensation in the solar plexus, reflecting tension in the diaphragm. There may be chest discomfort, pangs of grief or sadness in the Heart chakra. Notice tension in the throat or jaw, notice aches or other tension in the temples. And every time you notice these things, gently bring your attention back to the breath, once again noticing the in-breath and the out-breath and the slow deep rhythm of the breathing, the movement of air through the nostrils and mouth.

Continue meditating this way for fifteen or twenty minutes before slowly bringing yourself back to the room, taking a few minutes to rest quietly as you gradually return to your normal waking state.

This is all you have to do; and in fact this is far more than most meditations will consist of. Meditation is essentially the art of doing nothing, focusing inward more and more until you become deeply quiet and deeply, effortlessly attentive. I like to think of those photographs I have seen of lionesses in Africa, lying absolutely lank on low tree branches, a couple of their powerful legs dangling; just hanging there, eyes open, not a scrap of tension or holding. You know — but could not guess from looking — what power and alertness is also hanging there, just a split second from fully manifesting itself if the need should arise. This is deep, alert relaxation. The lioness is charging her batteries. She is 'meditating' after her own fashion.

The lioness's mind is likely empty of unnecessary thoughts, wishes and dreams, or regrets concerning what did not happen last week. Being human, however, you will likely find that when you meditate, thoughts keep arising, taking you here, there and everywhere. With time and perseverance, these thoughts will begin to calm down and you will find yourself — just when you least expect it — in a state in which you are aware of few thoughts. There is not much going on in the mind yet, strangely, you are calm and relaxed and wide awake.

This is the fourth state of consciousness, called relaxed awareness or *turiya*, mentioned earlier on. Do not take this experience to be anything special; just accept it as another experience. If you take it to be something special, you will probably try to hold onto it, and you will immediately find yourself in thrall to your ego and thinking again. The paradox is that the moment you notice you are in a place of absolute quietness or, arguably, the moment just *before* you notice it, you are no longer in it.

For this reason and others, it is best not to try to achieve anything in meditation. Just take it as it comes, thoughts or no thoughts, quiet or not quiet, dynamic or not dynamic. It does not matter. Do not concern yourself either way. So long as your meditation does not encourage mind/body dissociation, all meditations are good. The only thing that matters is the regularity of practice because it is through regularity of practice that you learn the art of relaxed awareness, a state of inner calm no matter what is going on.

HURDLES: EFFORT, EXPECTATION & FALLING ASLEEP

Some of the things that bedevil beginning meditators are effort, expectation and falling asleep. The first, *effort*, is the ego's idea that if something is to be achieved, it could be achieved a bit faster with effort. Indeed, the idea that effort is required to achieve something is so ingrained in many people that even when their meditation has been going well for some time, sooner or later a bit of effort tends to creep in. In time, a little effort becomes a lot of effort and, eventually, the meditation is likely to suffer.

The second, closely related to the first, is *expectation*. If you have had a good experience, then an expectation creeps into subsequent meditations that you will achieve the same state, or an even better one. That expectation, or desire, becomes a thought that creates tension by replacing being in the moment with desire for something other. So do not try and do not expect anything in particular. Be with what is, instead of waiting for something preconceived. It will not happen that way. Again: knowledge is the thing that prevents us from seeing what is right in front of us. Forget what happened last meditation, so that you can be present for the one you are in. In other words, just take it as it comes.

The third, *falling asleep* during meditation, is not really a problem. Many people are sleep-deprived these days; so if you are someone who needs sleep, any relaxation may immediately take you there; and that in itself is not a bad thing. Just make sure that you are seated comfortably, because many months can pass this way before you gradually realize that, even as you are sleeping, you are *aware* that you are asleep. A seed awareness remains, an awakening awareness that can be regarded as another doorway into *turiya*. In fact, being *awake while asleep* is just another way of describing the state of relaxed awareness. So if you are falling asleep, do not worry about it in the slightest. Just welcome the deep relaxation, trust that your body needs the rest, realize that this is one of the ways it knows how to get it and continue with your practice.

DYNAMISM

Dynamic meditation has been discussed fully in chapter 13, but a few words here might be pertinent. The important thing is to build dynamism on an experience of silence. Once a state of relaxed awareness has been achieved, you are ready to allow some dynamism to enter the picture. This is because you are looking for spontaneous movements, not those that are suggested by the intellect or manifested through the will. And there is a huge difference. Dynamism spontaneously breaks down the containment barriers and, in so doing, can help you resolve blocks. Activity engendered by the intellect, on the other hand, generally achieves very little and may even accentuate existing blocks.

Dynamic activity can be facilitated by no more than an intention to allow movements that would otherwise be considered unacceptable. Such movements can be quite bizarre at first, since early sessions may manifest long-held-back feelings of repressed sexuality, rage, terror and grief. This, of course, is why a sacred space is so vital. Such expression is not socially acceptable (for the very good reason that most people are carrying similar loads and so are made extremely uneasy by the sight of what might look very much like the feelings they are working hard not to look at in themselves). But that is not to say their expression is not permissible. In sacred space, they can be expressed and their expression honoured.

THE MAP

Let us finish this section by building a kind of map — a simple listing of some of the steps involved in the process of re-establishing an unbroken field.

- ▼ *Trust that things are right* even when they appear to be wrong.
- ▼ Meditate on *intention* and *moving toward* — try to experience their meanings clearly.
- ▼ *Move*, experientially, *toward difficulties* when they arise.
- ▼ *Explore dynamism in meditation.*
- ▼ *Retrieve projected energy* (which is likely to be allied to your constitutional type — e.g., Water: fear; Wood: anger; Fire: sadness; Earth: worry; and Metal: grief) to reintegrate your shadow (i.e., to heal the persona/shadow dualism).
- ▼ *Trust your body*: let your mind roam your body and let your body be apparent in your mind; investigate places in the body where the mind feels it cannot or will not go; give

your body passive, quiet attention; do not try to use your mind to fix it; instead let the body speak; be curious about it (this will help to heal the mind/body dualism).

▼ *Learn to let go*: a good way to practise this in meditation is to think of every out-breath as your last breath (to heal the life/death dualism).

▼ *Learn to transmute and redistribute sexual energy* through dynamic meditation, tai chi, qi gong and other practices (to heal the love/sex dualism).

▼ *Meditate regularly* (to heal the existential dualism).

▼ *Express your wholeness in the world with an open Heart* to keep energy flowing freely on all levels.

It is not a simple thing to put these suggestions into practice. Some could take a lifetime to truly realize. But remember as you contemplate the list that it in no way represents a linear sequence of tasks but is in fact a map, an interconnected whole, each item of which relates to all the others, and will respond to any movement in, or attention to, the others.

THE UNBROKEN FIELD

There is a big but simple secret that can be very freeing, and it is this: *respecting social strictures does not mean we have to repress our energies.* There is a third way. It is possible to live in the world and not compromise our essential wholeness. By exploring and developing dynamism in sacred space, we can experience our totality by paying homage to our otherwise inexpressible energies, so they are less likely to manifest themselves through illness.

As the root meaning of holy is whole; to do these things and to experience wholeness by doing them is in fact entirely appropriate to sacred space. With practice, we tend to feel more and more whole and connected and, simultaneously, the sense of alienation recedes. No longer afflicted by the feeling of separation, we rediscover ourselves to be part of the unbroken field.

APPENDIX 1

VOID EXPLORATION / DIA

HOW TO PREPARE FOR THE EXPERIENCE

The following is a sketch of the verbal instructions given to people contemplating their first Dynamic Interactive Acu-Bodywork (DIA) experience.

PREPARATION

Wear loose-fitting clothing, no make-up. Remove jewellery (necklaces, earrings, rings with projecting or sharp contours, etc.), watches, belts — anything that can snag or that might inhibit your movements. Eat lightly or not at all. Plan to take a couple of hours afterwards to relax and integrate your experience. Plan to have someone drive you home, if possible.

PURPOSE

The intent is to *explore* rather than suppress your symptoms. With this in mind, try to flow with and support whatever your body wants to do during the process. Complete freedom of expression is really important. You should go with every impulse, whether it be emotional, movement or positional (e.g., your body may want to adopt a position reflective of an injury mechanism). *Dynamic* and *interactive* mean the key to success lies in active participation.

FORMAT

DIA usually begins with the insertion of a couple of acupuncture needles in your hands and feet while you lie comfortably on a mattress on the floor supported by pillows and covered with a blanket if you wish. This will generally be followed by a systematic palpation of the body for tender or symptomatic points, using acupressure. You are part of a witness/explorer team, not a passive recipient of a procedure. Your job is to breathe into any pain you experience, and allow the pain to speak through spontaneous sound and movement.

It is important to remember that there is no right or wrong way to do it. You are not there to please the witness. Spontaneity is the key and it is absolutely okay if nothing happens. In the case of a dual exploration (when two people share the same room for their experiences), try to stay focused on yourself even if the other explorer is making a lot of noise. You can certainly allow the sound to touch you emotionally but resist the urge to be pulled into rescuing or judging the other person.

THE STOP COMMAND

This type of exploration requires that you trust us enough to go into unknown mind-body territories with us. It is important that you know that you can stop the process at any time. 'STOP' is the magic word.

DIA is interactive, not adversarial; you should not try to grin and bear it. You are free to call a halt to whatever is going on if you are having difficulty coping or find yourself fighting the pain. When and if you say STOP, you can choose to have softer acupressure, or simply move on to other points.

Try not to overuse the STOP instruction. You are learning a new skill — like learning to ski, or riding a bicycle. Sometimes it is best just to keep going and look for rhythm. Above all, resist the temptation to stop the process at any point to try to understand it. Trying to understand is getting out of direct experience and into your head and that tends to break up the dynamics of the process.

BREATHWORK

From the beginning, you will be encouraged to breathe more deeply and regularly. Deeper breathing facilitates greater *presence* and so supports the exploration. Some common phenomena associated with deeper breathing include:

▼ Dizziness after about a minute
▼ The feeling that you do not want to carry on
▼ An altered state: a more present-moment attitude; less concern with day-to-day problems; more in the body; breathing becomes effortless.
▼ Numbness, tingling, spasms in the hands, wrists or elsewhere, tightness around the mouth, etc.

SIGNS OF ENERGY MOVEMENT

▼ Myoclonic shaking — involves limbs and/or body shaking or jerking rhythmically or otherwise. This can be interpreted as an energy release and as tension leaving the body. It can feel as if there is an electric current running in the body.
▼ Emotional release — reflects a letting go, often associated with shaking.
▼ Mental imagery — reflects previous experiences, often related to the particular area of the body being explored.

The sessions generally last about an hour. Please remember that you may need some time to just sit and relax afterwards. Your response to void exploration can vary from one session to the next and it is best to have some time afterward to integrate whatever experience you may have had.

SELECTED ACUPUNCTURE POINTS

Organ	Source Point	Energy Axis	Pinyin	Translation	Location
Kidney	KI-3	Shao Yin	Taixi	Great Creek	Between medial malleolus and Achilles' tendon
Heart	HT-7	Shao Yin	Shenmen	Spirit's Door	Ulna side of ventral wrist crease
Small Intestine	SI-4	Tai Yang	Wangu	Wrist Bone	Ulna side of wrist, between 5th metacarpal and Hamate bone
Bladder	BL-64	Tai Yang	Jinggu	Capital Bone	Base of 5th metatarsal
Spleen	SP-3	Tai Yin	Taibai	Big White	Behind 1st metatarsal head
Lung	LU-9	Tai Yin	Taiyuan	Great Abyss	Radial side of ventral wrist crease
Large Intestine	LI-4	Yang Ming	Hegu	Adjoining Valleys	Between 1st and 2nd metacarpals
Stomach	ST-42	Yang Ming	Chongyang	Pouring Yang	Middle of back of foot
Liver	LV-3	Jue Yin	Taichong	Great Pouring	In web between 1st and 2nd toes
Pericardium	PC-7	Jue Yin	Daling	Big Tomb	Middle of ventral wrist crease
Triple Heater	TH-4	Shao Yang	Yangchi	Pool of Yang	In the dorsal wrist crease between 3rd and 4th metacarpals
Gall Bladder	GB-40	Shao Yang	Qiuxu	Wilderness Mound	Just anterior/inferior to lateral malleolus

Table 1: Organ source points

Point	Pinyin	Translation	Location
LI-4	Hegu	Adjoining Valleys	1st interdigital space, hands
LV-3	Taichong	Great Pouring	1st interdigital space, feet

Table 2: The Four Gates

Zone	Point	Pinyin	Translation	Location
Back Zone	SI-3	Houxi	Back Creek	Lateral to 5th metacarpal at end of transverse crease made when fist is clenched
	BL-62	Shenmai	Extending Vessel	Just below lateral malleolus
Lateral Zone	GB-41	Zulinqi	Near Tears on the Foot	Between 3rd and 4th metatarsals
	TH-5	Waiguan	Outer Gate	1 inch proximal to dorsal wrist crease between radius and ulna
Ventral Zone	KI-6	Zhaohai	Shining Sea	Just below medial malleolus
	LU-7	Lieque	Broken Sequence	1.5 inches proximal to styloid process, on the radius
Chong Mai	SP-4	Gongsun	Grandfather Grandson	Anterior-inferior margin of 1st metatarsal, proximal end
	PC-6	Neiguan	Inner Gate	1 inch proximal to ventral wrist crease between radius and ulna

Table 3: Points Used to Access the Curious Meridians

APPENDIX 3

FRENCH ENERGETICS:
THE EIGHT CHARACTER TYPES

Requena describes in detail the way his eight character types arise out of his six temperaments. The schema are fairly complex but may prove interesting to readers who want to understand another way in which the constitutional attributes of the various energy vectors can be derived.

ACTIVE/NON-ACTIVE : YANG/YIN

The first classification polarizes *active* and *non-active* (perhaps more usefully conceived as *doing* and *being*) and refers to the yin and yang aspects of the six energy circuits. The yang axes (Tai Yang, Shao Yang and Yang Ming) are all classified as *active* temperaments, while the yin axes (Tai Yin, Shao Yin and Jue Yin) are all classified as *non-active*.

This simply means that yang temperament types tend to mobilize their energy more easily, are more inclined to physical action and tend to be more gregarious, while yin types tend to be slower to act and generally stiller, tend to concentrate their energies inwardly and are more inclined to be self-contained.

EMOTIONAL/NON-EMOTIONAL :
FEELING/DETACHMENT

The second set of qualities — *emotional/non-emotional* — refers to the degree to which an individual engages the world from a feeling place. Although the Fire element, containing as it does the Heart energy, is readily understandable as an emotional centre, in this system emotionality is considered a dominant feature of three elements — Water, Wood and Fire. As a group they might be understood as *emergent* energies, that aspect of the five phases in which the energetic vectors are moving out of the universal toward the personal — that is, pre-birth (Water, the universal), youth (Wood, developing ego) and midlife (Fire, maturing ego).

By contrast, the late-summer Earth and the autumnal Metal elements are considered non-emotional and might be understood as expressions of the return from personal to universal, which manifests as increasing ego detachment. Perhaps a better word for Earth and Metal energies might be *spiritual*, in which case the dichotomy could be thought of as feeling versus detachment.

PRIMARY/SECONDARY : REACTIVE/THOUGHTFUL

The third division — *primary/secondary* — refers to the way an individual reacts to situations, whether immediately, reflexively and reactively, or in a slower and more thoughtful manner. Berger says the primary individual focuses on what is happening, while the secondary looks to what has happened and what will happen, the history and the consequences. The primary temperament is allied to Wood and Earth sectors, while the secondary is ascribed to Water and Metal. The Fire sector is doubled: it produces primary types when associated with Wood and secondary when associated with Water. The primary organs of the Fire element are the Triple Heater and the Pericardium which, you may recall, are the outer Heart protectors. Their guardian function — to turn away potential difficulties before they can penetrate to bruise the deeper recesses of the Heart — makes it logical that they would be more reactive.

The six circuits (Tai Yang, Shao Yang, etc., plus the two extras

provided by distinguishing Metal and Earth types in the Yang
Ming and Tai Yin circuits) and their associated characteristics produce eight psycho-physiological types shown in the following table.

CHARACTER TYPE	ORGAN PAIR	TEMPERAMENT	PERSONALITY / DISPOSITION
TAI YANG	Small Intestine and Bladder	Active, Emotional, Secondary	Passionate nature, intense
SHAO YANG	Triple Heater and Gall Bladder	Active, Emotional, Primary	Enthusiastic, often quick-tempered
YANG MING — Earth	Stomach and Large Intestine	Active, Non-emotional, Primary	Sanguine, cheerful, confident
YANG MING — Metal	Large Intestine and Stomach	Active, Non-emotional, Secondary	Phlegmatic, cold, composed
TAI YIN — Earth	Spleen and Lungs	Non-active, Non-emotional, Primary	Amorphous, indifferent, seeks company
TAI YIN — Metal	Lungs and Spleen	Non-active, Non-emotional, Secondary	Apathetic, inward, taciturn
JUE YIN	Pericardium and Liver	Non-active, Emotional, Primary	Nervous, sensitive, volatile
SHAO YIN	Heart and Kidney	Non-active, Emotional, Secondary	Sentimental, sensitive, low self-image

Table 1: The eight character types

The eight character types include not only Tai Yin–Earth and Tai
Yin–Metal but also Yang Ming–Earth and Yang Ming–Metal, as
mentioned above. And while this certainly has its usefulness, in
my experience it seems to overemphasize the Yang Ming and Tai
Yin, without adding much to the simplicity of the three circuits
and six energy axes.

GLOSSARY

CARPOPEDAL SPASM: A flexion contraction or cramping of the hands and feet sometimes induced by hyperventilation. (*See* chapter 15, Everyday Life Meditations.)

CHAOS (or RIGIDITY) OF RESISTED SURRENDER: Refers to the pathological effects of a blocked Metal sector. In this situation, energy from the Earth sector is diverted around Metal into the Water sector, often resulting in physical stiffness and enforced helplessness. As the individual grows increasingly rigid, an equivalent chaos tends to manifest in the family and caregivers who find themselves responsible for the sufferer's personal care. (*See* chapter 9, Energy Diversion, and chapter 21, The Earth–Metal Sectors.)

CHONG MAI (or, CHONG MO) and CHONG MAI BLOCK: Chinese medicine conceives of the *Chong Mai* as a central energetic pillar which supplies original energy (*yuan qi*) to all the other meridians. It also connects the Heart (4th chakra) energetically with the genitals (2nd chakra). A *Chong Mai* block between these two chakras is very common, constituting what Western psychology has called a love/sex split. (*See* chapter 8, The Chakras and chapter 16, Sexual Healing Meditations.)

COGNITIVE DISSONANCE: When an experience contradicts the rational mind's belief or expectation about how life is, then the mind is thrown into confusion. It appears to have to choose either: to reject the experience and maintain its belief; or, to alter its belief to accept the experience. A third way, which involves accepting both poles of the contradiction simultaneously, results in ego transcendence and the expansion of mind into Mind. Cognitive dissonance is a common difficulty encountered during the struggle for healing and has to be negotiated if healing is to be realized. (*See* chapter 8, The Chakras)

COMPARTMENTALIZATION: Ego containment and dissociation strategies lead to field compartmentalization. The compartments may be largely *somatic* such as in regional pain syndromes, or *psychic* such as in multiple personality syndromes, or mixed (psychosomatic), leading to a wide variety of pain syndromes and psychic disturbances (*See* chapter 3, Qi and Blood Stagnation).

CONSTITUTIONAL TYPES: According to the five element tradition of Chinese medicine, each individual has a personality predisposition which reflects the quality of energy present in a particular season of the year. These types are classified as Wood (spring), Fire (summer), Earth (centre), Metal (autumn) and

Water (winter). (*See* chapter 5, The Five Elements and chapter 6, The Six Temperaments).

CONTAINMENT BARRIERS: The borders between field compartments. These barriers will often be structured in the body as physically palpable tension bands and/or temperature differences. (*See* chapter 2, Fragmentation of the Field and chapter 3, Qi and Blood Stagnation.)

DISSOCIATION: The ego strategy of moving consciousness away from areas of the body that are painful or otherwise unpalatable (*See* chapter 3, Qi and Blood Stagnation.)

DOWNSTREAM EFFECT: A quantity of blocked energy has been released in one part of the body but becomes trapped or blocked again in another part of the body. (*See* chapter 14, Downstream Effects.)

DUPUYTREN'S CONTRACTURE: A medical term for thickening of the fascial tissue in the hands, commonly manifesting as a nodular or cord-like fibrosis in the tendon sheaths of one or both hands and tightness and flexion contractions of the ring and little fingers. (*See* chapter 19, Water–Fire Sectors.)

EGO-DEVELOPMENT: The maturational process from infancy to young adulthood, in which we establish a viable and functional identity in the world. (*See* chapter 3, Qi and Blood Stagnation, chapter 7, The Heart/Mind Split and chapter 10, Intention.)

ENANTIODROMIA: A phenomenon in which a person's values and beliefs literally turn upside-down, like the hanged man in the Tarot deck. It frequently follows a period of cognitive dissonance and represents the stage prior to the full integration of such dissonance (*See* chapter 4, Transcendence and Transformation.)

ENTRAINMENT: The tendency of adjacent vibrational phenomena to adopt the same or related frequencies in the way one string on an instrument will tend to vibrate in harmony with an adjacent one. (*See* chapter 1, The Field of Energy and chapter 10, Intention.)

ENFORCED HELPLESSNESS: The effect of a blocked Metal sector. In this situation, energy from the Earth sector is diverted around Metal into the Water sector, often resulting in physical stiffness and enforced helplessness. As the individual grows increasingly rigid, an equivalent chaos tends to manifest in the family and friends who find themselves responsible as caregivers. (*See* chapter 9, Energy Diversion, and chapter 21, Earth–Metal Sectors; *see also* CHAOS OF RESISTED SURRENDER).

EXPLORER-WITNESS CONTINUUM (or VOYAGER-WITNESS CONTINUUM): A non-hierarchical, unitary DIA relationship, as compared to the more familiar, practitioner-client relationship which is hierarchical and dualistic. In using the term explorer-witness, I am attempting to underscore the non-dual nature of the healing work. (*See* the introduction and chapter 17, Acupuncture Techniques.)

FIELD: An informational pattern of waves and troughs which surrounds an object. The field around the body is electromagnetic and represents the sum total of all the tiny electromagnetic fields around each individual ion (hydrogen, sodium, potassium ions, e.g.). (*See* chapter 1, The Field of Energy.)

FIELD AWARENESS (in meditation, e.g.): An inner attention in which the meditator is aware of the self as a field of experience, of fluidity, fluctuation and change, rather than a physical object (*See* chapter 1, The Field of Energy.)

FIELD COHERENCE: A phenomenon in which various bodily rhythms become synchronized with each other and also with natural rhythms outside the physical body. Studies have employed EEG results to demonstrate increased brainwave coherence in long-term meditators. (*See* chapter 4, Transcendence and Transformation.)

FIVE ELEMENTS or FIVE PHASES: The aspect of Chinese medicine that deals with personality types and their relationship to the seasons of the year. Some practitioners and theorists feel that the cyclical and seasonal aspects of the constitutional types (*see* CONSTITUTIONAL TYPES) are more important than the elements. The five elements are occasionally referred to as the five phases for this reason. Five phases emphasizes the condition of change which is fundamental to Chinese philosophy and thus to Chinese medicine. We have chosen to use the more familiar translation, five elements. (*See* chapter 5, Five Elements.)

GOLDEN GATE, THE: A mythical pass which connects material life and the Tao. It is sometimes also called the door of death and the gate of birth. (*See* chapter 10, Intention.)

INTENT or INTENTION: Represents the directional vector set by the mind, whether it be toward difficulties or away from them. In the normal course of events, the ego's intent is pre-set to move away from symptoms; and this intention has to be reversed before healing can occur. (*See* chapter 10, Intention.)

INTERFERENCE PATTERNS: Refers to a complex pattern of waves and troughs in a field. An example can be found in the image of overlapping circles created on the surface of a pond by two adjacent sticks wiggled in the water. (*See* chapter 1, The Field of Energy; and note the icon of overlapping circles at the chapter heads.)

JOYLESS LABOUR: Refers to the result of a blocked Fire sector. In this situation, energy from the Wood sector is diverted around Fire into the Earth sector, with the result that the individual often works for security rather than passion. (*See* chapter 9, Energy Diversion.)

KRIYA: The movements and postures adopted by Yogic aspirants who are channelling rising kundalini energy. (*See* chapter 13, Dynamic Meditation.)

LAW OF CURE, THE: Formulated by Constantine Hering (1800–1880), one of the founders of American homeopathy, the Law of Cure states that symptoms are resolved from within to without, from innermost to outermost, from top to bottom and in reverse order in which they occurred (i.e. backwards chronologically). (*See* Chapter 14, Downstream Effects.)

MEISSNER EFFECT: A phenomenon in physics in which increasing coherence in an energy field is accompanied by increasing resistance of the field to outside interference. Such coherence in the body's energy field can bring about increased well-being, a strengthened immune system and a remarkable resistance to disease. Chinese medicine refers to this coherent energy state as *Zhen Qi* (or true qi). (*See* chapter 1, The Field of Energy and chapter 4, Transcendence and Transformation; *see also* SUPERCONDUCTANCE)

MIND/BODY BLOCK: A common condition in which the ego has separated itself from the body. It might be considered a cerebral compartmentalization. In its extreme form, the block can manifest as a hot-cold differential across the neck. (*See* chapter 2, Fragmentation of the Field.)

MUSCULAR TENSION BANDS: Tight muscular bands which reflect the body compartmentalization. Wilhelm Reich referred to this phenomenon as muscular armouring and understood it to occur in horizontal segments or bands. Three very common bands occur in the pelvis, the diaphragm and the upper chest. (*See* chapter 2, Fragmentation of the Field and chapter 3, Qi and Blood Stagnation.)

MYOCLONIC SHAKING: An energetic release of muscular tension which takes the form of a vibration of the limbs, trunk or neck. The shaking can range from a fine shivering to gross or spasmodic physical movements. (*See* chapter 11, Dynamic Interactive Acu-Bodywork).

MYOFASCIAL TENSEGROUS MATRIX: Myofascial is a term used to refer collectively to the body's muscle (*myo-*) and connective tissue (*fascia*). Bones and myofascial tissue together make up a myofascial tensegrous matrix, a stable yet flexible system which is capable of carrying vibrational information. (*See* chapter 1, The Field of Energy and chapter 14, Downstream Effects.)

NEUROMA: A swelling of the sheath of a nerve, often in the feet but can be anywhere. They are often painful. (*See* chapter 19, The Water–Fire Sectors.)

OEDEMA: Tissue swelling from fluid extravasation into the interstitial spaces. Oedema of the lower legs is more common in elderly people or those with heart failure. (*See* chapter 19, The Water–Fire Sectors.)

ORIGINAL ENERGY: That quality of energy which is resident in the infant before the ego gets around to setting limits on what is and is not acceptable. Chinese medicine calls this energy the *yuan qi*. (*See* chapter 4, Transcendence and Transformation; under Fragmentation and Original Energy; *see also* SHADOW WORK.)

PALLIATIVE CARE: Care offered to people when there is no chance of a cure and death is the likely outcome. Palliative care emphasizes compassionate symptom relief rather than disease treatment. (*See* chapter 18, Cancer and the Death Mystery.)

QI GONG: A system of exercise ranging from formal meditation to postures and movements, each designed to enliven and promote the flow of qi in the body. Qi gong is similar to tai chi (taiji) but tends to be more repetitive and to focus on developing certain qualities of energy. (*See* chapter 8, The Chakras.)

REFERENT: A recognizable experience with which to understand a word or concept. For example the word 'dog' needs a referent (a dog) before the word is understood. With regard to specific meditation experiences, a referent is the particular experience itself, identified as such by a reliable witness. Once this referent experience is identified, it can be more easily recognized both in future meditations and in other aspects of life. (*See* chapter 10, Intention and chapter 11, Dynamic Interactive Acu-Bodywork.)

SAN JIAO: (also known as Triple Warmer, Triple Heater, Triple Burner and Triple Energizer): The space in which the physical structure of the body exists and the spaces in between things in the body, such as the interstitial spaces. It also refers to the three major body cavities, the chest, the abdomen and the pelvis. These three cavities are often separated from each other by tension bands and so can become pathologically compartmentalized. In Chinese medicine, the *san jiao* is responsible for distributing original energy (*yuan qi*) evenly throughout the body via the various energy meridians. (*See* chapter 5, The Five Elements.)

SASMITA SAMADHI: In the Advaita Vedanta tradition, *sasmita samadhi* refers to the penultimate state of consciousness in which the knower (*purusha*) has totally differentiated his beingness from his body (*prikiti*). Beyond *sasmita samadhi* lies the ultimate state in which there is complete unity of knower and known. (See chapter 4, Transcendence and Transformation.)

SHADOW: Jung described the shadow this way in *The Archetypes and the Collective Unconscious*: 'The shadow personifies everything that the subject refuses to acknowledge about himself and yet is always thrusting itself upon him directly or indirectly — for instance, inferior traits of character.' In another text, he says, '... the shadow (is) that hidden, repressed, for the most part inferior and guilt-laden personality whose ultimate ramifications reach back into the realm of our animal ancestors...' (*See* chapter 2, Fragmentation of the Field and chapter10, Intention.)

SOMATIC: Refers to the physical body, as opposed to the psyche or mind. The term 'psycho-somatic' is often used to denote an illness considered largely mental in origin, though expressed vicariously through physical symptoms. (*See* chapter 3, Qi and Blood Stagnation.)

STARVATION IN THE MIDST OF PLENTY: Refers to the situation of blocked Earth energy. In this situation, energy from the Fire sector diverts around Earth into the Metal sector, where it manifests as a false asceticism and anxiety due to the inability to receive. One common physical manifestation is diabetes. (*See* chapter 5, The Five Elements.)

SUPERCONDUCTANCE: A phenomenon of highly ordered systems such as super-cooled metals, in which semi-conducting crystals are brought into a highly ordered state by being cooled to very low temperatures. Biological systems have many semi-conducting systems. (*See* chapter 1, The Field of Energy; *see also* the MEISSNER EFFECT and *ZHEN QI.*)

SUPER-HEALTH: Refers to the Meissner effect and the *zhen qi*. When an individual achieves this state of his qi, then he or she usually enjoys abundant good health. (*See* chapter 1, The Field of Energy and chapter 4, Transcendence and Transformation.)

TAI CHI (TAIJI): (Though the Chinese should be rendered *tai ji* or *taiji* in English, it has for so long been written *tai chi* that we decided to leave it in this interim spelling for ease of reading.) Tai chi means something like 'supreme ultimate' in recognition of its great power to work with the energy systems of the body, to build health and to honour and explore the body-mind's nature. (*See* chapter 8, The Chakras.)

TENSEGROUS: A system which has both solid and elastic parts arranged in such a way as to produce a flexible structure. The body is a tensegrous structure, the myofascial matrix forming the elastic aspect and the bones forming the solid struts. Such a system is relatively stable, but capable of absorbing impacts and transmitting vibrational information. (*See* chapter 1, The Field of Energy and chapter 15, Everyday Life Meditations.)

TRANSCENDENCE: The process in consciousness in which opposites can be integrated without generating pathology. It is the means by which *transformation* becomes stabilized and integrated in consciousness (as *transformation*, in its turn, is the foundation of *transcendence*). (*See* chapter 4, Transcendence and Transformation.)

TRANSFORMATION: Refers to the process in which a previously unrecognized reverse-polarity energy vector is contacted and directly experienced. If the new perspective is sustained for any length of time it could be called an enantiodromia. Transformation is the foundation of *transcendence*; and *transcendence* is the means by which *transformation* becomes stabilized and integrated in consciousness. (*See* chapter 4, Transcendence and Transformation.)

TRIPLE HEATER: *See SAN JIAO.*

TURIYA: The fourth, or ground, state of consciousness which transcends the waking, dreaming and deep sleep states. (*See* chapter 4, Transcendence and Transformation.)

UNBOUNDED CHAOS: Refers to a blocked Wood sector. In this situation, Water energy is diverted around Wood into the Fire sector, resulting in a pattern of chaotic behaviour, ranging from simple acting out to frank delusions. (*See* chapter 5, The Five Elements.)

VECTOR: Vector has been adapted from mathematics to indicate energy having three aspects: directionality, movement and force. It is therefore something more than a trajectory or a pathway. (*See* chapter 4, Transformation and Transcendence and chapter 9, Energy Diversion.)

VIOLENT TRANSFORMATION: Refers to the effect of a blocked Water sector. In this situation, energy from the Metal sector bypasses Water to impact in the Wood sector. Such a diversion is frequently the situation in cancer. (*See* chapter 5, The Five Elements.)

VOID: A state of consciousness in which we are aware of inner and outer, subjective and objective simultaneously. It is similar, perhaps, to the Zen notion of beginner's mind, the always fresh mind of unmediated perception, but refers more specifically to the context in which the state arises. The void, as I am using the term, is accessed through DIA, while beginner's mind is cultivated through meditation. (*See* chapter 10, Intention.)

WIND: Though unseen, the presence of wind in the natural world can be inferred through its effects, such as movement in the branches of trees. Likewise in Chinese medicine, 'Wind' is inferred in disorders involving abnormal movement, like tremors, tics or muscles spasms. In the five elements, Wind is associated with the Wood element, which is said to control the smooth flow of qi. (*See* Chapter 20, The Wood–Fire Sectors)

ZHEN QI: Authentic qi, or true qi: the energy of an integrated individual who has, through inner work and sustained personal cultivation, achieved an unbroken field. (*See* chapter 1, The Field of Energy.)

BIBLIOGRAPHY

Aron, Elaine and Arthur. *The Maharshi Effect: a revolution through meditation*. Walpole, NH: Stillpoint Publications, 1986.

Berger, Gaston. *Traité pratique d'analyse du caractère*. Paris: Presses Universitaires de France, (1950) 1974.

Bly, Robert. *Iron John: a book about men*. New York: Addison-Wesley, 1990.

Burr, Harold Saxon. *Blueprint for Immortality: the electric patterns of life*. Saffron Walden: C.W. Daniel, 1972.

Campbell, Joseph. *This Business of the Gods: in conversation with Fraser Boa*. Caledon East, Ontario: Windrose Films, 1989.

Choa, Kok Sui. *Pranic Healing*. York Beach, Maine: Samuel Weiser,1990.

Connolly, Diane M. *Traditional Acupuncture: the law of five elements*. Columbia, MD: Traditional Acupuncture Institute, 1994.

Crichton, Michael. *Travels*. New York: Harper Collins, 1988.

Deadman P. and M. Al-Khafaji. "A Brief Discussion of the Points of the Window of Heaven." *Journal of Chinese Medicine*. vol. 43, 1993.

Dossey, Larry. *Healing Beyond the Body: medicine and the infinite reach of the mind*. Boston and London: Shambhala, 2001.

Dossey, Larry. *Reinventing Medicine: beyond mind-body to a new era of healing*. San Francisco: Harper, 1999.

Greenwood, Michael T and Peter Nunn. *Paradox and Healing: medicine, mythology and transformation*. Victoria, BC: Paradox Publishing, 1992.

Greenwood, Michael T. *Braving the Void: journeys into healing*. Victoria, BC: Paradox Publishing, 1997.

Hammer Leon. *Dragon Rises, Red Bird Flies: psychology, energy and Chinese medicine*. Barrytown, NY: Station Hill Press, 1990.

Hastings, Anne Stirling. *Body and Soul: sexuality on the brink of change*. New York: Plenum Press, 1996.

Helms, Joseph M. *Acupuncture Energetics: a clinical approach for physicians*. Berkeley: Medical Acupuncture Publishers, 1995.

Houston, Jean. *The Search for the Beloved: journeys in sacred psychology*. Los Angeles: Jeremy P. Tarcher, 1987.

Hunter, Marlene. *Making Peace with Chronic Pain: a whole-life strategy.* New York: Brunner/Mazel, 1996.

Jarrett, Lonny S. *Nourishing Destiny; the inner tradition of Chinese medicine.* Stockbridge, MA: Spirit Path Press, 1998.

Johnson, Robert A. *We: understanding the psychology of romantic love.* New York: Harper and Row, (1945) 1983.

Johnson, Will. *The Posture of Meditation: a practical guide for meditators of all traditions.* Boston, MA: Shambhala Publications, 1994.

Joy, W. Brugh. *Avalanche: heretical reflections on the dark and the light.* New York: Ballantine Publishing Group, 1990.

Joy, W. Brugh. *Joy's Way: a map for the transformational journey.* New York: Tarcher (G.P. Putnam's Sons), 1979.

Jung, Carl Gustav. *CG Jung, Psychological Reflections.* Edited by Jolande Jacobi. Princeton, NJ: Princeton University Press, 1973.

Jung, Carl Gustav. *Memories, Dreams, Reflections.* Recorded and edited by Aniela Jaffé. New York: Vintage Books (Random House), 1961.

Krishnamurti, J. *Talks and Dialogues.* NY: Avon Books, 1968.

Kurtz R, and H. Prestera. *The Body Reveals: an illustrated guide to the psychology of the body.* New York: Harper and Row, 1976.

Leadbeater, C.W. *The Chakras.* London: The Theosophical Publishing House, 1969.

Lowen, Alexander. *Depression and the Body.* Toronto: Longmans, 1972.

Mindell, Arnold. *Dreambody: the body's role in revealing the self.* Portland, Oregon: Lao Tse Press, 1998.

Mindell, Arnold. *The Shaman's Body: a new shamanism for transforming health, relationships and the community.* San Francisco: Harper, 1993.

Morgan, Marlo. *Mutant Message Down Under.* Lees Summit, MO: MM Co., 1991.

Nisargadatta Maharaj, Sri. *I am That: talks with Sri Nisargadatta Maharaj.* translated by Maurice Frydman. Durham, NC: The Acorn Press, 1973.

Osbourne, Arthur. *Be Still, it is the Wind that Sings.* Tiruvannamalai, Tamil Nadu: Sri Ramanasramam, 2000.

Oschman, James L. & Nora H. Oschman. *Readings on the Scientific Basis of Bodywork, Energetic, and Movement Therapies.* Dover, NH: N.O.R.A., 1997.

Oschman, James L. *Energy Medicine: The Scientific Basis.* Edinburgh: Elsevier/Harcourt Brace and Company/Churchill Livingstone, 2000.

Pascal, Blaise. *Pensées.* edited by L. Brunschvicg. Paris, 1909.

Pert, Candace. *Molecules of Emotion: the science behind mind-body medicine*. New York: Touchstone (Simon & Schuster), 1997.

Pomeranz, Bruce and Gabriel Stux. *Acupuncture: textbook and atlas*. Berlin, Heidelberg, New York: Springer-Verlag, 1987.

Requena, Yves. *Terrains and Pathology in Acupuncture*. Brookline, MA: Paradigm, 1986.

Sagar, Stephen M. *Restored Harmony: an evidence-based approach for integrating Traditional Chinese Medicine into complementary cancer care*. Hamilton, Ont.: Dreaming DragonFly Communications, 2001.

Stein, Robert. *Incest and Human Love: the betrayal of the soul in psychotherapy*. Dallas, Texas: Spring Publications, (1973) 1984.

Suzuki, Shunryu. *Zen Mind, Beginner's Mind*. NY & Tokyo: Weatherhill, (1970) 1977.

Talks with Sri Ramana Maharshi. Tiruvannamalai, Tamil Nadu: Sri Ramanasramam, 2000.

Wang, Zhi Gang. "Taoism and self cultivation." *Journal of Chinese Medicine*. vol.37, 1991.

Wilber, Ken. *The Spectrum of Consciousness*. Wheaton, IL and Chennai (Madras) India: Quest Books, Theosophical Publishing House, (1977) 1993.

White, John, ed. *Kundalini: Evolution and Enlightenment*. St. Paul, Minnesota: Paragon House, (1979) 1990.

Worsley, J.R. *Classical Five-Element Acupuncture, Vol. 3. The Five Elements and the Officials*. Charlottesville, VA: The Worsley Institute of Classical Five-Element Acupuncture, 1998.

Yogananda, Paramahansa. *Autobiography of a Yogi*. Los Angeles: Self-Realization Fellowship, (1946) 1969.

Yogananda, Paramahansa. *The Divine Romance: collected talks and essays on realizing God in daily life*. Los Angeles: Self Realization Fellowship, 1986.

Yutang, Lin, ed. *The Wisdom of China and India*. New York: Random House, 1942.

Index

italicized page numbers indicate a figure or table where there are numerous other page references, **bold face** indicates a major entry, or definition
CT = constitutional type

397

399